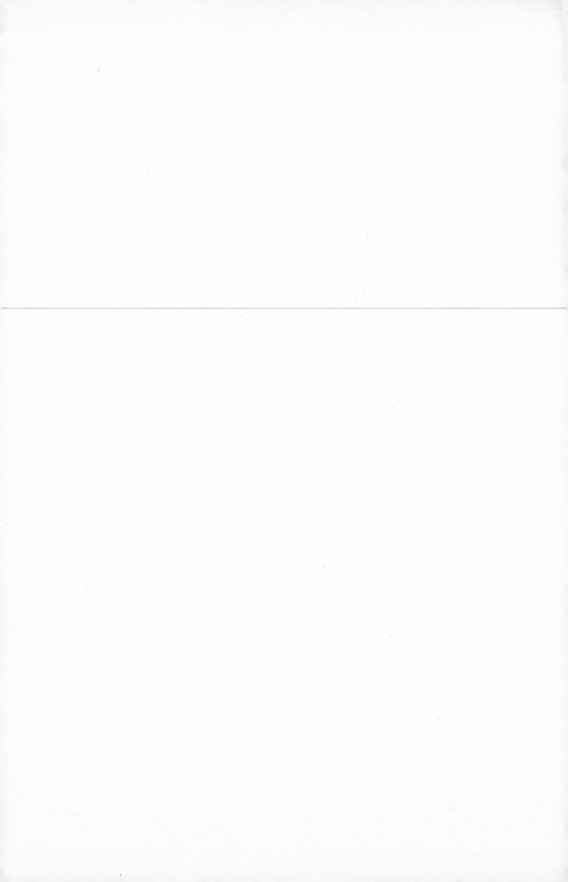

Also by John Case
DIGITAL FUTURE
UNDERSTANDING INFLATION
ENTERPRISE *(with Eric Sevareid)*

JOHN CASE

The Resurgence of

FROM THE GROUND UP

American Entrepreneurship

SIMON & SCHUSTER
NEW YORK / LONDON / TORONTO
SYDNEY / TOKYO / SINGAPORE

SIMON & SCHUSTER
Simon & Schuster Building
Rockefeller Center
1230 Avenue of the Americas
New York, New York 10020

10 9 8 7 6 5 4 3 2 1

Library of Congress Cataloging-in-Publication Data

Case, John
  From the ground up : the resurgence of American entrepreneurship /
John Case.
     p. cm.
  Includes bibliographical references and index.
  1. Small business—United States. 2. New business enterprises—United
States. 3. Entrepreneurship—United States. 4. Organizational change—
United States. 5. Economic security—United States. I. Title.
HD2346.U5C33 1992
338′.04′0973—dc20   91-37972
                                                                         CIP
ISBN: 0-671-68308-X

To the memory of my mother,
JOSEPHINE YOUNG CASE

Contents

Foreword

SOMETIMES we don't recognize what has happened until we look back on it. So it is with the changes that shook American business in the 1980s.

The decade brought a curious mixture of nervousness and excitement to economic life. On the one hand, we wrung our hands over the decline of older industries, and over our seeming inability to compete with the Japanese (or the Taiwanese, or the Koreans). We watched the stock market anxiously; when it plummeted, in October 1987, we were quick to anticipate a lasting crash. We wondered when the government deficit or some of Wall Street's more egregious shenanigans would catch up with us.

We noticed, too, that many of our biggest corporations were in rough shape. Some of the giant companies we once thought of as dominating world markets were staring glumly at red ink. Others were going on frantic acquisition-and-divestiture binges, leaving us uncertain about what they did for a living. (B.F. Goodrich sold off its tire-making operation, Singer its sewing-machine division.) Some corporations proved themselves lean and mean by shuttering plants and sacking employees. Others—presumably not lean or mean enough—ran to the government for protection from imports. Companies as big as Gulf Oil and RCA were swallowed by still-larger companies. Other giants, such as TWA, were taken over by upstart financiers. Faced with such carnage, how could we be sanguine about the future of the American economy?

And yet: despite our nervousness, despite the plight of the big corporations, despite blistering competition from abroad, the business world of the 1980s showed a remarkable amount of life. The Great American Job Machine, as the editorial writers began calling our high-employment economy, somehow found work for all the baby boomers (19 million new jobs between 1980 and 1989), at a time when employment in other industrial nations was growing slowly or not at all. Silicon Valley and similar high-tech hotbeds around the country continued to pioneer ever more radical new technologies, even though some of the older electronics companies were struggling. The states once known as the Rust Belt found themselves booming, though many of the mills and factories shut down earlier in the decade never reopened. Business itself enjoyed a kind of cultural revival. To be sure, Wall Street's excesses frequently turned our stomachs. But working for a company—particularly a young, innovative company—once more became an honorable and exciting thing to do.

Why the contradictions? The argument I'll make in this book can be summarized pretty simply. All such developments, both frightening and encouraging, were symptoms of a twenty-year change in the American business landscape—a change with dramatic implications for the 1990s and beyond.

In the past, it paid a company to grow very, very large. The economic environment was stable, and the United States was securely in the international driver's seat. American companies that were big enough could, with three or four others, dominate world markets. They could build huge factories, snap up subsidiaries, crank out more and more goods. They could also—no small matter—provide stable, high-paying jobs, often for employees' entire working lives. Business was predictable, and for the most part we took the business world for granted.

In the 1970s this stability began to crumble. Oil prices and other costs began spiraling out of control. Overseas competitors began gobbling up market share. Some industries found themselves facing stringent new regulations, while others faced the unknown prospects of deregulation. Amid all these uncertainties appeared a pervasive new technology, microelectronics, that would have upset the marketplace all by itself.

Like a series of seismic shocks, these changes began reshaping the business landscape. Large corporations floundered. They downsized and divested, redrew their organizational charts, and (as they liked to say) redefined their missions. Some fell victim to the takeover wars. Meanwhile, newer and smaller companies sprouted up and nosed their way into niches opened up by the economic tremors. Gradually, without most of us seeing what was happening, these new companies began playing a critical role in our economy. As we'll see, they reshaped whole industries, from semiconductors and steel to trucking and telecommunications.

I don't argue—I don't think anyone would—that big companies, the General Electrics and General Motors of the world, were in their death throes. But I do think the 1980s brought the beginnings of a new kind of economy. Willy-nilly, Americans began looking for jobs and opportunities outside the ranks of the nation's largest corporations. Willy-nilly, businesspeople began learning to survive in a marketplace in which the fiercest competitors were companies they had scarcely heard of. Throughout the 1980s people with ideas or inventions flocked to create new businesses. So did people who were simply fed up with the new uncertainties of corporate life. The big companies were still there. But they weren't where the action was.

From the Ground Up is the story of this new economy: where it came from, how we first learned of it, and what made it different, both in older parts of the business world and in newer ones. It's a story that turned out to be more complex than I had first suspected. In years past, businesses could be fit into a few simple taxonomies. There were large companies and small ones, customers and suppliers, manufacturers and service companies. Inside a company there were management and labor, or owners and workers.

In the new economy, as the stories in this book show, none of these categories could be drawn so neatly. The new companies I visited went about their business differently. They were often managed in ways that would make a traditional boss's hair stand on end. The larger issues raised by the new economy weren't neat, either. What we Americans gained in opportunity—lots of innovative, highly competitive new enterprises to work for—we lost in stability. During the 1980s we did tolerably well economically, yet we regarded the future with trepidation because it was so uncertain. When the economy slowed down in the early 1990s, we were gloomier still. We forgot that business cycles are just business cycles—and that the long-term outlook for American business was probably brighter than ten years earlier.

One final word on what you'll find within. This book is a work of journalism, not of economics. I have learned a great deal from economists, but I'm not one of them. Besides, though we frequently think of the economy as an abstraction (and economists generally treat it as such), it could scarcely be less abstract. "The economy" is shorthand for a million different businesses and marketplaces, each of them populated by people trying, for better or worse, to do their jobs, to produce goods and services that other people want to buy, and in the process to make a living or a profit. When the structure of the economy changes, as I believe it has, we all have to get used to new ways of working and doing business.

From the Ground Up is about these new ways.

1

Discovery

At some point in our lives, most of us get a picture in our heads of what the economy—the business landscape—looks like.

I remember, for example, my seventh-grade cit. ed. class at Hamilton Central School in Hamilton, New York. It was called cit. ed.—citizenship education—because, so my brother Sam told me, the New York State legislature had decided that "social studies" sounded too much like "socialism." This was the 1950s. The teacher was Mrs. Ames, an agreeable woman with firm ideas about pedagogy. I will never forget the Turning Point of the Revolutionary War, because Mrs. Ames went around the room, all thirty of us, and asked each boy and girl to stand and tell her that the Battle of Saratoga was the Turning Point of the Revolutionary War. Why? Because it ruined the Threefold Plan and convinced the French to help us. (If you don't know what the Threefold Plan was, ask a seventh grader.) Educators take note: Repeat the same point often enough and a kid will remember it three decades later.

At any rate, before we got to the Revolutionary War we had to study New York State. That was when I first began learning about the economy, though I didn't know the word and Mrs. Ames didn't try to teach it to us. We learned What New York State Made. Rochester: cameras. Syracuse and Schenectady: electrical equipment. Corning: glass.

15

We kids figured we knew who made what anyway. Cars, for example. We could tell a Ford from a Chevrolet and a Bel Air from an Impala. Sam, from whom I learned even more than from Mrs. Ames, taught me to identify Hudsons, Studebakers, Nashes, and the obscure cars made by Kaiser-Frazer, which was industrialist Henry J. Kaiser's ill-fated challenge to the Big Three. But no one I knew owned any of these second-rate vehicles. Real cars were made by General Motors, Ford, and Chrysler. Everything else had similar provenance. Kitchen appliances came from General Electric and Westinghouse, tires from Firestone and Goodyear, breakfast cereals from Kellogg and General Mills. If your family bought a new TV, kids wanted to know—after how big it was—if it was a Zenith or an RCA or a Magnavox.

So by the time Mrs. Ames began teaching us about Rochester and Schenectady, we knew it wasn't cities that made things, it was companies. Rochester was Kodak. Syracuse and Schenectady: General Electric. Corning: Corning Glass Works. Like everyone else in those days, we took it for granted that the work of America was done mainly by huge corporations, enterprises that had probably always been there and would certainly always be there. They were the companies that sponsored TV shows and bought ads in *Life,* that grown-ups talked about or worked for, and that made the stuff you saw around the house.

THE GALBRAITH MODEL

The understanding that we were dutifully drinking in was, of course, correct. The big corporations dominated the business world. Indeed, they were getting bigger with every passing year. In 1954 the 500 companies on *Fortune* magazine's first list of the largest industrial corporations collectively took in $137 billion, equivalent to 37 percent of the gross national product. Five years later the figures were $197 billion and 40 percent. The trend continued as I left Mrs. Ames in Hamilton and went, eventually, to college. In 1969 the Fortune 500 collected $445 billion, equivalent to 46 percent of the GNP.

Even more striking was the growth, both absolute and relative, in big-company employment. In 1954 the Fortune 500 employed roughly 8 million people, equivalent to almost half the manufacturing work force. In 1959 the figure was more than 9 million, the fraction more than half. By 1969 the 500 employed close to 15 million people, equivalent to almost three-fourths of the manufacturing work force.

Most Americans gave this situation little thought; it appeared to be the natural order of things. Those who did found it worrisome. Liberals, of whom there were many in the 1960s, fretted about big business's power vis-à-vis labor, consumers, and the government itself. Conservatives worried about monopoly. John N. Mitchell, the Wall Street bond lawyer who became Richard Nixon's attorney general and gained lasting notoriety in the Watergate era, gave a speech to the Georgia Bar Association in 1969 that might have been written by Ralph Nader. The danger posed by concentrated corporate power to our economic, political, and social structure, he said, could not be overestimated. "Concentration of this magnitude is likely to eliminate existing and future competition . . . It creates nation-wide marketing, managerial and financing structures whose enormous physical and psychological resources pose substantial barriers to smaller firms wishing to participate in a competitive market.

"And, finally, super-concentration creates a 'community of interest' which discourages competition among large firms and establishes a tone in the marketplace for more and more mergers.

"This leaves us with the unacceptable probability that the nation's manufacturing and financial assets will continue to be concentrated in the hands of fewer and fewer people. . . ."

Worrisome or taken for granted, the ever-growing size of America's dominant corporations was still not difficult to understand. All you had to do—and many, many people did so—was read Professor Galbraith.

By the late 1960s, John Kenneth Galbraith was not just an economist but a phenomenon. His 1958 book, *The Affluent Society*, had been a huge best-seller. In the 1960s, by one biographer's count, he produced "8 nonfiction works, a novel [actually two, one under a pseudonym], 32 magazine articles, 54 book reviews, 35 letters to the editor, 8 introductions to books, numerous lectures, and major speeches for Lyndon Johnson and Edward, Robert, and John F. Kennedy." He served as JFK's ambassador to India, as chairman of Americans for Democratic Action, and as president of the American Economic Association. When *The New Industrial State* was published, in 1967, a Senate subcommittee organized hearings at which the best-selling book's ideas were both attacked and defended. Galbraith owed some of his influence to his lucid prose and acid wit, a combination that made his books a pleasure to read rather than a chore. Pleasurable reading was generally unknown in economics. But much of his appeal reflected the power of his ideas—and the fact that, alone among academic economists, he was able to explain why the business landscape looked the way it did.

The New Industrial State's explanation of the large corporation turned on two notions largely ignored by conventional economics: planning and power. Bringing modern, technologically complex goods to market, Galbraith observed, required a long period of time, a considerable investment of capital and specialized knowledge, and a good deal of organization. Henry Ford, so ran the economist's famous example, could produce his first cars simply. With only a little backing from investors, he could buy his materials on the open market, hire a few men to help him build the vehicles, and then see how they sold. But when the Ford Motor Company introduced the Mustang, in 1964, the car represented years of planning and millions of dollars' worth of investment. The company needed to know exactly where its parts and supplies were coming from, how high its costs would be, and how many Mustangs it could reasonably expect to sell. It had to plan the operation both extensively and intensively.

But planning alone wasn't enough. The company might *plan* to hire so many workers, and buy so much steel and so many mirrors, and it might *like* to sell, say, 100,000 cars the first year, but to realize its expectations Ford needed a measure of control over all the possible variables. Supply and labor contracts had to be negotiated and nailed down. Distribution systems had to be in place. Money had to be spent on consumer research, on marketing strategies, and on advertising. If Ford could control some of the variables directly—say, by owning its suppliers—so much the better. If it could influence other variables simply by being big, so much the better again.

Conventional economics attributed corporate giantism to economies of scale—the ability to lower costs by producing in large volume. "But the present view," wrote Galbraith, referring to his own, "also explains what the older explanations don't explain. That is, why General Motors is not only large enough to afford the best size of automobile plant but is large enough to afford a dozen or more of the best size. . . . The size of General Motors is in the service not of monopoly or the economies of scale but of planning. And for this planning—control of supply, control of demand, provision of capital, minimization of risk—there is no clear upper limit to the desirable size. It could be that the bigger the better." Galbraith heaped derision on those who, like Mitchell, railed against the anticompetitive nature of big business and invoked the threat of antitrust laws. "To suppose that there are grounds for antitrust prosecution whenever three, four, or a half dozen firms dominate a market is to suppose that the very fabric of American capitalism is illegal."

In Galbraith's view, the business world could be divided into two essential parts. One included the big manufacturing companies, utilities, transportation and communications firms, and so on—every enterprise that depended on sophisticated technology and required large-scale organization. This was the modern, dynamic sector of the economy, the part that was growing and shaping the rest. The other sector was small business, i.e., everything that was left over. In a later book, Galbraith acknowledged that he had paid insufficient attention to small business in *The New Industrial State*. But it scarcely mattered. "Small and traditional proprietors" were confined to the fringes of the marketplace. Entrepreneurs ran personal and professional service firms, small job shops, establishments such as corner stores and gas stations that survived only because their proprietors worked impossibly long days for ridiculously little money. Indeed, Galbraith couldn't resist a note of condescension toward the small-business man. His vaunted independence, wrote the professor, "is often the caution, conformity, obeisance, even servility, of a man whose livelihood is at the mercy of his customers. His is often the freedom of a man who is pecked to death by ducks."

Like any popular sage, Galbraith both reflected and fashioned his era's understanding of the economy. Every kid knew there were a lot of big companies out there. People who paid attention to such matters saw them getting bigger, and Galbraith cogently explained why that should be so. With little to challenge it, this picture of the business landscape was embedded in American heads.

This made it both surprising and suspect when, at the end of the 1970s, we began hearing that those giant companies were no longer playing as dominant a role as we had come to expect. The first bearer of the news was a man named David L. Birch.

BIRCH'S CHALLENGE

You don't need a license to practice economics. That was fortunate for David Birch: he had an undergraduate degree in physics and a doctorate in business administration. Most people who learned of his work assumed that he was an economist and referred to him as such. I learned he wasn't a *real* economist (having neither a Ph.D. in economics nor a job in an academic economics department) when I was writing an article about him and began talking to real economists. Some loved his work and some hated it. All prefaced their remarks by saying, "Of course, David Birch isn't an economist."

Had he been one, he wouldn't have done what he did. But we'll get to that.

Birch was a curious mixture of academic and entrepreneur. A resident of suburban Boston, he maintained one office at the Massachusetts Institute of Technology, in Cambridge, where he had established a research entity called the Program on Neighborhood and Regional Change. He had another office in a stylish industrial park at the other end of Cambridge. There, he had set up a small company called Cognetics Inc., which sold business information to corporate clients. I arranged to meet him at Cognetics one day in 1988. In preparation, I put aside my customary notebook and armed myself with a tape recorder; I had heard Birch speak several times already, and I knew he talked the way my teenage sons ate: rapidly and voluminously.

When I arrived, he got right to the point, which was to explain the origins of his surprising research into the economy.

"I majored in engineering and applied physics at Harvard, class of 1959. Afterwards I went in the air force. Then I worked for RCA for a while, out here at Hanscom Field. I was assigned to the intercept of the Ballistic Missile Early Warning System—BMEWS, pronounced *bemuse*. RCA's task was to develop identification systems so you had a fail-safe method of identifying friend or foe. My team's job was to see if we could outfox the systems. We'd send these F-102 or F-104 fighters out and bring 'em back in again against BMEWS and see if we could get through without triggering an alarm.

"It was really fun. I did it for a year and a half, then went to the Harvard Business School, then went to work for General Dynamics designing the resupply system for a manned orbiting space station that was on the drawing boards. Later I did a similar thing for the Mariner spacecraft to Mars, out at the Jet Propulsion Laboratory in Pasadena. I must have driven across the country five times during all this. I was out at the JPL twice, with stints at Harvard in between. I got my doctorate in 1967, something like that."

Most people with Birch's experience and interests would have been clambering up an aerospace company's corporate ladder. But he found himself worrying about other matters entirely. "At that point, it was obvious that our cities were a mess. People were getting shot. The world was coming unglued. I began to get interested in the problems of the cities, trying to understand how they were changing." Leaving his budding career with the military-industrial complex, he took a part-time job teaching at the Harvard Business School and began figuring out how to apply his training and skills to urban problems. As a physicist-turned-systems-engineer, Birch had always seen his job as investigating "the particles"—the many tiny parts and subsystems that made up the early warning system, or the orbiter, or the spacecraft. To understand or change the whole system you had to know how those parts fit together. That, he decided, was the way he would approach social science. Having scared up some research money, he set out to study the city of New Haven, Connecticut.

Or rather its particles. "We started building histories of businesses in New Haven, to understand how they moved around. We interviewed hundreds of residents to see why they chose a neighborhood. We interviewed builders to see why they built in the places they did. I became a sworn agent of the Census Bureau and was allowed access to every census record for New Haven. I matched those up with bank records to see how people used money. We were always trying to understand individuals—what people did and why they did it. Then we would aggregate those data into neighborhoods, and aggregate neighborhoods into the city." Gradually, Birch built a modest reputation as an urban-affairs researcher, and found himself able to win research grants, mostly from federal agencies. Leaving Harvard, he affiliated with the Massachusetts Institute of Technology and began a study of why people move from one city to another.

Around him, society was changing. By now it was the 1970s, and headlines told of inflation, recession, the boom in the Sun Belt, the onslaught of Japanese-made products. America's most pressing problems were no longer just in the cities; now they seemed to emanate from the economic system itself. Birch's new migration research pointed in the same direction. Millions of people were moving. (Texas alone gained nearly a half-million residents from migration between 1970 and 1975.) When you asked people why they moved, most of them said they had moved because they had, or hoped to find, a new job. To Birch, the data suggested mammoth, wrenching change in the economy, with jobs vanishing by the thousands from one region and materializing in another. Still thinking about the particles, he realized that some *companies* must be shrinking, or giving up the ghost, while others were growing. Some might be moving, too. Were there any patterns? Maybe locally owned companies tended to stay in one place, while absentee-owned companies were footloose. Or maybe that notion was just a myth. In any event, he quickly discovered that no one had systematic data capable of answering that question or any other he might want to ask about where jobs were coming from. No one, in fact, had even thought to ask the question.

As far as economists were concerned (for Birch had ventured from the ill-defined realm of urban affairs into what most people would think of as economics), such questions scarcely existed. The generation of jobs, like many other issues, was a matter readily explained by theory, and thus not very interesting. Jobs are created when the level of demand in the economy is sufficiently high. Or, as another angle of economic vision would put it, jobs are created when employers find that additional workers produce more in revenues than they require in wages. Economists might worry about how to affect overall demand or the aggregate wage level, but they rarely thought much about individual companies, industries, or regions, which were no doubt behaving (if you had all the relevant information) as theory said they would.

There were practical obstacles as well. Government agencies that collected data about businesses, such as the Internal Revenue Service and the Census Bureau, were prohibited by law from releasing information about individual companies. Most private sources of business information tracked large, publicly traded concerns—those of interest to investors—and ignored the rest of the economy. Moreover, anyone who could gather up data might reasonably be daunted by the prospect of sorting through it. Computers were common in universities by the 1960s, but computing time was expensive and programming cumbersome. Enterprising economists might be using computers to run equations comparing inflation rates with, say, changes in the money supply. None had tried to compile and analyze a large database of information about individual businesses.

But then, Birch wasn't an economist.

He had none of the economist's preconceptions about what he should study or how he should study it. When he wanted to know where jobs were coming from, or why some seemed to be disappearing, his instinct was not to theorize but to locate information about individual companies, see which ones had grown and which had shrunk, and then analyze the characteristics of both groups. Nor did the logistical problems of manipulating so much data faze him. A scientist by training, he figured he could somehow find and utilize whatever computing power he needed. At MIT in the 1970s, he had negotiated a deal giving his researchers and programmers full access to the university's computers between 2:00 A.M. and 6:00 A.M. Like gnomes, they would cart their tapes of migration information over to the vacant computer center, work all night, and leave as the sun was coming up. Later, as computers got cheaper, Birch was able to buy a pair of 32-bit Perkin-Elmer superminicomputers. They were less powerful and much more expensive than many of today's personal computers, but they put an end to the midnight treks, and they gave him in-house data-processing capability that few other social scientists had.

Birch felt confident—rightly so, as it happened—that he could get funding for research on where jobs were coming from, and that his computers could handle the voluminous information he wanted to get. Where he'd get the information itself, he wasn't so sure. Ideally, he'd like data about every company in America over time: how many employees it had, what industry it was in, who owned it, and so on. But the government wasn't handing out such data, and Birch could hardly start from scratch. Finally, recalling his New Haven days, when he had learned a little about the city's companies by looking at their Dun & Bradstreet records, he put in a call to Dun & Bradstreet's Boston office.

The Dun & Bradstreet Corporation, headquartered in New York City, traces its ancestry back to 1841, when a man named Lewis Tappan started a credit reporting bureau he called the Mercantile Agency. Robert Graham Dun took over the agency in 1859 and gave it his own name; in 1933, R.G. Dun & Company merged with a competitor that was also named for its founder, John M. Bradstreet.

A century and a half after Tappan, D&B had become a multibillion-dollar purveyor of business information, numbering among its many subsidiaries the A.C. Nielsen Company (which rates TV shows), Moody's Investors Services (which rates bonds), and several other divisions. "Chances are," wrote the *Wall Street Journal,* "D&B knows how many bottles of bleach your local supermarket stocks. It knows what television shows Americans are watching. It monitors hundreds of corporate and municipal bond offerings. One of its almost 30 divisions even ferrets out the most promising spots for striking oil." The company's oldest product—a line of business in which it enjoyed a near-monopoly—was the credit information it maintained on millions of American businesses. Some 80,000 companies subscribed to this database; D&B received an average of 90,000 inquiries a day for information on would-be borrowers and credit customers.

The D&B representative who met with Birch, Dennis Jacques, would later recall for me his early discussions with Birch. "He was asking a *lot* of questions. How was our data collected? How was it filed? We told him we had information we'd been gathering for 150 years, and in the 1960s we'd started to automate it. By 1969 we had all the files on computer.

"No one else had called in looking for historical data on a national scale, going back and trying to create a time series. I thought it was pretty exciting. If he wanted to build some type of database or analytical tool to study growth, this was the way to do it. Management, well, they were a little skeptical at first. You know, 'What does this guy want these old files for? Nobody ever asks for those.' We didn't know how to sell them because nobody'd ever asked for them before. It's a typical thing; you go to a big corporation with something out of the ordinary, that's what happens. Later, quite a few D&B upper management people took an interest in what he was doing."

Birch and Jacques came to terms: Birch would lease individual business records from D&B, records that would indicate not only financial information on the business but its size, ownership, date founded, and so on. Birch decided he would start a few years back— say, 1969—and buy information in chunks, then program his computer to track what had happened to individual enterprises. In 1974 he ordered data from 1969 and 1972. The next year he bought data

for 1974, and later for 1976. (Biannual samplings, he felt, were sufficient for his purposes, and D&B declined to sell him records less than
a year old). The information arrived in cartons full of magnetic
computer tape, thirty or forty tapes for each year.

Firing up the Perkin-Elmers, Birch began the long, slow process
of finding out what the tapes could tell him.

Like a historian stumbling on an undiscovered cache of docu-
ments, Birch was at once excited and nervous. Buried somewhere in
the millions of records should be fundamental information about the
dynamics of the American economy—about which companies were
growing and which shrinking, and what distinguished one group
from the other. The voluminous data would be his first glimpse into
what he thought of as the hidden economy, the millions of companies
whose stocks aren't traded on any exchange and who rarely appear
in anyone's news stories. But he worried about how good the numbers really were. D&B did have a strong interest in accuracy, because
credibility was essential to its business. But the company wasn't a
federal agency, nor was it trying to compile a census. And even
diligent data gatherers, he knew, can founder on many rocks: figuring
out what to list, learning how to get the best information, making
sure that it is entered and maintained accurately. Birch's confidence
level sank when, partway through the research, a company president
Birch was interviewing confided that he never told D&B the truth.
When his company was small, he said it was bigger. When it began
growing, he understated the growth; he didn't want anyone else to
know how successful he was.

So Birch wrestled with the data. It took years. "We learned that
the best way to find problems was to decrease the size of the universe
you're studying—to increase the grain, the level of detail. When you
got down to a county or a neighborhood, you uncovered problems
that had been buried in the averages." He compared D&B's listings
for several Connecticut counties with the Census Bureau's County
Business Patterns, which tabulates the number of business establishments in each county. He investigated how D&B treated companies
with more than one branch. (That seemingly small issue would turn
out to be a bone of more contention than Birch could have imagined
at the time.) He learned to identify subsidiaries, as opposed to independent companies, and to watch for "new" companies that were

merely existing companies that had changed their legal status. When he was through, he thought he had a pretty good idea of what D&B's list could and could not tell him.

It was, he emphasized, a sample of the business universe, not a complete census of it—although the 5.6 million business establishments he came up with when he combined the records from all four years probably accounted for the vast majority of incorporated enterprises at the time. Manufacturing concerns were overrepresented, since nearly all of them required credit ratings. Trade and service businesses were underrepresented until, in the mid-1970s, D&B made a deliberate effort to improve coverage in this area. Many small professional-service firms (doctors' offices, consultants, etc.) and many nonprofits never appeared in the file at all, because they rarely bought anything on credit. Small businesses as a group, however, were not underrepresented. Since they were less stable than large ones, prospective suppliers were quicker to demand credit ratings.

One big failing of D&B's listings from an analytic perspective was the firm's undercoverage of new businesses. A lot of new businesses must be starting every year, Birch surmised, to replace all those whose deaths and disappearances D&B diligently recorded. "I spent a lot of time worrying about the undercoverage of start-ups. It takes D&B a long time to absorb all the firms that start in a given year. They just aren't in the file. We actually built a large computer simulation to estimate the extent of the problem, given all the data sources we could bring to bear. We looked at new-incorporation statistics, actual employment in an area, number of establishments in an area, company death rates. Then we'd impute what the start-up rate had to be to make it all come out right. It was like the computer simulations I used to do to optimize spacecraft design, an elaborate process to get relatively few numbers. But it held up well. To test it, we actually called on every start-up company we could find in New Haven, walking down the streets and knocking on doors."

Eventually, Birch had numbers that he thought corresponded pretty well to the real world: a consolidated sample of businesses from 1969 to 1976, edited for accuracy to the best of his ability and capable of being corrected for the undercoverage of new companies; in all, a statistical portrait, particle by particle, of the American economy. His first major report on all this data was due at the Commerce Department, which was then funding his research, in December 1979. Birch called his report *The Job Generation Process*.

The document—50-plus pages of text accompanied by 240 pages of computer-generated tables—was a measured academic study, replete with cautions about the limitations of the data and seemingly devoid of earthshaking conclusions. Birch broke down job growth into its component parts: jobs created by new businesses, by expansions, and by companies moving into an area; jobs lost by discontinuances, contractions, and by companies moving out. Then he analyzed how important each of these factors was and what characterized companies in each category. He looked at the data by region; he looked at it by industry. Not surprisingly, the text focused on the pressing economic questions of the day. Were companies leaving the North for the Sun Belt in droves? (No. "Runaway" shops accounted for a minuscule portion of employment change.) Were companies opening up new, presumably nonunion branches in the South? (Yes, especially in manufacturing.) Were regions' economic destinies controlled by distant corporations? (To a significant extent. But patterns were different in different sectors of the economy.) The tables seemed to index the data by every conceivable cross-classification. A typical table would be headed, "Components of [Employment] Change 1969–1976. Region: North Central. Industry: Services. [Company] Size: 0-20 [Employees]."

But the real news, so to speak, lay in one short section of the paper that Birch said he added almost as an afterthought. He had made sure to compile subsidiaries' records into the totals for their corporate parents, so that a Sears distribution center, say, was counted as part of the big retailer, not as a separate business. Now he asked how big all those companies were. Did most job growth come from larger companies, or from smaller ones?

It was a startling statistic in an otherwise unremarkable study. Of the several million new jobs added to the American economy between 1969 and 1976, roughly 80 percent of them were created by companies with fewer than 100 employees, and *nearly two-thirds by companies with fewer than twenty employees*. In regions such as the Northeast, large companies were actually shrinking, meaning that smaller businesses had generated all of the net new jobs.

"It is the thousands of anonymous smaller firms," wrote Birch, "that are carrying all the burden in the older sections of our country—and the lion's share in the growing areas as well." He sent off copies of his report to the Commerce Department and to other contacts in Washington; across the top of each he penciled, "Thought you might be interested in this." Not long after, he wrote an op-ed piece for the *New York Times* on his conclusions. "Think small," it advised.

WAS BIRCH RIGHT?

Official Washington in 1980 was not a happy place.

It was the time of the decade's second energy crisis, this one touched off by the overthrow of the shah of Iran, and of President Jimmy Carter's "malaise" speech ("The erosion of our confidence in the future is threatening to destroy the social and political fabric of America"). Over at the Federal Reserve Bank, chairman Paul Volcker had announced a new policy designed to curb inflation, which was then well into double digits. The Fed would henceforth allow interest rates to rise uncontrolled. Pretty soon, indeed, the prime rate was closing in on 20 percent. But political frustration over the sorry state of the economy focused on the Fortune 500 as much as on the Fed. The oil giants, glutted with cash, were accused of having engineered the energy crises. The auto companies, floundering, seemed to be caving in to the Japanese. Chrysler nearly went broke and had to be bailed out by the government.

And what did it say right here in this paper that had been funded by the government and written by a professor at MIT? By implication, it seemed to say, *Forget the Fortune 500.* They aren't creating many new jobs; they might as well be folding up their tents. The life in this economy, the dynamism, the leading edge belongs to the small companies, the entrepreneurs, the family businesses. These are the enterprises that made this country great.

Now, that was the kind of thinking a politician could get behind.

"After the Chrysler rescue was enacted, I was selected to be chairman of the [House Banking Committee's] economic stabilization subcommittee," remembered James J. Blanchard, then a young Democratic representative from suburban Detroit (and later governor of Michigan). "I decided to launch a set of hearings on the dynamics of the U.S. economy. At that time, everybody was debating industrial policy and wondering how many more companies we would have to bail out.

"But I quickly found that the whole clamor for industrial policy was almost irrelevant to the growing sectors of the economy. As David Birch and others were saying, what we had to look at was the rate of business growth. You didn't want to be developing policies designed for the Fortune 500 when the rest of the [business] world was providing most of the new jobs."

Suddenly Birch's phone was ringing. He testified before congressional committees. He began meeting with a group of younger representatives and senators dubbed Atari Democrats, after the company that brought the first video games to market. Recognizing a good thing when it saw one, Carter's Small Business Administration promptly named Birch Researcher of the Year and gave him an award. Washington's reaction was echoed in other policy-oriented circles, regardless of political hue. The influential conservative journal *The Public Interest* asked Birch to write up his research for publication. State economic-development officials began asking him to speak. And what an appealing message he brought them! If Birch was right, they could forget about begging General Motors to locate its next plant in their state. They could get rid of those large and controversial tax breaks that big companies always seemed to expect when they built a new facility. Instead, the officials could develop plans for encouraging *entrepreneurship*.

Percolating outward from the original paper, Birch's once-cautious account was oversimplified to the point where it seemed to turn conventional, Galbraith-inspired thinking on its head. Big companies: shrinking, collapsing, yesterday's news. Small companies: growing, proliferating, the businesses of tomorrow. For politicians it was a convenient picture. Still, a sober-minded observer had to wonder. Birch was using data that had never been used for research purposes before. His findings challenged a fundamental, decades-old understanding of the way the economy worked. Besides—sorry, but it had to be said—he wasn't even an economist.

It was only a matter of time, in other words, before his view of the economy would be targeted for attack. Ironically, it was hit first by friendly fire.

In 1978, the Small Business Administration's new Office of Advocacy had begun looking for data on small companies, only to find exactly what Birch had found: no one collected such information on a national level except the IRS, and the IRS wasn't sharing. When Birch's research hit the headlines, the SBA decided it, too, would get Dun & Bradstreet's records, starting with the years 1978 and 1980.

Rather than maintain the database itself, however, the agency would contract with the venerable, well-respected, and therefore credible Brookings Institution. "Brookings had instant name recognition," recalled Bruce Phillips, a senior economist with the SBA's Office of Economic Research, "and we wanted a contractor that would be unimpeachable." At Brookings, two researchers named Catherine Armington and Marjorie Odle were given the job of editing and analyzing the raw data. Armington and Odle essentially started over, working out procedures of their own for filling in D&B's various gaps. They published their results in early 1982.

If Birch had been hot only a year or two earlier, he now seemed to catch a quick chill. Birch said most of the new jobs come from small companies? Nonsense, reported Armington and Odle, only about 40 percent do—roughly equivalent to small business's share of the economy. Birch's error, they suggested, was to count "establishments," or places of business, rather than companies. If you counted every "business office of the telephone company, or the local cannery of a large food-processing company" as a small business, maybe you could come up with Birch's conclusion that eight out of ten new jobs originated with small companies. But if you did it the right way, you got much more modest numbers. "A significant portion of the growing small *establishments* are branches or subsidiaries of large *firms,* and when employment growth is measured by the size of the firm rather than by the size of the individual establishment a sharply different picture of the role of small business in the job-creation process emerges." Translation: Birch is all wet.

So. Think how *you'd* feel if you were running the Office of Advocacy, of all things, for the Small Business Administration, and you'd just spent a lot of money on a database that you thought would trumpet small companies' importance in the economy. What did you get for your money? Ouch. "There's no question it was embarrassing," said the SBA's Phillips. Catherine Armington chuckled when asked about the SBA's reaction. "We were told we'd essentially be banned from Washington if we didn't stop talking to reporters." Birch, up in Cambridge, was peeved. He began preparing a detailed response, which he issued in spring 1983.

But the damage had been done, and at least some scholars decided that Brookings had proved Birch wrong. As late as 1988 two Harvard economists were writing in the *Washington Post* that Birch had counted establishments, not companies, and that a "report by the

Brookings Institution" had discredited his numbers. It was a refrain I heard from others when, also in 1988, I set out to write that article on Birch.

I volunteered for the job because I was a little confused myself. The background was this. I had spent several years by then writing for *Inc.*, a magazine for people who own or manage small, growing companies. (*Inc.* itself was an example of what Birch was talking about: started in 1979 by a man named Bernard Goldhirsh, it quickly grew to a nationwide circulation of 650,000, roughly the same as *Fortune*'s. In the process it created a hundred or so new jobs, my own included.) The magazine had discovered Birch early on, publishing a lengthy interview with him and engaging him to write a monthly column. Its writers and editors, for the most part, subscribed to his views about the economic importance of small companies. So, of course, did a lot of other people. Despite the Brookings study, Birch's message reached many receptive ears as the decade wore on. *Inc.* helped spread the word.

Even so, there were whispers. Dun & Bradstreet data is lousy, some researchers charged. Dun & Bradstreet data is excellent, said an expert in the field, but Birch draws conclusions from it that even D&B can't draw. And what about that Brookings study? Some observers believed it had discredited Birch; others pooh-poohed it. Birch himself issued puzzling, seemingly contradictory, statements. Small companies create 80 percent of new jobs? A *Wall Street Journal* article quoted him saying that 80 percent was a "silly number" that meant "almost nothing."

All this was intriguing enough. More intriguing still—and a subject neither I nor anyone else at *Inc.* knew much about—was the report that other researchers around the country were beginning to follow in Birch's methodological footsteps, analyzing the economy not by looking at gross unemployment rates, trade balances, and so on, but by compiling big computerized databases on individual businesses. Maybe they were finding out how right, or how wrong, Birch was. To me, that was a matter of no small interest. Despite my years at *Inc.*, I had a soft spot for the Galbraithian analysis that had seen me not only through college but through the 1970s, when I was editing a political-affairs quarterly. If the world was really different now, I would need to be convinced.

So I met with Birch and listened to his life story that day at

Cognetics. I also talked with one of the Brookings researchers, with many of the people doing Birch-like research (most of whom weren't economists, either), and with regular economists. I wrote my article; and when I realized that the article had only scratched the surface of what people were learning about the changing business landscape, I wrote several more. Slowly, I began to grasp why Birch and other researchers in the field so often spoke of a "new" economy. More and more Americans, so it seemed, were working and doing business in a marketplace in which large size no longer guaranteed survival, in which the points of reference that had helped us grasp the economic world since seventh grade were fading—and in which the new opportunities, the jobs and the growth, lay with companies we had never heard of.

A few fundamental findings marked the boundaries of this change.

First: *The several hundred companies described by John Kenneth Galbraith as "the heartland of the modern economy"—big, stable manufacturing corporations—had declined, both in size and in stability.* Frankly, I don't think this reflects poorly on Professor Galbraith, who as this book went to press was in his eighties and still writing. His analysis dated back to the 1960s, and the years since then have not been economically tranquil. Besides, he was the one who reminded observers of the economy to study the structures and institutions of the real world, not just the constructs of economic theory.

At any rate, the figures for the 1980s were hard to argue with.

In 1979 the Fortune 500 registered $1.4 trillion in sales, equivalent to 58 percent of GNP, and employed 16.2 million workers, equivalent to more than three-fourths of the manufacturing work force. The years 1981 and 1982 were recession years, and not surprisingly the big corporations laid off workers. But then something happened that had never happened before. The economy picked up, but the 500 continued to dwindle in importance. Every year thereafter their sales either inched upward or actually declined, rarely keeping pace with the growth of the economy as a whole. And every year but one (1984) their collective work force got smaller. By 1989 their combined sales totaled slightly less than $2.2 trillion, by then equivalent to only about 42 percent of GNP. Total employees amounted to only 12.5 million, about three-fifths of the manufacturing work force.

To put the matter more starkly: between 1979 and 1989 the

American economy *added* nearly 19 million new jobs. The Fortune 500 *lost* 3.7 million.

To be sure, *Fortune*'s famous list is of the 500 largest manufacturing companies, and manufacturing employment didn't grow much in the 1980s. (Contrary to popular belief, it didn't decline much either.) But this was a phenomenon of size, not just of economic sector. Consider the "Service 500," a supplementary listing of service-industry companies begun by the magazine in the early 1980s. Between 1982 and 1989 employment in these 500 companies rose by 2 million, or 18 percent, only a small fraction of overall job growth in service-producing industries. In services, at any rate, the 500 largest companies employed less than 15 percent of workers.

Stability was lacking as well.

Fortune's first listing of the industrial 500 appeared in 1955, in the midst of Eisenhower-era calm. During the next quarter-century fewer than ten companies a year, on average, dropped off the list. There was no reason for the number to be any higher. Takeovers were unknown then, and a position on the magazine's list virtually assured profitability. "Big corporations," wrote Galbraith, "do not lose money." In 1957, he observed, there was a mild recession, yet not one of the 100 largest industrial corporations failed to return a profit. In 1964, a prosperous year, the top 100 again all made money, and only seven companies among the whole 500 were in the red. What a contrast with 1988! That year—so profitable, on the whole, that *Fortune* gleefully headlined its report "The Biggest Blow-Out Ever"—*forty-two* of the 500 companies lost money, eleven of them for the second successive year. The conglomerate LTV, number 56 on the list, lost $3 billion. What with shrinking, being acquired, or deciding to get out of manufacturing, some 143 companies had disappeared from the list between 1983 and 1988—about twenty-eight a year, on average.

Make no mistake: the American economy in the 1980s continued to be influenced mightily by its largest corporations, and the United States became home to more and more operations run by other countries' largest enterprises. We were not returning to the era of workshops and family-run factories. But the fundamental postwar trend—the same group of huge corporations getting ever bigger and more dominant—came to an end.

Second: *Newer, smaller businesses took up the economic slack.*

A large number of companies were started in the 1980s. A large number of small businesses grew, some of them into good-size concerns. And, yes, all these companies as a group did account for a disproportionate share of new jobs.

When the dust stirred up between Brookings and Birch had settled, a couple of facts became clear. One, Birch had not made a boneheaded play and confused establishments with companies; he had indeed performed the laborious task of linking up all the individual establishment records provided by D&B with those of their corporate parents. Two, the Brookings researchers had made some blunders of their own, notably in assuming that no overseas jobs were included in the employment totals reported for large, multinational corporations. That said, differences remained. The Dun & Bradstreet data were, after all, pretty raw, and turning the millions of records into useful statistics required a series of decisions about how to fill in gaps, search out errors, and reconcile the list with guideposts such as the Labor Department's figures on total employment. Make different decisions along the way and you'd come out with different figures.*

The particulars of the dispute, however, were soon buried by the sands of time. With Ronald Reagan in the White House, the SBA no longer wanted Brookings—an institute identified with the Democrats—as its contractor. Never mind: in good Washington fashion, Catherine Armington and Marjorie Odle moved over to an organization called Applied Systems Institute and proceeded to win a new contract for managing the database. Working with SBA economists, they continued to refine their methodologies and to collect data every two years.

The findings? Both Birch and the SBA discovered that there was no consistent figure, and hence no way of saying that small companies always accounted for x percent of new jobs. In some years they might be responsible for 100 percent of new jobs. In other years—when bigger businesses were expanding—the proportion would be smaller.

---

*The task has always been complicated by periodic changes in D&B's data-gathering procedures. Birch observed that between 1976 and 1978 D&B had purged its lists of approximately 800,000 records that hadn't been accessed or updated in five years. These "spurious deaths" of companies made the file virtually unusable for the two-year period. Catherine Armington, coauthor of the Brookings study, remembered an opposite glitch in 1985: D&B made a special effort to enumerate all the branches of the 3,000 largest companies and suddenly came up with something like 73,000 "new" branches. "We had to review the whole database and impose constant rules that would supersede D&B's where necessary," she said.

That explained Birch's otherwise cryptic comment that 80 percent was a "silly number." The years 1978 and 1980, which Armington and Odle studied, marked a period when bigger companies were growing. That helped account for the gap between their original work and Birch's.

Even the SBA's relatively conservative methodology, however, turned up one consistent finding: since 1976, small companies were more important job generators than large ones. Businesses with fewer than 500 workers employed roughly half the work force, for example, but accounted for about three-fifths of the new jobs on average. Those with fewer than 100, or fewer than twenty, showed a similar disproportion. The figure varied from place to place as well as from time period to time period. But few serious students of the subject doubted the importance of small companies in creating new jobs.*

Third: *The new importance of entrepreneurship and small-company growth was suggested by other statistics, some of them even put forth by real economists.*

• Dun & Bradstreet's count of new incorporations rose from 264,000 in 1970 to 534,000 in 1980—and then to 684,000 in 1988. The "new incorps" figure is never a good measure of real new businesses, since some unknown fraction of them are entities incorporated only for legal or tax purposes (a neighborhood association, say, or an unincorporated business deciding to incorporate). Even so, the trend line was hard to ignore.

• Economists William A. Brock, of the University of Wisconsin, and David S. Evans, of Fordham University, analyzed a rough-and-ready measure of firm size, obtained by taking America's gross national product (corrected for inflation) and dividing it by the number of companies filing tax returns. GNP per company, so to speak, rose

---

*Employers Large and Small, a 1990 book by Charles Brown (of the University of Michigan) and James Hamilton and James Medoff (of Harvard), was seen by its authors and in press accounts as an attack on Birch. But it didn't really dispute this conclusion. "Small business's share of new jobs," said the authors, "is clearly impressive."

The three scholars did point out that small-company jobs might not be long lasting, and that many jobs apparently created by "small" companies were actually created by *new* companies that remained small only for a while. They also argued that small companies shouldn't get special treatment from the government. Birch himself wouldn't disagree with any of these points. Except for a gratuitous repetition of the canard that Birch confused companies with establishments, the book was less an attack on Birch than on advocates of small business, who frequently availed themselves of Birch's numbers.

steadily for most of the postwar era, from $150,000 in 1947 to $245,000 in 1980. This was consistent with the notion of the big getting bigger. Then the trend turned downward; by 1987 the figure was only $210,000.

• According to an analysis by Zoltan J. Acs and David B. Audretsch, editors of the journal *Small Business Economics,* small companies' share of sales in the economy was gradually creeping upward in the 1980s. This phenomenon was partly due to the growth of service industries, in which companies tend to be smaller, on average, than in other sectors. But even in manufacturing—historically the segment of the economy most dominated by big companies—small companies' share of sales rose more than five percentage points between 1976 and 1986.

• Research on state and regional economies—some utilizing independent, non-D&B data—bore out Birch's findings. A 1981 study by Michael B. Teitz and his colleagues at the University of California at Berkeley concluded that small companies "dominate" job generation in California. A 1989 study by John E. Jackson, of the University of Michigan, found new and small companies accounting for four-fifths of Michigan's new jobs.

• The change seemed to be international in scope. In 1985 the Organization for Economic Cooperation and Development, in Europe, concluded that "small firms have been particularly important in net job growth over the past 10 or 15 years." A 1987 survey for the International Institute for Labour Studies, in Geneva, found that "most countries" in the industrialized non-Communist world had experienced a post–World War II decline in small-company employment, followed by a rise beginning in the 1970s.

Now this is all pretty abstract, not to mention hard to believe. *Wait a minute,* I hear you say. *Surely companies were getting bigger, not smaller, during the 1980s. What about all those giant mergers and buyouts I read about? What about Time Warner, RJR Nabisco, and Chevron snapping up Gulf Oil?* Bear with me: we'll get to mergers and takeovers in the next chapter. In the meantime, remember that a few big combinations were just that, a few big combinations. Remember, too, that mergers and buyouts often resulted in a big company being broken up into its component parts (selling off assets, Wall Street called it).

As for the abstractness of all those statistics, I sympathize—which is why, a year or so after talking with Birch, I decided to visit a man named Sammis B. White, in Milwaukee. White was one of several researchers around the country who were utilizing Birch's methods to learn more about regional economies. I had heard that his approach was more refined than most, and that he was in the midst of what would probably be the definitive study of the Milwaukee area.

THE MILWAUKEE STUDY

In Milwaukee, the changing economy was anything but abstract.

One of the city's biggest companies at the start of the 1980s, for example, was Allis-Chalmers Corporation. Allis-Chalmers made farm machinery, diesel engines, and other heavy equipment. In 1979 it employed nearly 30,000 people and racked up close to $2 billion in sales, which made it number 175 on the Fortune 500. In West Allis (a Milwaukee suburb so close to downtown it might as well be part of the city proper), the company's giant plants covered some 125 acres.

Then: *pffft*.

Hit by recessions, Japanese competition, and assorted other megatrends, Allis-Chalmers went broke. Divisions that anyone wanted were sold off, the others shut down. When I was visiting Milwaukee, in late 1989, the company was little more than a shell, with ten employees in West Allis and forty more operating a repair facility in Houston. Revenues that year came to $3.2 million, about the same as two McDonald's outlets.

Other big Milwaukee employers also ran into trouble during the decade. Allen-Bradley Company, the giant manufacturer of industrial controls, was sold off to Rockwell International after a bitter internal battle. Schlitz—the beer that made Milwaukee famous—was ignominiously bought out by Stroh and its operations moved out of the city. Among them these big companies were responsible for thousands of lost jobs.

And yet somehow, incredibly, things seemed pretty good.

As the 1980s came to an end, Milwaukee's downtown wasn't sliding into Lake Michigan, as some had once predicted. On the contrary, it was coming off a five-year building boom, the likes of which hadn't been seen for decades. Unemployment was down to around 4 percent, a full percentage point below the national rate. Some suburban counties were seeing so much industrial and commercial development that companies could scarcely find enough workers. No one could entirely explain what was happening. Which industries were fueling all this growth? What companies were leading it?

Like Birch, Sam White was an unlikely explorer of such questions. Appointed to the University of Wisconsin's urban-planning department, he had spent most of his professional career pursuing ordinary interests for a planner: housing, neighborhood revitalization, and so forth. He hadn't even been interested in the business landscape until he saw it collapsing in the recession of the early 1980s. But a study of welfare recipients that he undertook for the county of Milwaukee underscored the disastrous implications of the collapse. "Things were so bad, the welfare population had increased by a factor of four. And 85 percent of them, we found, had held a steady, full-time job. We heard heartbreaking stories. 'I've been a responsible citizen. I've worked all my life. I was making $10, $12 an hour.' "

White wanted to understand that disintegration, and he wanted to understand why, later in the decade, the economy seemed to be reviving despite the continuing troubles of companies such as Allis-Chalmers. He had read Birch's work, and he wondered if small companies were playing as important a part in Milwaukee as they seemed to be nationally. Then, in 1986, he heard through the academic grapevine of data that might provide some answers.

The state of Wisconsin, like every state, maintains an unemployment insurance system. As part of the system, every company with at least one employee has to file a quarterly report. On it they are supposed to report the business they're in, how many employees they have at each location, and how much their payroll comes to.

Right there, White figured, would be the information he needed to understand the paradox of Milwaukee's economy. By looking at the records he could see which companies and industries were growing and which were shrinking. And the data might be even better than Dun & Bradstreet's. After all, every company operating in the state had to report its employment under penalty of law.

So he began making arrangements. The state of Wisconsin agreed to provide the data—ten years' worth of records covering nearly 50,000 businesses in the Milwaukee area. The cost was nominal, and the only stipulation was that White couldn't release information on individual companies. The University of Wisconsin agreed to provide computer time and graduate assistants. Organizations such as the Federal Reserve Bank of Chicago chipped in to help cover other expenses.

Then White began scrutinizing the data—and, like Birch, he found problems.

A company with plants all over the state would list all of its employees in its Milwaukee headquarters, creating the illusion of a huge downtown installation. Blips would appear: a sudden jump of 1,000 employees from one year to the next, in a company or institution White knew hadn't changed much. It was just the kind of discrepancy and inconsistency that Birch had wrestled with—the kind that some believed compromised Dun & Bradstreet's data.

Birch, working on a national scale, could write programs to correct or compensate for patterns of irregularity, and could check a few of the biggest, most obviously screwed-up records.

White, since he was focusing on only one metropolitan area, decided to call up the companies with questionable records. All of them.

Well, almost all. "If we called them all up, we'd still be on the phone," he said. There were 46,436 private- and public-sector establishments in the Milwaukee-area ten-year files, 30,000 or so for any given year. Undaunted, White had his graduate students analyze the records. Then they hit the phones. They called up or otherwise checked every manufacturing company, every company with more than fifty employees at one location, and every company that grew by more than twenty employees in one year. The calls—there were thousands of them—covered an estimated 70 percent of the region's employment and virtually all of the records that might be significant sources of error. When the graduate students were through, they had compiled a database of metropolitan business activity that no one, not even a real economist, could charge with gross inaccuracy.

When I visited in 1989, the analysis of this cleaned-up database was in full swing. White and his students had already produced papers tracking employment and payroll changes, by industry, in the city and in the suburbs. They had studied the industrial city of West Allis in detail, and graduate student Bill McMahon had produced a report on nearby Racine. For the moment, they were limiting themselves to the analysis of establishments, or places of business. Later they planned to analyze the data by company, linking branches into a single record for each enterprise.

Slowly, White's operation had begun to create a picture—and at least a partial explanation—of Milwaukee's puzzling economy. You could see the contours most plainly in a relatively small space, such as the city of West Allis.

By rights, West Allis should have been an economic basket case, a candidate for federal disaster relief. Anyone could see the reason just by driving down Greenfield Avenue: there was the huge Allis-Chalmers complex, or what was left of it, mostly shuttered and empty. Between 1979 and 1987 the collapse of Allis-Chalmers had eliminated close to 4,000 jobs in the city. West Allis as a whole, White and his colleagues found, had lost more than 8,000 factory jobs, or 56 percent of its manufacturing employment.

Overall employment in West Allis, however, had dropped only 10 percent. The city was enjoying nearly 4,000 new jobs in services, including almost 1,000 in health services and 2,600 in the diverse category known as business services. Nearly all of these jobs were in small establishments: the average size of a place of business in West Allis's service industries in 1987 was nineteen employees.

Surprisingly, manufacturing in West Allis was far from dead. While big companies had collapsed, smaller manufacturers were growing—in printing, in metalworking machinery, and several other industries. Total employment in small establishments (fewer than 250 employees) was growing as well. And the *number* of small establishments was increasing.

It was the phenomenon that David Birch had discovered—in spades. *All* of West Allis's loss in jobs was due to the decline at Allis-Chalmers and a few other big companies. *All* the new jobs came from smaller companies.

As West Allis went, so went the whole region. White's figures showed that essentially all of the jobs lost by the Milwaukee metropolitan area had been in large business establishments. The largest manufacturers had lost about 50,000 jobs between 1979 and 1987, a drop of 44 percent, and midsize manufacturers had declined by 5,000 jobs. Every other size category of business, in both manufacturing and services, showed an increase in employment. In manufacturing, employment in companies with fewer than twenty workers rose 28 percent. In services, growth was strongest in the 100- to 250-employee range, and weakest in the more-than-500 range. One county in the region, Waukesha, to the west of the city, actually gained 229 new manufacturing companies and about 4,000 manufacturing jobs, along with 1,242 new service-industry businesses and more than 21,000 service-industry jobs.

If you were seeking a visible symbol of the change, you needed to look no farther than the old Schlitz brewery, not far from downtown. In the early 1950s it had been the largest brewery in the world; thirty years later, when Stroh acquired Schlitz, it was shut down. Redeveloped shortly before I visited, the plant was now occupied by a cable television company, a health-care organization, a construction business, a restaurant, and several nonprofits.

"There are as many jobs in that building now," said Tim Sheehy of the Metropolitan Milwaukee Association of Commerce, "as there were when Schlitz was there. But a lot of them are with smaller organizations."

Something, it was plain, had happened to the business landscape we used to know.

Companies that had once dominated the marketplace were declining in importance. A host of smaller businesses seemed to be flourishing. The dynamism—the growth—in the economy seemed to have shifted from large to small, from the familiar to the not-so-familiar. To Galbraith, the large corporations were "the part of the economy which, automatically, we identify with modern industrial society." That was no longer true.

But the research of Birch, White, and the others raised sizable questions. What had happened to the Fortune 500? Why were smaller companies apparently prospering when big, seemingly more powerful ones were floundering? Who were these smaller businesses, anyway? It seemed unlikely that they were just video stores and fast-food eateries; plenty, after all, were in manufacturing. But could small businesses of any sort provide the innovation and technological sophistication that drive a modern economy? Could they provide not just jobs but wealth, growth, and opportunities?

To answer these questions is to understand much about the tremors and convulsions that have shaken American business to the core during the past twenty years. To learn about the sometimes-obscure world of thriving small companies is to get a glimpse of the economic landscape we're likely to be living and working in for some time to come.

2

The End
of the Corporate Era

E VEN FROM the sidelines—let alone if your job was on
the line—the turbulence that shook corporate America during the
1980s was something to behold.

Huge companies were bought out or taken over, thereby vanishing as independent entities. Gulf Oil was swallowed up by Chevron,
Kraft Foods by Philip Morris, RCA by General Electric. Other huge
companies clung tenuously to independence, often by paying off
would-be predators. Gillette fought off two takeover attempts in as
many years, taking on massive amounts of debt to do so. Goodyear's
continuing independence cost its shareholders $93 million.

A few companies, such as newly merged Time Inc. and Warner
Communications, tried to turn themselves into world-straddling
giants. Others sought desperately to shrink, both by trimming their
operations ("downsizing") and by selling off whole divisions (divestiture). The surgery could be radical. Bethlehem Steel dwindled from
nearly 100,000 employees in 1979 to 30,500 in 1989. Exxon, according
to *Fortune,* "closed nine refineries, slashed tanker capacity by 25%,
shed more than 10,000 service stations, and trimmed more than
24,000 employees" in just two years. (It wound up the decade with a
work force only three-fifths as large as what it had started with.)
Singer—a company instantly and automatically identified with sew-
ing—got rid of its sewing-machine division. Then Singer itself was
taken over and dismantled.

The 1980s also taught us the words *leveraged buyout,* or LBO. In some LBOs, divisions of companies were bought up by their managers, thus creating separate, smaller, privately held enterprises. In others, whole corporations were "taken private" by LBO specialists such as the Wall Street firm of Kohlberg Kravis Roberts & Company. The owners of these newly private companies often sold off chunks of them to pay down the big debts they'd taken on to make the purchase. (Remember the *l* in LBO; these deals were called "leveraged" for a reason.) KKR, which engineered a buyout of the just-merged R.J. Reynolds and Nabisco, peddled $5 billion worth of the company's operations within a year of taking it over. (The Del Monte Foods division alone brought $1.5 billion.) Back in 1979, according to figures compiled by Harvard Business School professor Michael C. Jensen, there were 75 leveraged buyouts, with a total value (in 1988 dollars) of $1.4 billion. Nine years later there were 214, with a total value of $77 billion.

Looking back on this mercurial decade, *Fortune* could hardly believe what was happening. It was "a new era of rapid rise and ruin," the magazine announced in its 1989 listing of the 500 largest industrial corporations. "Modern business has never seen anything like it." Writer John Paul Newport, Jr., pointed out that 143 companies that had been on the list five years earlier were missing from the current list—including more than 100 acquired, merged, or taken private. "It was eat or be eaten." And then there was the dramatic number that reflected all the sell-offs, layoffs, bust-ups, and downsizings: the Fortune 500 as a group employed 3.7 million fewer people in 1989 than in 1979, though the economy had added nearly 19 million new jobs.

What *was* going on here, anyway? To the managers and employees involved, the convulsions were devastating; to the rest of us, unnerving. Mostly we blamed the avaricious takeover artists and mergers-and-acquisitions specialists, Wall Street hustlers who seemed to make such a killing on every transaction. They were "paper entrepreneurs," charged critics such as Harvard's Robert B. Reich: all they did was rearrange our economy's assets rather than add to them. And they were pushing deal after deal. "Paper entrepreneurs have discovered there is no necessary limit to the amount of service they can urge on their customers and thereupon provide. Deals thus have become more plentiful, and larger."

The critics were partly right: any time millions can be made by arranging a sale, there will be plenty of eager salespeople. But the view that Wall Street greedheads were responsible for all the corporate restructuring begged a few questions. Avarice was not invented in the 1980s. Why did the takeover wave happen then and not before? What had happened to the economic power—the seeming invulnerability—of large corporations? How did companies that had once ruled the economic roost find themselves ready for the plucking?

Answering these questions—explaining the disintegration of corporate America—will take us back at least twenty-five years. For takeovers and other corporate restructurings were, at their roots, manifestations not just of greed or fancy financial footwork but of fundamental, long-term changes in the marketplace. And it's all those changes, not takeovers alone, that laid the groundwork for a new economy.

THE UPHEAVALS

In the mid-1960s, America's big corporations sat astride the economic world. Fun facts to know and tell: All but two of the world's twenty biggest companies were American. The United States produced more manufactured goods than the next nine industrial nations put together. General Motors (one company) earned as much in profits as the ten biggest companies of France, Great Britain, and West Germany *combined* (that's thirty companies). In 1967 an influential French journalist named Jean-Jacques Servan-Schreiber published a book called *Le défi américain (The American Challenge);* in it he predicted that the third-biggest industrial power, after the United States and the Soviet Union, would soon be U.S. corporations based in Europe. Servan-Schreiber hadn't forgotten Japan; he asserted that both Japan and Sweden would do well in the future. They just wouldn't be "strong enough to deal with the U.S. as equals, nor [would] they be truly competitive." So much for his crystal ball.

Here at home, big companies were spreading their tentacles. R.J. Reynolds diversified from cigarettes into foodstuffs and freight shipping, Borden from dairy products into glue, fabrics, plastics, chemicals, toilet preparations, and surgical appliances. ITT's Harold Geneen, *conglomerateur extraordinaire,* acquired Avis Rent-a-Car, Sheraton, Continental Baking, Levitt & Sons (the builders of Levittowns), and nearly fifty other companies. A series of little-noticed buyouts and combinations in textiles, agriculture, petroleum, and home appliances led to more and more domination of those industries by the biggest companies. Overall, the number of large acquisitions rose from 800 or 900 a year in the early 1960s to well over 2,000 by decade's end. Optimism ruled: the economy was booming and the stock market was high. A decade that was tumultuous in so many other respects was at least placid economically: Times were good.

Then came the 1970s.

The 1970s don't have a distinctive identity, like the revolutionary 1960s or the yuppified 1980s. But they were nonetheless unusual: they were years of mind-bending economic disruption. Let me refresh your memory—or, if you were born after 1965, add to it.

The decade got off to a rocky start. Inflation was up, thanks largely to the Vietnam War; oddly, so was unemployment. The post–World War II system of international trade, with other nations' currencies roughly pegged to the dollar, was no longer working; too many dollars were accumulating overseas, and the dollar had to be devalued. A series of agricultural disasters in 1971 and 1972 drove up the price of food. Still, these were ordinary calamities. In time, governments and businesses would have corrected or adapted to the problems.

As the years wore on, however, it became plain that the marketplace—the economic environment—wasn't just shifting slightly, it was undergoing a series of upheavals. Three in particular stand out. One was the continuing turmoil in the macroeconomy, meaning overall levels of prices and output. The second was the dramatic rise in international competition. The third was a revolution in technology.

The Macroeconomy. By most calculations, the troubles affecting the nation's economy as a whole began with the Organization of Petroleum Exporting Countries.

OPEC, the brainchild of a Venezuelan oil lawyer named Juan Pablo Perez Alfonso, had been around since 1960, but its attempts to control the international oil market had never amounted to much. Then, on October 6, 1973, the Jewish Day of Atonement, Egyptian president Anwar el-Sadat, later to be hailed by President Jimmy Carter as a man of peace, launched a surprise attack on Israel. Events unfolded quickly.

"In the initial fighting" (the chronology is detailed in Steven A.

Schneider's definitive study, *The Oil Price Revolution*), "Israel suffered heavy losses of troops and equipment and quickly turned to the United States to replace its supplies."

Though nervous about antagonizing the Arab world, from which it imported a small but rapidly growing percentage of its oil, the United States agreed to resupply Israel.

Meeting in Kuwait on October 17, the Arab oil ministers called for production cutbacks and voluntary, country-by-country embargoes on exports to the United States. Saudi Arabia, by far the largest oil producer, held off, hoping to convince the United States to moderate its support of Israel.

On October 19, President Nixon sent Congress a message asking for $2.2 billion in additional military assistance to Israel.

On October 20, Saudi Arabia banned oil shipments to America.

The immediate effects of the embargo were simple: shortages, reflected in long lines of cars at gas stations, and sharp price hikes. Between 1972 and 1974 the average price of fuel oil jumped 80 percent, the price of gasoline close to 50 percent. But the short-term fallout paled beside the long-term effects. Though hardly anyone had noticed, the United States had been importing more and more of its oil over the years—and so was vulnerable, as it had never been before, to a cartel such as OPEC. For its part, OPEC was delighted to find it was now capable of controlling the international price of crude, and began doing just that. All during the 1970s the price of oil went up. In 1970 the price of crude averaged about $3 a barrel. Ten years later, right after an OPEC meeting in Venezuela, the newspapers were reporting an average price for crude of over $30.

As the United States began shipping money to the OPEC nations, its own economy staggered. A recession in 1974 and 1975 was accompanied by inflation rates that hadn't been seen since right after World War II. (The phrase *double-digit inflation* made its unhappy appearance.) Incomes stagnated: real wages fell in 1974 and again in 1975, declining more than a trivial amount for the first time since the Depression. The value of the dollar on international markets fell, recovered, fell again. All such turmoil led otherwise sensible people to think that, if Judgment Day weren't at hand, it was at least on its way. "Among business leaders, fear is developing that a gathering crisis will turn the nation decisively toward socialist patterns," reported a sober *U.S. News & World Report* in July 1976. "One indication: a *Harvard Business Review* poll of readers—most of them corporate executives—who by a big majority foresaw a shift to a more communal and planned society."

Paranoia in the executive suites? Maybe. But there was a perverse logic to the fear, because corporate executives found themselves living out a peculiar nightmare, unlike anything they had known. Energy costs were skyrocketing. Spot shortages cropped up. "We always assumed that if we could sell [a product], we could get the raw materials," said an International Harvester executive in 1974. "That is just no longer true." Inflation fed on itself: scrambling to keep up, workers demanded higher wages and suppliers charged higher prices. Consumer behavior grew erratic, alternating between nervous belt-tightening and unrestrained borrowing and spending. With costs rising and demand uncertain, profits fell. The stock market sank into a kind of stupor.

So what should a manager do? Invest in new plants and bring out new products now, or wait until things improved? Who knew when that would be? The passing years brought only more chaos. In early 1979, Iranian revolutionaries deposed the shah and interrupted the flow of oil from Iran, resulting in more price hikes, more gas lines, and more inflation. Finally, in October 1979, the Fed made its famous move to curb inflation by letting interest rates rise virtually unchecked. The prime nearly tripled, peaking at around 20 percent. The real interest rate—meaning how much a loan cost after you allowed for inflation—went from *near zero* in 1979 to more than 9 percent in 1981.

The slump that followed was a fitting close to an already grim ten years. The Fed's draconian move worked: high interest rates discouraged borrowing, forced consumers and businesses to cut back drastically on spending, and thereby eased the pressure on prices. These cutbacks, in turn, led to a brutal recession, even worse than that of 1974 and 1975. In 1982 the national unemployment rate hit 10 percent. The gross national product (corrected for inflation), which in good times rises 3 percent to 4 percent a year, *fell* 2.5 percent. Local conditions could be worse still. In Michigan, one worker out of every six was unemployed.

International Competition. In 1972, my brother Jim, who lived upstairs from me at the time, bought a Datsun station wagon. This was considered a pretty radical move for a New Englander; only one other friend back then had a Japanese car. But those who bought them found that the cars were instant conversation pieces and lent their buyers an air of knowledgeable practicality ("Yeah, it handles like a European car. And the price!"). In the early 1970s Volkswagen was still the leading import, selling as many cars as Toyota and Nissan combined. But the Japanese were coming on strong, particularly in California, and they got a boost from OPEC. When the first oil shortage hit, Nissan discovered that its Datsun 1200 had been cited for best gas mileage by the U.S. Department of Transportation. The company immediately aired an ad portraying a Datsun being driven coast to coast, complete with a team of independent experts to certify that it had made a then-incredible 40 miles a gallon on the trip. The tag line: "Datsun saves." By 1975 Toyota had passed Volkswagen, with Nissan close behind, and imported cars as a group accounted for 18 percent of the market, three times their share only ten years earlier.

As Japanese cars began flooding the market, so did Japanese radios, TV sets, record players, cameras, and dozens of other products—even machine tools, an industry whose story is knowledgeably told by Max Holland in his 1989 book, *When the Machine Stopped.* As late as the early 1960s both German and American machine-tool makers were enjoying a booming market *in Japan.* Japanese companies fought back, getting help both from the Ministry of International Trade and Industry (MITI) and from friendly U.S. companies willing to license their technology; by 1965 they had reclaimed much of their domestic market. But the victory looked pyrrhic. Japan's home market was so sluggish, and competition in the industry so intense, that many machine-tool companies went broke. MITI in 1965 declared the industry one of the "sick men" of the Japanese economy.

What turned the industry around wasn't the efforts of MITI (though it tried) but the persistence of individual tool builders such as Yamazaki Machinery. Like other Japanese companies at the time, Yamazaki concentrated on inexpensive, standard-model machine tools, becoming known in the United States for low-priced engine lathes. But the company also invested heavily in state-of-the-art numerical-control machine tools, and in the early 1970s bought more licenses from U.S. companies, boosting its technological capabilities still further. Soon Yamazaki was offering technically sophisticated tools that, according to Holland's account, were both "more reliable and considerably less expensive than American equivalents." (In 1976, for example, the company was selling a machining center for roughly half what its U.S. licensor charged for a similar product.) Nor was Yamazaki alone. By 1978 imported machine tools were occupying up to 22 percent of the market, with Japan "rapidly supplanting Germany as the number-one supplier of tools to the U.S. market."

In the 20 years since Americans first noticed the Japanese as competitors, we have heard many explanations for their preeminence in manufacturing. But the case studies of Japanese industry that are now beginning to appear suggest nothing magical. The Japanese government's efforts to foster innovation, and to protect Japan's industries from too much international competition, surely helped. But the companies themselves, fiercely competitive with one another, demonstrated an amazing willingness to experiment and to learn. The reward, of course, was the huge, lucrative American marketplace. The first Toyota sold in the United States bombed so badly that the company withdrew from the market for three years. The first Yamazaki lathes, sent here in 1962, were rejected as unsatisfactory in quality by the U.S. distributor. American corporations, in their heyday, could take their country's market for granted; all they had to do, so it seemed, was what they had always done. The Japanese knew they didn't have a prayer unless they could somehow learn to make goods that were higher in quality and lower in price than their U.S.-made counterparts. Like Avis, they tried harder.

Anyway, the Japanese were soon joined by others. In 1970 Americans imported not quite one-tenth of the goods they used. By 1980 that figure had grown to one-fifth and was still climbing. More and more imports were coming from South Korea, Taiwan, Singapore, Hong Kong, and China. Contrary to what we're sometimes told, the United States was not taking a shellacking in every industry; exports, too, rose rapidly, although not as rapidly as imports. And from the point of view of consumers, the imports were generally beneficial: the Japanese and other overseas suppliers provided us with cheap, high-quality goods. That's why we bought from them.

From a large corporation's point of view, however, what mattered was neither the United States's relative position in international trade (which got most of the attention in Washington) nor whatever benefits consumers might be enjoying from the growth in imports. What mattered was that suddenly the corporation's products were facing blistering new competition, both at home and abroad. By 1980, Harvard's Reich calculated, "more than 70 percent of all the goods produced in the United States were actively competing with foreign-made goods." American companies weren't used to this: most had competed only with each other. Now they were up against enterprises whose executives faced different sets of costs, and who had learned different lessons about how to play the game.

Technology. In the 1950s and 1960s the most visible new technologies were self-contained inventions, and were therefore easily dominated by a single company or small group of companies (Polaroid cameras, Xerox copiers, RCA's "compatible color" TV systems). For a while that was even true of computers, with IBM and a handful of competitors making machines for a small number of customers. In the mid-1960s there were roughly 30,000 computers in use in the United States. Nearly all were owned or used by large organizations, because the computers of the day were cost-effective only when large amounts of information needed to be processed.

The proliferation of minicomputers in the late 1960s began to undermine that state of affairs, and by 1976 the number of computers in the United States had increased sevenfold. But the true turning point in the computer revolution was the invention of the microprocessor, the "computer on a chip" introduced to the market by Intel Corporation in 1971. (Once, in the middle 1970s, an electronics executive speaking to a convention audience wanted to dramatize how much things had changed in his industry; he pulled eighteen microprocessors from his pocket and tossed them into the startled crowd. Twenty years earlier, he explained, the computing power represented by those chips would have cost $18 million.)

Soon engineers and businesspeople were arguing about the ramifications. Computers themselves could be made much smaller and cheaper than anyone had ever dreamed. The first "personal computer," the MITS Altair, was advertised to electronics hobbyists in January 1975; the Apple II followed in 1977. Would *every* business soon have its own computer? Every home? The possibilities boggled the mind. Maybe more important, some computing power could now be cheaply built into any number of other products and manufacturing processes. Silicon chips could substitute for electrical switches, relays, controls. They could be programmed to run machinery and automobile engines. They could be hooked into home furnaces, appliances, telephones, television sets. Who knew the limits?

We're used to regarding this ongoing technological revolution from the citizen's perspective, either marveling at the wonders or worrying how we'll cope with machines we can't understand. But let's look at it from the perspective of an executive back then, sitting

atop a corporation that had probably spent a lot of money on old—
and no doubt more expensive—technologies. From this vantage
point, microchips were ants at the economic picnic, upsetting the
stability of the marketplace in a number of ways:

• *Whole categories of existing products and services could rapidly become obsolete.* Since 1975 we have seen the virtual demise of
mechanical cash registers, rotary-dial telephones, electric typewriters,
mechanical adding machines, reel-to-reel tape recorders, home-movie
cameras, and all sorts of industrial instruments and controls. Progress? To a company watching its market evaporate, it could look like
a catastrophe. (Western Union, which had hung on for most of the
telephone age, lost more than $1 billion in 1988 because it failed to
anticipate the effect of fax machines on its hitherto-profitable telex
network.)

• *Adroit new companies could elbow aside established manufacturers who didn't move fast enough.* Minicomputers were introduced not by established computer makers but by new enterprises
such as Digital Equipment Corporation. Microcomputers—personal
computers—were introduced by another generation of entrepreneurs.
With the exception of IBM, no established computer company has
made a dent in the personal-computer market. It's not because there
wasn't any room there; as late as 1985 new personal-computer manufacturers were still entering the business.

Microelectronics affected other nooks and crannies of the marketplace, over time, in similar ways. A *Business Week* clip in my files,
from 1976, reports that Bru-Der Instrument Corporation was under-
cutting the makers of conventional taxi meters with a cheaper electronic model. A 1989 clip, from the *New York Times,* tells how
International Game Technology came to dominate the Nevada slot-
machine business because the old-line leader, Bally Manufacturing
Corporation, "was slow to adopt the computer technology that revo-
lutionized gaming machines."

• *Big companies had to begin placing bets on the new technology, only some of which would pay off.* Appliance maker Amana
Corporation, a subsidiary of Raytheon, gambled on a microproces-
sor-controlled microwave oven (the "Touchmatic"), which it
brought out in 1975. Bingo: Its oven sales rose 62 percent that year
and even more in 1976. ("Nothing in the appliance industry has ever
taken off like the Touchmatic," exulted Amana vice-president Richard D. Maxwell.) Texas Instruments, a large and highly sophisticated

electronics company whose engineers had matched Intel virtually step for step in the development of the microprocessor, spent millions in the 1970s in an effort to dominate the new digital-watch business. In 1976, with other companies' digitals up around $100, it shocked the industry by announcing a watch priced at $20. In 1977 it drove the price down to $10. Three years later TI was indeed a leader in watches, doing an estimated $70 million a year—and was making so little money it decided to quit the business entirely, idling more than 2,000 workers. The company's strategy, observed *The Economist,* "drove TI way down to the bottom of the market, to compete with watches from Japan, and then with even cheaper models assembled in Hong Kong."

Any one of these three phenomena would have upset the economic environment. Together they amounted to a tidal wave of turmoil. Worse, other unsettling trends seemed to magnify the upheavals. One was a new wave of regulation. Companies that had learned to live with traditional regulatory agencies, such as the Federal Trade Commission, now found themselves confronting the Environmental Protection Agency (1970), the Occupational Safety and Health Administration (1971), the Consumer Product Safety Commission (1970), the Magnuson-Moss Warranty Act (1975), which beefed up the FTC's consumer-protection powers, and the Employee Retirement Income Security Act (1974), which was the first in a series of increasingly restrictive laws governing pension funds and other benefits. All of these new agencies were venturing onto untrodden ground, which meant that no one could foresee what they would actually do—or, indeed, how long they would last. You might support the goals of any or all of them, but there was no doubt they added to the uncertainty of doing business.

The wave of deregulation at the end of the decade had a similarly destabilizing effect. "Deregulation" as it was implemented in the late 1970s didn't mean getting rid of environmental and social regulatory agencies such as OSHA (as plenty of recalcitrant businesspeople would have liked); it meant abolishing "economic" regulators such as the Civil Aeronautics Board, which apportioned air routes and set air-fares. Airlines, trucking companies, banks, railroads, and telecommunications companies were all abruptly escorted out of their cozy regulated environments into the harsh weather of competition. And all those businesses, in turn, were major providers of services to other companies, who found themselves facing bewildering arrays of new "products" in transportation, communication, and financial services. Gone were the days when a manager could order a telephone system just by calling the only phone company in town.

THE UNRAVELING

To understand the effects of all this turbulence on U.S. business, remember what John Kenneth Galbraith taught us about the corporate system.

A large corporation, Galbraith said, sought control over its marketplace. That was the essential logic of size: the bigger you were, the more resources you could bring to bear on just this task. Suppliers could be dominated or bought up, and labor commandeered with the promise of high wages. Big, technologically sophisticated plants could pour out products by the truckload, and heavy marketing budgets could (usually) persuade consumers to snap them up. Predictable costs, predictable revenues, predictable profits: exactly what shareholders liked to see, and exactly what the astute head of a big company could regularly deliver. Competitors, most of them American, faced similar costs and business conditions. Since no big company was likely to be driven out of business, "competition" meant jostling for a point or two of market share.

The catch in this logic, of course, was that big investments in managing the marketplace—new factories, new products, new marketing blitzes—would pay off only so long as everything else in the environment remained stable. Costs couldn't change. Competitors and consumers had to keep on doing pretty much what they had done in the past. In the 1970s such stability vanished. Because of the economic situation, consumers began behaving unpredictably and costs went haywire. Competitors from Japan and elsewhere entered the market, playing by different rules. Suddenly, big investments might as easily lead to big losses as to big gains. Size might even be a handicap: a large corporation might be too slow to adapt to the new conditions.

The sources of uncertainty affected executives of different industries in different ways. Say that you're running an auto company. You're under attack by imports, which are providing consumers with choices they have never had before. You're not sure what buyers are looking for, anyway. Do they want fuel-efficient cars? Small, four-cylinder cars accounted for 2 percent of U.S. production in 1970, jumped to 12 percent in 1974, fell to half that in 1977, and skyrocketed to 29 percent by 1980. Such uncertainties were one cause of Chrysler Corporation's brush with bankruptcy in 1979.

Or, say that you're in the steel business. You're facing recessions, which you might be used to, and foreign competition, which you're surely not used to. Imports of steel-mill products rose nearly 50 percent between 1970 and 1981. Are you likely to realize, amid the onslaught of imports, that Americans aren't using as much steel per dollar of GNP as they once did—partly because Detroit is making smaller, lighter cars?

Or suppose you run one of the many giant companies that supply the construction industry. Your raw-materials costs are suddenly hard to predict, and your business is being battered both by recessions and by high interest rates. Housing starts plummeted in the mid-1970s, rose, plummeted again. Fewer homes were started in 1982 than in any year since 1946—*even though roughly half the huge baby-boom generation was then between 25 and 35.*

Since real-life experience is more instructive than supposition, consider the sorry position of the men—there were several of them—who ran, or tried to run, a company once known as Radio Corporation of America. It was a company so hard hit by the decade's events that it stands as a sort of symbol for America's business decline. Conveniently, it also shows how disastrous the interplay of all the upheavals could be.

In the late 1960s, Robert W. Sarnoff was slowly taking control of RCA from his father, David Sarnoff, who was grudgingly relinquishing it. The younger Sarnoff, known as Bob or Bobby, turned fifty in 1968. He was pudgy and amiable, and had a reputation for having a short attention span. Had he been named Smith, observes historian Robert Sobel, "he doubtless wouldn't have gone to the top at RCA, or perhaps anywhere else, and everyone (including him) knew it, or at least behaved as though this were so." But never mind. "General" David Sarnoff, as the father liked to be called, had built RCA into one of America's premier technology-based companies, and had run it as his own. Son Bobby was the designated heir, and no one was really expected to quibble.

Besides, how much trouble could Bobby Sarnoff get the company into? Except for an ill-conceived venture into the computer business, everything RCA touched seemed golden.

It was far and away the largest producer of color television sets; fearing antitrust problems more than competition, it even sold picture tubes to other companies. It was a major manufacturer of black-and-white sets, radios, record players, and tape recorders. It owned NBC, then the largest network, and was a familiar name in the recording industry. A prime defense contractor, it made high-tech equipment such as space communications and guidance systems. Even its forays into conglomerate building—*de rigueur* for a big company back then—looked classy. In 1966 it bought Random House, one of the nation's top-ranked publishers. A year later it acquired Hertz Corporation, number one in rental cars. Though RCA was already a giant in 1959, ranking number 24 on the Fortune 500, it grew steadily throughout the 1960s, more than doubling its sales and adding 42,000 employees worldwide. By 1969 it ranked number 21. It was an archetypal market-dominating American company.

For a while, Bobby Sarnoff played around, his father nervously looking on. He changed the name of the company from Radio Corporation of America to just plain RCA. He got rid of the old logotype (three letters in a circle with a lightning bolt coming out of the *A*) and replaced it with a 1960s-modern, block-letter RCA logo. But by 1971, when his father died, Bob was readying the company for yet another decade of growth. He sold off the money-losing computer division, absorbing a big loss. He invested heavily in new consumer-electronics plants in Europe, getting set for what RCA executives figured would be the next monster market for color TVs. There were hints in the air of dramatic technological breakthroughs. For example, the company invited journalists to its newly christened David Sarnoff Research Center in Princeton, New Jersey, and showed them a prototype video product called HoloTape. Soon, promised Bob Sarnoff, consumers would be able to buy a HoloTape player for about $400, and half-hour-long "program albums" for $10 apiece. Surely HoloTape would create nearly as big a market as color TV itself.

On one level, the history of RCA in the following decade resembled a who's-in-charge-here situation comedy. The company had had a reputation for Byzantine internal politics under General Sarnoff. Even so, the boardroom farces of the 1970s were extreme:

• In November 1975 RCA's board of directors abruptly refused to renew Bob Sarnoff's contract as chairman and chief executive officer. The most visible reason was the company's shoddy performance during the recession: declining earnings in two successive years. A more important reason was that Sarnoff, after a brave start, seemed to have lost interest in running the company. His favorite activity: accompanying his wife, diva Anna Moffo, on concert tours. When the board began discussing his ouster, he was traveling in the Far East.

• Sarnoff's successor was Anthony Conrad, a career RCA man who had been second in command. Less than a year after his appointment, Conrad announced to the board that, gosh, he somehow had forgotten to file personal income-tax returns for the previous several years, and now he was being investigated by the IRS. The board accepted his resignation that day. (Why Conrad failed to file the tax returns never became clear. It wasn't money; he owed the government only $20,000, and for that was forced out of a job that paid $300,000. Since Conrad died in 1984, we may never know.)

• Edgar H. Griffiths took over from Conrad, and for a while business reporters decided that RCA's troubles were over. "How Ed Griffiths Brought RCA Back into Focus" was the title of a glowing 1978 piece in *Fortune*. In 1980 *Forbes* chimed in with "Upturn at RCA: It's for Real." Despite rumors to the contrary, announced writers Robert J. Flaherty and Anne Bagamery, "Griffiths is not about to be fired; he is firmly in the saddle." RCA, they gushed, was "a dream of a company," perfectly poised for a revival in the 1980s. Griffiths could then retire on "a flood of rising earnings."

• Alas, Griffiths was already on the way out. As became clear later, he had lost the board's confidence, in part because of his emphasis on short-term profits and his refusal to do any long-range planning. In early 1981 his resignation was formally accepted and a new chairman appointed: Thornton Bradshaw, an RCA director who was president of Atlantic Richfield Company. "A Peacemaker Comes to RCA," announced *Fortune*. (Bradshaw, as it happened, would be RCA's last chairman, peaceable or otherwise; I'll explain why shortly.)

So there was plenty of bumbling in the executive suites. But underlying the comings and goings was a sorrier tale; of a once-dominant company utterly unable to cope with a rapidly changing marketplace.

Aside from NBC, the heart of RCA's business in the 1960s was the manufacture and sale of color TV sets. The company had introduced color in 1954, and for several years thereafter had swallowed losses on what *Business Week* called "the most complex consumer product ever developed." But by 1960 it had turned the corner, and for the next several years the color market exploded. Though Zenith and other U.S. competitors began to eat away at its market share, RCA remained the industry's dominant player.

With dominance, to be sure, came a certain amount of arrogance, which would come back to haunt the company. RCA had long supplied Sears, Roebuck & Company with black-and-white TV sets to be sold under the giant retailer's own label. In 1963 Sears asked RCA to supply it with large numbers of color sets on a similar basis. No dice, said David Sarnoff. Sell them under the RCA label or not at all. When other U.S. manufacturers gave the same response, Sears made a deal with Sanyo, giving the Japanese their first toehold in the American market. "From 1963 to 1977," writes Sobel, "Sears purchased 6.5 million Japanese TV sets from Sanyo and later Toshiba, worth more than $700 million." RCA didn't seem to care about Japanese competition, maybe because the Japanese manufacturers had licensed much of their technology from—who else?—RCA. (Under a license arrangement, one company buys the right to use another's technology.) In 1962 alone the company licensed various electronics patents to thirty-two different Japanese companies; it licensed its color cathode-ray tube to Mitsubishi. A list of all of RCA's technology licenses to Japan during the 1960s runs on for several pages.

But RCA then failed to keep up with changes in television technology, which was rapidly being affected by the microelectronics revolution. In the early 1970s television makers could finally do away with vacuum tubes; microelectronics had progressed to the point where color sets could be economically produced with semiconductor-based integrated circuits ("solid state"). By 1971 Japanese manufacturers had converted 90 percent of their production equipment to solid state, while RCA didn't offer a solid-state product line until 1973. The conversion offered the Japanese several advantages: compactness, reliability, and, above all, a chance to automate production. By 1979 Japanese manufacturers needed between fifty-one and seventy-six minutes of labor, on average, to produce a color set. American manufacturers such as RCA needed 2.7 hours.

The loss of preeminence in color TV might have been absorbed, if everything else had been on track. It wasn't. NBC had been derailed in the early 1970s, and spent the rest of the decade playing "genteel second fiddle to CBS." From 1975 on it trailed CBS and ABC in prime-time and daytime ratings, and its earnings were modest by comparison to archrival CBS. Hertz was hurt by the gas crunches, which cut down on travel and made the company's big cars less appealing for resale. In 1980, bludgeoned by car-rental price wars, a drop in air travel, and high interest rates, Hertz's earnings plummeted. Edgar Griffiths' major diversification move—buying a finance company known as CIT Financial—was completed just as interest rates took off, meaning that CIT's borrowings suddenly got much more expensive. Buying CIT, a company source told *Business Week,* "could be Griffiths' worst decision."

Then there was that HoloTape. Or rather there wasn't that HoloTape, since even when Bobby Sarnoff demonstrated it to journalists a decade earlier, it was only a prototype with no immediate commercial possibilities. (The picture ranged from "poor" to "lousy," said George Brown, an RCA engineer.) But in the 1970s there was video in the air: the prospect of something, a tape player or a disc player or a device not yet imagined, that could play movies or other recorded programs over a TV set and that would be cheap enough for large numbers of American families to put in their homes. RCA, which had once been a world leader in every form of consumer electronics and had plenty of money to spend, might reasonably have been expected to come out with such a product first. The product might even have saved the company.

RCA, in fact, had been investigating a variety of technologies: HoloTape, which utilized a laser to produce TV images from holograms; magnetic tape; and a video disc something like an ordinary record. HoloTape was stillborn. Magnetic tape (the sort that would ultimately be used in a videocassette recorder) seemed unpromising. A tape playback head capable of handling all the information on a videotape had to be a piece of precision equipment, and RCA concluded that manufacturing the heads to the necessary tolerances would be prohibitively expensive. (The Japanese, of course, were even then deciding that the necessary tolerances *could* be obtained, and were learning ways, mostly involving new integrated-circuit technology, of bringing the cost down.) The wave of the future, RCA decided, was the videodisc, a phonographlike system that would play movies recorded on discs. As early as 1975 the company was announcing plans to market disc players for $400—some year soon.

When Griffiths replaced Conrad, he pushed the date back. Griffiths was "somewhat more cautious than . . . his predecessors," said *Forbes*. He was "reluctant to bring [the videodisc] to market," observed *Business Week*. The reason was that introducing a product of this sort would be hideously expensive: as with television itself, there could be no mass market until sufficient programming (i.e., discs) was available. And the cautious Griffiths was making his mark not by spending money but by trimming expenses. "Suppose you put $100 million at risk to market [it]," he mused. "And suppose at the end of that expense you couldn't declare yourself a failure or a success. So you spend another $100 million. How many years will it take to build the market, and what will it cost?" Rather than take such a risk, he postponed the introduction of videodiscs again and again.

Postponing the introduction of a new technology may make sense if you are trying to bring costs down, or if you are waiting for demand to build. Postponing the introduction of a new technology while a competing technology establishes itself—well, that has to rank high on the honor roll of management muck-ups.

Griffiths had given up on manufacturing a tape player. But watching the new Japanese VCRs begin to catch on, he figured RCA should hedge its bet on discs. So he cut a deal with Matsushita to market the Japanese company's VHS-format recorders in the United States. The deal had its limitations. RCA's license wasn't exclusive, and as a reseller the company earned only a small share of the profits from the machine. Even so, it was something of a landmark in VCR history. VHS-format recorders were cheaper, and could fit more on a single tape, than Sony's pioneering Betamax system. With RCA's still-strong marketing muscle behind it, the VHS format took off, and by 1978 RCA had passed Sony as the number-one marketer of VCRs.

Never mind that RCA could see firsthand the explosive growth in the VCR market; it now decided to introduce the videodisc, and in no small way. It persuaded Zenith, Sears, J.C. Penney, and CBS to adopt its disc system. It predicted that it would sell 200,000 players and 2 million videodiscs in 1981 alone. (This was to be the chief source of that "flood of rising earnings" *Forbes* saw chairman Griffiths retiring on.) On February 25, 1981, RCA engineered a massive nationwide rollout of the new product. The players themselves sold for $499.95. They came with a disc catalog of 100 titles that ranged in price from $15 to $30.

This venture, of course, was over shortly after it began. Postponed so long, the once-innovative videodisc now had to compete with a well-established VCR industry, and with a growing number of stores renting prerecorded movies on tape, not on disc. Unlike a VCR, the videodisc player couldn't record. Unlike competing disc systems, RCA's had no glitzy technological capabilities, such as stop action or computerized search (so that you could skip around in a how-to program, for example). It was a movie player pure and simple; but anyone who wanted to watch movies at home could now buy a VCR for only a little more money and rent films for a few dollars a night. By October one dealer told the press, "No RCA VideoDisc players have been sold here in five months, and they no longer are kept on hand." In March 1983, after reporting videodisc losses of roughly $100 million in *both* 1981 and 1982, company president Robert R. Frederick asserted that "under no foreseeable circumstances" would RCA abandon videodiscs, a sure sign that abandonment was under consideration. The end came only a year later, with chairman Thornton F. Bradshaw making the announcement. RCA's losses on its videodisc venture, said Bradshaw, came to $580 million.

With hindsight, executives such as RCA's can look like buffoons—at once arrogant and overcautious, technologically inept and managerially foolish. It's worth remembering that RCA wasn't alone in its blundering. Chrysler had to be bailed out by the government, and the whole U.S. consumer-electronics industry was destroyed by the Japanese, not just RCA's portion of it. It's also worth remembering that the people running U.S. corporations had no preparation for the technological and economic disruptions they encountered in the 1970s. Many, to be sure, reacted without much foresight. But foresight is almost always a scarce commodity, in business as in every other human endeavor.

THE RECKONING

What happens when companies as large as RCA make such a devastating series of blunders?

Some go bankrupt, like Allis-Chalmers, or nearly so, like Chrysler. Others, like RCA itself, may muddle through for a while, making money on some divisions, losing it on others, and hoping that the bottom line each year comes up black rather than red. If it weren't for the stock market, many more troubled American corporations might have muddled through the 1980s, until they either learned to adapt to the new conditions or were driven under for good.

If it weren't for the stock market. Nearly all big companies, of course, are owned by investors, who trade their shares of ownership on Wall Street's stock exchanges. And what does a company's stock sell for? The price reflects supply and demand at any given moment. Supply and demand, in turn, reflect investors' best guesses about the company's earnings in the future. If you think the future holds growth and higher profits for your company, you won't be quick to sell your stock. If you're not sanguine, you'll put your money in treasury bills, or in gold, or under the mattress. Stock prices will rise and fall accordingly.

For twenty-five years after World War II—even in the so-called go-go years of the 1960s—the stock market was a pretty quiet place. A typical day in 1965 might see 6 million shares change hands on the New York Stock Exchange, compared with close to 200 million today. Stocks in the country's largest companies—the blue chips— seemed not only safe but lucrative, and indeed rose in value over the long term. That was the financial reflection of the big companies' ever-increasing market dominance. Not surprisingly, stock prices were high relative to companies' intrinsic worth. In 1965, for example, a share of stock in a typical industrial company was trading for more than twice its nominal value on the company's books. A share of RCA might be worth $30 in book value, but it could cost more than $60, because it represented a share of the company's future earnings as well as its present assets. And in a Galbraithian economy, RCA was almost guaranteed to do well in the future.

Not surprisingly, that kind of stock market couldn't survive the 1970s.

The market was agitated even in the early years of the decade: prices plunged in 1970, rose, then plunged again in 1974 after the first oil crisis. But as the decade wore on, a deeper and more significant trend became apparent. Investors weren't happy about what was happening at any given moment. And they were positively gloomy about the future. The energy situation seemed out of control. So did inflation. Competition in the marketplace was stiffening; more and more companies were losing business to the Japanese and other overseas antagonists. The trajectory of new technology was itself unpredictable; certainly no one could know which companies would best be able to capitalize on it.

So stock prices not only bounced around, they declined, over time, relative to what companies were worth as measured by their balance sheets. The gap between companies' book value and market value began to close. By the end of the 1970s, the average company was selling for something close to its book value; many were selling for less. (Indeed, if you adjusted corporate assets and liabilities for the effects of inflation, as economists Philip Cagan and Robert E. Lipsey undertook to do, the average company's market value in 1977 was only half its book value.)

"Stock prices got so low," explained Jeff Madrick, a veteran journalist who chronicled the takeover wave in his book *Taking America,* "that if all the debt were paid off, many companies had cash and accounts receivable enough to exceed [their] market value." This was the financial reflection of the chaotic marketplace of the 1970s.

Ponder the implications of this state of affairs. *If you could buy a company, particularly one that the stock market didn't like, you would acquire a bundle of debts and assets for a relatively modest amount. You could pay off the debts, and right away, never mind what you might earn in the future, you would have assets worth more than what you paid for the company.* An environment more conducive to takeovers is hard to imagine.

To be sure, companies had always bought up other companies. But the acquisitions were usually friendly, and required agreement on both sides; the few that were unfriendly, such as some of the mergers engineered by conglomerate builder Charles Bluhdorn of Gulf + Western during the 1960s, were looked at askance, both by respectable corporate executives and by Wall Street's biggest investment banks. Now, there was every incentive for big corporations to go shopping, whether or not the potential acquiree liked the idea. How long could respectability (what Galbraith once called the Convenient Social Virtue) hold out against such compelling economics?

Not long. In 1974 a well-established and eminently respectable company called International Nickel Company, or INCO, bid for an old-line Philadelphia battery maker known as ESB—and immediately let it be known that the bid would go forward whether or not ESB's managers agreed to the acquisition (they didn't). INCO's investment banker, moreover, was the top-of-the-line Wall Street firm Morgan

Stanley & Company, a direct descendant of J.P. Morgan's financial empire. A year later conglomerate builder Harry Gray of United Technologies mounted a hostile bid—his first—for Otis Elevator. It was a textbook illustration of the economic logic involved: Otis's stock, worth $38 a share on the books, was selling for only $32.

Soon both the pace of takeovers and the size of the deals began to pick up. Babcock & Wilcox, a maker of coal-burning boilers and nuclear reactors, became the object in 1977 of the "most frenzied bidding contest Wall Street had ever seen," with the eventual winner paying $750 million for the company, $240 million more than the initial bid. (The winner, an oil-rig manufacturer named J. Ray McDermott & Company, may ultimately have rued its victory. It seems that Babcock & Wilcox had built the Three Mile Island nuclear plant, whose notorious accident took place only a little more than a year later.) In 1977 the total value of merger transactions was $22 billion; in 1978, $34 billion. By 1981 it was up to $83 billion. The biggest single transaction that year was Du Pont's takeover of Conoco, then the ninth-largest oil company, for $6.8 billion.

In 1982 takeovers finally spilled over from the business pages to the headlines and gossip magazines. That was the year that Bendix Corporation's chief, William Agee, with paramour Mary Cunningham at his side, made his bid for Martin Marietta. The financial aspects of the deal were as soap-operatic as the personal aspects. Agee compiled a secret list of takeover targets, designated by code names such as Earth, Wind, and Fire. When he made his bid for Martin Marietta, the company promptly turned around and made an offer for Bendix. (This was the so-called Pac-Man defense.) Martin Marietta's "white knight" (a third company called in to aid one side) was Harry Gray of United Technologies. Agee's white knight was Gray's chief rival, Edward Hennessy of Allied Corporation. When there appeared no way out of the impasse, Agee agreed to sell Bendix to Allied—and shortly thereafter Hennessy eased Agee out of his job. "Hennessy says that when he saw [Agee] and Mary Cunningham on the cover of *People* magazine," notes Madrick, "he had had it."

By the end of 1982 two distinct phenomena had impressed themselves on the minds of corporate America's executives. First, thanks to the severe recession, business had gone from pretty bad to terrible. *Fortune*'s 1983 listing of the 500 largest corporations, reflecting year-end figures for 1982, read like a dirge. A 6 percent drop in the companies' total sales, only the second sales decline since the magazine began compiling the figures. A whopping 27 percent decline in profits, "the largest earnings dip in the 29-year history of the 500." Fifty-eight companies reported losses—another record—including two that lost more than $1 billion apiece (International Harvester and Bethlehem Steel). The Dow-Jones Industrial Average, which better than any other number reflects the stock market's appraisal of America's largest companies, averaged around 880 in 1982, roughly one-third of what it would be only seven years later. RCA's stock bottomed out at around $17 a share, less than one-third of its 1967 high—and that's with no correction for the blistering inflation that had occurred in the interim.

Second, the takeover wave had by now developed a massive momentum of its own. Even during the 1970s, factors other than low stock prices had contributed to the growth of hostile takeovers. Inflation increased companies' cash flow, for example, even while it raised the cost of building new plants. Better in so uncertain an environment to buy someone else's plant—particularly since it was likely to be a bargain. By the early 1980s, moreover, the phenomenon had snowballed, to a point where the charges of Robert Reich and others about "paper entrepreneurs" began to ring true. Mergers-and-acquisitions specialists had discovered they could make millions of dollars in a single transaction. They had acquired the skills to find and pull off deal after deal, the sums ever larger and the transactions accomplished ever more quickly. Banks and investment pools were willing to provide mountains of cash to finance the takeovers, and the newly prominent "risk arbitrageurs," or "arbs," were quick to speculate on any company that seemed likely to be put "in play." Then, too, a new breed of independent takeover artist—exemplified by T. Boone Pickens and Carl Icahn—had appeared on the scene. With war chests often raised by junk-bond specialist Michael Milken of Drexel Burnham Lambert, they could afford to go after companies as big as Gulf Oil and TWA.

No one, so it seemed, was safe.

For the executive of a large corporation, the lesson of the takeover wave was both simple and compelling: Do something *right now* to improve your company's business and get the stock price up, or risk losing both your company and your job. No longer could a corporation expect to muddle through simply because it was big. The new strategies of business management that appeared during the

1980s—the strategies that led to all of the subsequent restructur-ings—stemmed from that realization.

One strategy, of course, was to run to Washington. Lockheed had been bailed out by government loan guarantees in 1971; mindful of the precedent, Chrysler went hat in hand to Congress in 1979. But bailout was a solution only *in extremis,* and other companies relied on the tried-and-true method of seeking protection from imports. Auto, steel, and machine-tool companies sought quotas on Japanese products. The textile and apparel industries leaned heavily on Con-gress to pass the so-called Jenkins bill, mandating cutbacks on im-ports from Taiwan, Hong Kong, South Korea, and nine other coun-tries. Executives of semiconductor companies began frequenting Washington as early as 1981 to ask the government to ban what they claimed was the Japanese practice of "dumping," or selling chips in the United States below cost. No amount of government assistance, of course, could make a company immune to takeover. But any amount helped, if only because it might boost a company's profits and thus its stock price.

(None of these business leaders, apparently, had learned what might be called The Lesson of John Nevin. As chairman and chief executive officer of Zenith, Nevin spent much of the 1970s leading the charge against Japanese TV manufacturers, only to be eased out by Zenith's board in 1979. Why? "He became leader in anti-Japan move-ment," reported the industry publication *Television Digest* in its clipped style, and "was openly criticized by financial analysts for spending too much of his time and Zenith's money battling issue in courts and at various govt. hearings. All stop-Japan proceedings he launched were essentially failures. . . ." In 1988 Nevin quit trying: as the new chief executive of Firestone Tire & Rubber, he presided over the sale of Firestone to the Japanese company Bridgestone.)

A second strategy was to give up and allow your company to be swallowed up by a friendly buyer. RCA was so vulnerable to a takeover that it had little other choice. Like most big companies, it incorporated many diverse businesses under one corporate roof. But in the new economic climate—with every business under some kind of threat from the marketplace turmoil—investors weren't optimis-tic, and so the corporation's total market value was less than its individual pieces might be worth. *Fortune*'s A. F. Ehrbar pointed out as much in a 1982 article with the forthright title, "Splitting Up RCA." With the stock at 17, RCA's market value figured out to just under $2 billion. But NBC alone was worth an estimated $1 billion, Hertz $500 million, and the company's other divisions $1.5 billion. They were worth so little put together because investors, as a group, didn't believe RCA's management could do a good job running them.

RCA managed to resist being taken over for a while; when Agee's Bendix began buying up stock, chairman Thornton Bradshaw issued a prickly (and effective) statement opining that "Mr. Agee has not demonstrated the ability to manage his own affairs, let alone someone else's." Still, the future looked chancy. Raider Irwin L. Jacobs began buying RCA stock. The Bass brothers, of Texas, were said to be interested. In March 1985 Bradshaw officially stepped down as CEO, with company president Robert Frederick taking his place, though Bradshaw stayed on as chairman. The rumor that year was that RCA, which had sold off both CIT and Hertz, would soon make a major acquisition, probably MCA, the entertainment giant. Discussions, however, fell apart.

Then, late that fall, General Electric chairman John Welch, looking for acquisitions of his own, arranged a meeting with Bradshaw to discuss a buyout of RCA by GE.

Bradshaw was receptive, for reasons that aren't hard to fathom. "I had become increasingly worried . . . about the ability of RCA to compete in the new worldwide scene," he said later. He was no doubt worried about the share price as well; by 1985 the company's liquidation value was estimated to be at least twice the price of its stock. On December 5, Welch and Bradshaw met again, and this time the two men apparently resolved to go ahead. Gently—one hopes—Bradshaw broke the news to new president Frederick, who reportedly cast the only vote against the merger at the decisive board meeting on December 8.

RCA as an entity disappeared more quickly than anyone might have thought possible. "So large a company simply doesn't vanish into another," predicted Robert Sobel in 1986. "Moreover RCA will remain at Radio City, which will not be renamed GE Plaza." Again, a clouded crystal ball. General Electric promptly sold off RCA Records (now produced by the West German conglomerate Bertelsmann A.G.) and RCA's TV manufacturing operations (sets bearing the RCA and GE labels are made by Thomson Group, the state-owned French concern). The company's 1988 annual report listed GE Plastics, GE Medical Systems, and the names of other divisions; there was no mention of RCA, except that "the RCA brand" was to be added to the company's "existing GE, Monogram, and Hotpoint brand names." In 1988 the red RCA letters at the top of Rockefeller Center came down. Up went the initials GE.

A third strategy for a vulnerable company was to go on the attack. It was eat or be eaten, *Fortune* said, and some CEOs decided that they would rather be vultures than carrion. Cash-rich cigarette companies such as R.J. Reynolds and Philip Morris continued their diversification binges, for obvious reasons. (How long would you want *your* business to depend on a product accused of killing 390,000 Americans every year?) General Electric itself bought more than 300 businesses in addition to RCA in the 1980s, though it sold off more than 200. By 1990 GE was the fifth-largest industrial company in America, up from number 10 in 1980, though (because it had cut back its involvement in labor-intensive industries) it had 100,000 *fewer* employees.

The most celebrated big-getting-bigger merger of the 1980s was the combination of Time Inc. and Warner Communications, consummated in 1990. In a stroke of the pen, Time chairman J. Richard Munro and Warner boss Steve Ross created an entertainment giant with interests in books, magazines, movies, records, TV production, and cable TV programming and distribution. In principle, the new company was positioned to be a leader in all those fields—though if things didn't work out as planned, it would be vulnerable in the future to a classic bust-up takeover. (By late 1990, indeed, *Business Week* was pointedly wondering when the company would begin selling off divisions to reduce its mammoth debt load.)

At any rate, all three of these strategies had only limited appeal. Most companies, whatever their executives might wish for, couldn't really expect government protection. Most preferred to remain independent, and many had neither the cash nor the inclination to go on an acquisition spree. The most common strategic response to the vagaries of the 1970s, ironically, was not to grow bigger but to make the company smaller. Since this fourth strategy turned out to be the most far-reaching in its implications, it needs a longer explanation.

The news stories chronicling mergers and acquisitions such as Time Warner—particularly those in the popular press—made it seem as if all big companies were getting bigger. In fact, as people who followed the situation knew, the opposite was more often the case.

For one thing, takeovers themselves didn't automatically create monster companies. The hallmark of 1980s-style takeovers was leverage, meaning that would-be acquirers borrowed huge amounts of money to do their shopping. Typically, the assets of the target company would be pledged as collateral for the loan. But since those assets were often worth *more* than what had to be borrowed—remember RCA—the acquiring company usually wanted to get rid of some to repay most or all of the loan. This process often created a smaller company. When Pantry Pride bought Revlon, for example, CEO Ronald Perelman sold off Revlon's sizable prescription-drug business, leaving the new company smaller than the old. Before raider Paul Bilzerian was convicted of stock fraud, he essentially dismantled the Singer Company, taking it over and selling off eight of its twelve divisions.

But the real significance of such moves lay in their catalytic effect. Think about it: you run a large, diversified corporation. You're worried about raiders and other would-be acquirers—and you can't help noticing that they're discovering hidden value in the pieces of the giant corporations they're buying out. The lesson: Sell off before they get there.

This lesson represented a sea change in managerial thinking, which had held since the 1960s or before that big was good, bigger was better, and a diversified company was inherently more valuable than a more specialized one. "In the wake of so many mergers," observed Jeff Madrick, "it became recognized that diversification was not necessarily good; that individual businesses, especially if unrelated, could be managed better if independent and not part of a large conglomerate. Indeed, separate businesses were more valuable if managed independently, and a corporation could produce higher share prices by selling these individual businesses off." *Business Week,* in an influential cover story published in 1985, chronicled the effects of this realization. A "growing number of companies that once thought diversification and expansion were vital are abruptly changing course," wrote the magazine's Stewart Toy. "They are slimming down and narrowing their focus, lopping off divisions, and selling assets and product lines. . . . This riot of voluntary restructuring is something the U.S. has never seen before."

Toy's list of examples took nearly a page and included such onetime blue chips as International Harvester (selling off its farm-equipment division) and Dow Chemical (selling off its oil-field-services business). "All told," he wrote, "U.S. companies sold some 900

divisions and subsidiaries last year, a jump of 40% in four years."
One of the leaders in divestiture: ITT, which by the middle of the
decade had sold off 85 subsidiaries. (Later, it sold even its core
telecommunications business, though in this case the buyer was Alca-
tel N.V., a joint venture between ITT and a French company.) Gulf
+ Western, another 1960s-style conglomerate, got rid of scores of
businesses in the middle 1980s, including a billion-dollar sale of
several consumer- and industrial-products companies in 1985. Today
the company has renamed itself Paramount Communications Inc.,
reflecting its new focus on entertainment and communication; it still
owns Simon & Schuster, publishers of the book you are holding (or
at least it did when I was writing it). Said Paramount chief Martin S.
Davis: "Bigness is not a sign of strength. In fact, just the opposite is
true." (That belief, to be sure, didn't stop Davis from bidding for
Time Inc. when rumors of the Time Warner merger first surfaced.)

Corporate divisions were often sold off to other big companies.
But just as often they were sold to aggressive midsize companies, or
were divested in so-called management-led leveraged buyouts. The
latter process—in which a division's managers put up a little of their
own money, borrowed a lot, and bought the company—created a
host of smaller independent enterprises. "The most widespread
going-private transaction, the leveraged buyout," wrote Michael C.
Jensen of the Harvard Business School in 1989, "is becoming larger
and more frequent. In 1988, the total value of the 214 public-company
and divisional buyouts exceeded $77 billion—nearly one-third the
value of all mergers and acquisitions."

Jensen, who attracted some notice for his view that the publicly
held corporation had "outlived its usefulness," argued that managers
buying a division had built-in advantages over the previous owners.
Their financial rewards depended solely on the performance of the
business they were running. They had no incentive to "milk" the
company, or to build up little empires of bureaucrats; indeed, because
of their high debt load, they had to run the business as efficiently as
possible. The available evidence supported Jensen's contention. A
statistical study by economists Frank R. Lichtenberg (of Columbia
University) and Donald Siegel (of the National Bureau of Economic
Research), using Census Bureau data, found that management-led
buyouts increased companies' productivity by about 20 percent. A
study of fifteen divested enterprises by merger specialist F. M. Scherer
showed that all but one did better on their own. A dramatic example

of this phenomenon was Springfield Remanufacturing Corporation, a Missouri enterprise that had once been a money-losing unit of International Harvester. Bought out in 1983 by a group of managers, the newly independent SRC grew steadily and made money; seven years later it was a profitable $65 million engine-remanufacturing company employing about 600 people.

Divestiture wasn't the only method of shrinking a company; the 1980s were, after all, the decade of "lean and mean." The term covered a variety of strategies. Nearly every large corporation trimmed its administrative staff. (GM in one two-year period slashed its salaried work force by 40,000, or 22 percent.) Many closed and consolidated plants, relying much more heavily than in the past on "outsourcing" (buying parts and services rather than making them). Companies had once grown large on what economists refer to as vertical integration, the ownership or control of every stage of the production process. Now they were *dis*integrating, depending on outside suppliers not only for parts and materials but for services such as building maintenance, cafeteria service, and engineering. The statistic that some analysts began watching as a measure of companies' efficiency was sales per employee—which also, of course, measures how much a company does under its own roof. Gillette in 1980 racked up sales of $68,000 per employee. In 1989 (after the company had weathered two takeover attempts and trimmed its work force), the figure was $127,000. Even allowing for inflation, that's better than a 25 percent jump.

By the end of the 1980s, the financial results of all the downsizing and divestiture could be seen: improved corporate performance, increased profits, and higher stock prices, with companies that had shrunk the most usually doing better than their larger competitors. "The biggest companies are the most profitable—on the basis of return-on-equity—in only 4 out of 67 industries in the *Business Week* Top 1000," the magazine reported in 1989. "Well over half the time, the biggest corporate player fails to attain even the industry average return on invested capital."

The large corporation had once typified the dominance of American business. Its size was both a cause and an effect of its power, the interplay reflected in the fact that the big generally got bigger. But the chaos of the marketplace had turned the equation upside down. In an unstable environment, size no longer brought power: it brought vulnerability. And most companies' answer to that vulnerability was to shrink or to break themselves up—or face takeover artists who would.

"Is your company too big?" asked *Business Week* in the 1989 cover story that seemed a fitting cap to the decade. "Are huge, sprawling corporations the dinosaurs of our economy? Are smaller, more nimble organizations our economy's salvation?

"Big vs. Small has become one big debate—and small seems to be winning."

As the decade came to a close, the takeover wave seemed spent. Michael Milken was headed for a prison term, and Wall Street was in a recession of its own. The economic restructuring, however, continued. Large companies continued to shuck or shut down divisions that looked somehow unpromising and to trim their work forces relentlessly. They remained wary of expansion.

From an economic perspective, in any event, the change had been accomplished. Big companies could no longer dominate the marketplace as they once had; they could no longer expect to grow larger and larger; they could no longer muscle their way into the many new niches that a dynamic economy is always creating. Most corporate leaders weren't even trying. As we'll see in the next chapter, they were ceding ground, for a number of good reasons, to newer and smaller companies.

3

New Business

TWENTY YEARS AGO it made sense to divide America's economic landscape into two broad segments. One was big business, which consisted of large, market-dominating corporations. The other was small business. "Making up the remainder of the economy," wrote John Kenneth Galbraith, "are around twelve million smaller firms, including about three million farmers whose total sales are less than those of the four largest industrial corporations; just under three million garages, service stations, repair firms, laundries, laundromats, restaurants, and other service establishments; two million small retail establishments; around nine hundred thousand construction firms; several hundred thousand small manufacturers; and an unspecified number serving the multivariate interests of an advanced society in what is collectively called vice."

This was a recognizable portrait of the America of 1970: it was Main Street USA, complete with a courtly nod toward ventures such as the numbers rackets that flourished in the days before state-run lotteries. Galbraith went on to point out some of the traits—other than size itself—that distinguished small enterprises from big ones. Unlike the giants, small companies rarely utilized sophisticated technology. They didn't have much of what he called organization—that is, the ability to marshal diverse resources and apply collective intelligence to the job at hand. They typically thrived in only a few sectors of the economy: "services" (those garages, laundries, restaurants);

creative endeavors (the architect's office, the craftsman's shop); and a few other markets in which "the entrepreneur, by reducing his own compensation, increasing his effort and—within limits—doing the same with his employees, can survive in competition with organization." Galbraith termed the latter phenomenon self-exploitation, and regarded it as an essential component of small-scale enterprise. How else could a small electrical manufacturer compete with General Electric, or a grocery-store owner with Grand Union, except by working long hours and paying starvation wages?

By the 1980s this handy bifurcation of the economy into big and small was becoming at once anachronistic and incomplete, like a division of the music world into classical and jazz. For one thing, too many visible, dynamic companies couldn't be squeezed into the Galbraith taxonomy. Sun Microsystems, The Limited, MCI Communications, and America West Airlines, to name only four examples, were giant corporations with thousands of employees, each as sophisticated in technology and organization as any company in America. But not one exhibited the kind of stability or market power Galbraith saw as characteristic of the large company. A similar disparity clouded the small-business side of the ledger. As David Birch showed, small companies accounted for a substantial fraction of new jobs, more than their share of economic activity would have led us to expect. It seemed unlikely that all these jobs could emanate from an unprecedented proliferation of service stations, laundromats, and repair firms. Where *were* they coming from?

Birch himself was curious about this last question, and set out to investigate it. He had come to think of his database as a kind of economic microscope: you could tell the computer to sort companies by industry, by region, by size, indeed by any available variable, and then to cross-reference and cross-index what it found. Turn up the magnification, so to speak, and you could see what was happening with printing establishments in Wisconsin or computer-service firms in Houston or all U.S. companies with more than 5,000 employees. Now, as he tried to figure out why small companies should be creating most of the jobs, he began focusing his lens on which businesses were growing and which were not. He also began adding up where all the new employment was coming from.

One fact leaped out at him right away. Despite what small-business advocates were claiming, despite Birch's own reputation as an evangelist for smaller enterprises, it was nevertheless undeniable:

Most small companies didn't grow at all. They provided work for their owners and a few other people; and, yes, maybe there were more such businesses than there used to be. The economy was continuing its long-term trend toward ever-greater employment in the service sector, and many service firms were tiny shops and offices. Still, these small, stable companies as a group had a marginal effect on net new employment. Allowing for the appropriate updates, they weren't so different from the small companies Galbraith had described.

Fact number two was equally striking: *Some companies, by contrast, seemed to start small and grow a great deal,* thereby providing work for large numbers of people. Michael B. Teitz, of the University of California, had found that between 12 percent and 15 percent of California's small companies accounted for the vast majority of the state's new jobs, just because they were growing so fast. Birch was finding comparable numbers on a national scale. The exact figures varied by region and by time period, as with all such research. But a relatively small group of businesses was indisputably creating most of the new employment.

A few of the companies in this group, he could see, grew so fast that they stopped being small, by any definition, very quickly. Compaq Computer was one example. Founded in 1981, it grew to more than $100 million in sales in its first year of operation, and by 1989 was employing nearly 10,000 people. Mrs. Fields Inc. was another. A decade after its 1977 founding, it had several hundred cookie stores sprinkled across the United States. But most growing companies revealed by the economic microscope weren't exploding like that; they were just growing. In the space of a few years they might expand from 5 to 15 employees, or from 15 to 50, or from 50 to 300. One year they might shrink, then they'd grow again the next year. ("There is a tendency for corporations to pulsate, rather than to sustain any particular growth pattern," Birch wrote in one of his studies.) By no stretch of the imagination were they in the same league as IBM or Sears. But they weren't the corner drugstore, either. They were obviously oriented toward growth, and indeed were responsible, as a group, for most of the new employment. Because they were expanding, many were likely to be doing something different from the competition—that is, they were likely to be both innovative and sophisticated in their operations. They didn't seem to belong on Galbraith's Main Street.

It wasn't hard for Birch, or indeed for anyone else, to figure out who some of these companies were. Some were ventures started by computer wizards and clever technology-oriented entrepreneurs—not just the Compaqs of the world, but the computer-parts suppliers, the distributors and retailers, the software developers, the systems houses. Others were businesses trading on the trends of the moment, from Ben and Jerry's Homemade Inc. (the ice-cream makers) to the dozens of new retailers gracing any up-to-date mall (Williams-Sonoma, The Sharper Image). Trouble was, all such obvious candidates combined accounted for only a fraction of the thousands and thousands of growing companies. Birch could see from his data that growing businesses could be found in all sorts of industries. They were in steel as well as electronics, machine tools as well as gourmet ice cream. They were in business services and wholesaling as well as in retailing. Many were in manufacturing, which was supposed to be a declining sector of the economy. A study by the Small Business Administration, based on its own Birch-like database, found that manufacturers with fewer than 500 employees added 1.4 million net new jobs between 1976 and 1986; larger manufacturers as a group abolished 140,000 jobs during the same period. Industries with the fastest-growing small-company employment share included primary metals, electronics, rubber and plastic products, chemicals, and machinery. Nor were these simply declining industries that large corporations were smart enough to get out of. Except for primary metals, every one of the industries was itself growing substantially.

At *Inc.* (which styled itself "the magazine for growing companies") we could see the growing-business phenomenon close up. Granted, plenty of the companies we wrote about were built on technology or trendiness: computer makers and medical-instrument pioneers on the one hand, hairstyling chains and weight-loss centers on the other. But many, many companies were in businesses devoid of such glitz. RailTex Inc., founded in 1977, grew to more than $16 million in sales by 1989. The company operated short-line railroads. Appliance Control Technology (ACT), started in 1986 by a refugee from Motorola, had 200 employees and $17 million in sales by 1989. ACT made control mechanisms for washing machines and microwave ovens. The fast-growing companies we uncovered sold insurance, hauled over-the-road freight, provided temporary-personnel services. They manufactured children's clothing, die-cast metal parts, and electronic circuit boards. Self-exploitation was not a word you would automatically choose to describe these enterprises. The owner of a small Indiana company that made filling machinery for the bottling industry paid his employees competitive wages and supplemented the wages with generous benefits and bonuses. He plowed money back into the business, equipping it with a state-of-the-art machine shop and a fleet of late-model delivery trucks. Then he took home more than $1 million a year in profits.

From all the evidence, the economic landscape had changed since Galbraith's day, and his once-useful taxonomy now had to make room for a new kind of company. Big business and small business, as he had defined them, were still around, if somewhat the worse for wear. But alongside them was a phenomenon, a third segment of the economy, that had burst into view only during the 1980s. To understand it, we need to focus an economic microscope of our own on three transformations in the very structure of American business, and on the sometimes surprising companies these transformations spawned.

THE SUPPLIERS

When large corporations began lopping off divisions in the late 1970s and early 1980s, they themselves created new companies. Before 1983 the people who rebuilt diesel engines for International Harvester would have turned up in Birch's statistics as employees of a giant, struggling multinational. After 1983 they showed up as employees of Springfield Remanufacturing Corporation, a small, growing business. The same was true of corporate-payroll trimming. A company that "downsized" by contracting out its pension-plan management or its cafeteria service was effectively transferring employees from its own payroll to the payroll of another company, usually smaller. The shrinking of big companies had indirect effects, too. In 1989 I visited a small, fast-growing machine-tool distributorship called Prime Technology Inc., in Grand Rapids, Michigan. One reason for Prime's rapid growth, explained owner Phil Pachulski, was the fact that its chief customers—large but newly lean corporations—no longer had many manufacturing engineers on staff. Seeing that lack, Prime had developed an engineering capacity of its own. It could now offer to design a complete system for manufacturing a given part, not just sell whatever machine tools the customer chanced to order.

All such changes began shifting the economic center of gravity from large corporations toward smaller ones. Though big organizations were still playing a pivotal role, more of the actual work was taking place under somebody else's corporate roof. But the shift wasn't occurring only on the margins of production; it permeated the manufacturing process itself. Growing companies were showing up in gritty, unglamorous industries because the way American businesses produced things was changing.

All manufacturers make some of their own parts and materials and buy others. Big manufacturers grew bigger, in the past, not only by making more and more goods but by acquiring more and more of their suppliers, thereby expanding their corporate umbrella. That trend reversed itself in the late 1970s and early 1980s: seeking flexibility in the face of so much uncertainty, companies began divesting themselves of suppliers rather than acquiring them, and began buying more of their parts on the outside ("outsourcing") rather than making them in-house. The texture of the relationship between customer and supplier changed as well, and with it the fundamental shape of the manufacturing economy.

Historically, big manufacturers and their outside suppliers inhabited a Galbraithian world. The big company was the repository of wealth, market power, technological sophistication, information, and planning. It designed both the products and their constituent parts. When it decided to buy, rather than make, a part, the engineering department sent the specs over to the purchasing department. Purchasing put the job out to bid, typically to a half-dozen or more vendors. Whoever bid the lowest got the work—for now. In the automotive industry, the usual contract was for one year. Suppliers frequently bid below cost, hoping to make money on production in later years. Often they didn't. "Even after a supplier has been selected to make a part, assemblers routinely line up alternate suppliers so the companies can be played against each other in the years to come," observed three MIT scholars who studied the auto business. "If the new model fails to sell as expected, a supplier may be dumped for a lower bidder."

The system kept most suppliers small, limited in capacity, and financially precarious. Few could afford any research and development; few could afford new technology. Their managers often knew little about running a business. In a 1977 questionnaire sent by two University of Michigan researchers to executives of auto-industry suppliers, "the vast majority indicated they did not make any distinction between fixed and variable expenses for pricing purposes. . . . Many had little idea of the success or failure of their pricing decisions until they received monthly or quarterly statements." In another study, the same researchers described a seminar in which managers of small metal-finishing companies were asked to estimate the cost of producing a particular part. The estimates ranged from $1.15 to $6.25. Many of the auto industry's suppliers were family-owned, observed Susan Rachel Helper, who studied the industry for her Harvard Ph.D. thesis, and the owner was often the only manager. "This person usually [ended] up focusing on the day-to-day details of the business, with little energy left over for more long-range tasks such as marketing, strategic planning, setting up a quality control system, technology scanning, or managerial recruiting."

So long as American manufacturers dominated their marketplaces, the system served the large companies well. In autos, Helper showed, the Big Three were able to earn substantial profits while forcing suppliers to compete for every nickel. With the advent of Japanese competition and the other uncertainties of the 1970s, however, the arrangement worked less well. Now U.S. manufacturers of all sorts were losing market share and suddenly had to come up with innovations in design, engineering, and manufacturing technology. They were expected to cut costs and boost quality levels by orders of magnitude.

Not surprisingly, many began emulating the practices of their Japanese competitors. They began experimenting with "just in time" inventory systems, with parts delivered to the factory in small lots. (The traditional American practice of stockpiling huge quantities of parts in adjacent storage areas was promptly dubbed the "just in case" system.) They undertook a new approach to quality control, attempting to build high quality into parts from the beginning, rather than simply weeding out defects after production. As in Japan, these changes alone put enormous demands on suppliers, who were now expected to manufacture to much stricter quality standards and to schedule production and delivery much more tightly. The big companies also began expecting their suppliers to do more engineering and design of parts, and to invest in new technology. (A 1990 report in *Business Week* said: "More and more with suppliers, Ford just specifies a part's function and lets the parts maker handle the design as well as the manufacturing.") The stick they wielded was the prospect of losing orders. The carrot was longer-term contracts, usually with higher margins than before. In autos, said Helper, the Big Three began negotiating multiyear contracts with parts suppliers, thereby giving the smaller companies both the incentive and the means to invest in new production technology.

These changes spawned a host of growing companies in otherwise old-line manufacturing industries. On one end of the size spectrum were businesses such as Prime Technology, the machine-tool distributor, which grew to two dozen employees by providing services to companies that hadn't needed them before. (In addition to its large customers, Prime served many smaller suppliers who didn't have the first idea how to do the kind of engineering their own customers were suddenly expecting.) At the other extreme was a company such as Magna International, headquartered near Toronto, which grew from several hundred employees in the mid-1970s to several thousand ten years later, nearly all of the growth due to contracts from the auto companies. (Magna was close to being an auto company itself; it was capable of designing and delivering dozens of different parts and subassemblies.) In between, in autos and nearly every other industry, were hundreds of parts suppliers, distributors, and engineering firms, all prospering from the large companies' cutbacks.

What had been a world with rich, market-dominating giants buying from small, unsophisticated suppliers was now turning into something quite different: a networklike system, in which manufacturing companies of varying sizes, each with specialized expertise, were beginning to collaborate on different stages of the production process. New companies came into being. Sleepy family businesses— the kind that once would have fit comfortably on Main Street— underwent a sort of metamorphosis. The neat division between small business and big was disappearing.

I learned how thoroughly these changes had permeated American manufacturing when I paid a series of visits, over a couple of years' time, to a company in Worcester, Massachusetts, called Kennedy Die Castings. Until then, I wouldn't have thought that a small, family-run, metal-parts maker would have shown up on anyone's list of growing, prosperous companies. Nor would I have imagined either Worcester or the die-casting industry to be the site of dramatic economic transformations. But the business landscape really was undergoing a series of upheavals, and manufacturing in particular had been shaken to the core. Maybe it shouldn't have been surprising that all the tumult had showed up in the day-to-day life of one small company.

Worcester is an aging industrial city an hour or so west of Boston. Its landscape resembles that of many New England mill towns: old factories now cordoned off by expressways, more bustle in the malls on the city's outskirts than in the once-elegant downtown district. Francis Kennedy, founder of Kennedy Die Castings, grew up in Rochdale, not far from Worcester, and graduated from Worcester Polytechnic Institute in 1930. He worked for General Electric for a couple of years, only to be laid off amid the deepening depression. He shipped out on a steamer to the South China Sea for another couple of years. Returning, he got a job in a woolen mill just west of Worcester, and by 1947 had worked his way up to chief engineer. One day in 1948, to his everlasting surprise, he arrived at work to find that the owner had decided to close the mill. Francis presided over the auction of the mill's equipment, then began wondering what to do next. Figuring he would rather be an owner than an employee this time around, he scanned the business ads in the newspaper. There he found a company that wanted to sell a die-casting machine for $5,000.

"My father," said Paul Kennedy, Francis's oldest son, "had to look up in the dictionary to see what 'die casting' was."

Die casting was, and is, a method of manufacturing metal parts. A die-casting machine injects molten metal under intense pressure into a mold—the die—where it quickly cools and solidifies. (A die-casting shop is a maelstrom of heat and noise; each "shot" of hot metal into the mold is complemented by the clatter of newly cast parts tossed into a waiting bin.) Francis was able to scrape together the money to buy the machine; he was also able to hire an experienced die-caster along with it. Soon the fledgling company was making zinc spools for wire recorders (predecessors of tape recorders) and cast-metal parts for the ends of Chevrolet brake cables. It grew for a while, mainly during the 1950s, peaking at fifty or sixty employees. Paul Kennedy and Bob Kennedy, two of Francis's sons, came to work for the company in the 1970s. Paul had also gone to Worcester Poly and had served in the army before joining his father in 1971. A gregarious man, he gravitated toward sales, and was soon spending much of his time on the road courting customers. Bob, three years younger, joined in 1977, after graduating from Holy Cross and spending seven years teaching school. Quieter by nature, he became the company's Mr. Inside to Paul's Mr. Outside.

The company they were working for could have been Galbraith's prototypical small manufacturer: a seat-of-the-pants operation housed in a decrepit mill and staffed mainly by the owner's relatives. "My uncle was receptionist, bookkeeper, and phone answerer," said Bob. "He had one desk. Paul had another; he was in charge of sales and production control. My father's desk was there, too. These were old-style offices: gray Steelcase desks.

"You'd come in in the morning and the first job was to mop the floor. Then you'd take production readings from the previous night and enter them in the book. You knew everything about what was going on. The production schedule was in your head—every customer's order, when pieces were due. Did a mold break? You'd substitute another part on the spot. My father, Paul, or I could walk by a machine and say, 'That's not running right.'"

Every Friday night Bob would take home Kennedy's file of customer orders and map out the next week's production schedule. Admittedly, it wasn't hard. The company was small, and in those days the only operations Kennedy performed were casting the parts and trimming off excess metal before shipping. Customers (mostly big manufacturers) typically maintained big parts inventories, and regardless of what they had ordered, or when, would call when they really needed a resupply. "In the past," said Paul, "the motto was, 'If they aren't calling, don't make it.'" Over time, the names of the customers changed. Wire recorders disappeared. Chevrolet took its business elsewhere. But Kennedy supplied Norton Company, itself headquartered in Worcester, with flanges for its grinding wheels. It supplied the Stanley Works, the big tool company, with handles for utility knives and cases for its chalk lines. Like thousands of other small manufacturers, it survived by doing today pretty much what it had done yesterday and the day before that.

But the same convulsions that shook large companies caused tremors all around the marketplace, and by the early 1980s the Kennedys were wondering if their business had a future. The country was in a recession. The buzzword of the day was *deindustrialization* (a subject that will come up later in this book). The automobile companies, though they were still the die-casting industry's single biggest customer, were not feeding new business to this particular group of suppliers. On the contrary: shaken by the energy crises and new government fuel-economy regulations, they were desperate to cut weight from their new models, and so they began replacing die-cast metal parts with plastic. Kennedy wasn't selling to the automobile industry at that point, but like other die-casting companies it was facing stiff competition from Asian firms. Sales dropped. In 1982, for the first time, the business lost money.

What frustrated Paul was that some parts of the economy seemed oblivious to the turmoil. This was Massachusetts, after all, not Michigan, and thriving computer makers such as Digital Equipment Corporation had plenty of work for small manufacturers. Trouble was, they wouldn't look at Kennedy, at least not more than once. Paul would take a prospective buyer on a tour through the run-down plant, the temperature up around 90 degrees because of the molten metal, and the buyer would say it was too dark, or too small, or too hot. (Several years later, Paul still fumed at the memory: "The place was *hot?* I was ready to kill them. It's a die-casting plant, and they're telling me it's hot?") Worse, companies such as Digital didn't want raw castings; they wanted finished, ready-to-assemble parts—which meant that the supplier would be expected to drill, tap, machine, plate or paint the metal as well as cast it.* Kennedy had never done that. They also expected modern methods of quality control, complete with full documentation. Kennedy had never worried much about formal quality control. If a customer got a bad batch of parts, the Kennedys knew, they could just ship 'em back.

Nor was it just the Digitals of the world that had different expectations. Even old-line customers such as Stanley were beginning to talk about higher standards, just-in-time deliveries, and the other symbols of the new era. "The marketplace was different," said Paul Kennedy, "Stanley's as well as Digital's. Stanley's competitors were now offshore and were beating them on price. Stanley had to win on something else, like quality. So they started placing new burdens on us. Every delivery on time, every time. They rated us. Our plant had been scared to death of delivering on time; we felt if they really wanted it, they'd call. And Stanley, like everybody else, was ratcheting up their quality standards. We had always had good quality; now they wanted *reported* good quality, with full documentation. We had to set up a formal quality-assurance department."

*"Drilling" means cutting a hole in a part; "tapping" means cutting a threaded hole, as for a bolt. "Machining" means milling or otherwise shaping the part; and "plating" means applying a metallic coating to it.

Slowly, over the next couple of years, Paul and his brother, who were gradually taking over from their father, began fashioning a plan. Suppose they could modernize their little company, put it in a bigger building and add to its capabilities? They could certainly take advantage of the computer industry's growth. And along with the new demands from old-line customers such as Stanley had come the prospect of significantly larger orders. Stanley had bought its own die-casting facility several years earlier, following the old precept of owning your sources of supply. But in the newly tumultuous marketplace, the big company was having trouble managing it. In 1985 it closed the facility down and began buying more from its suppliers. With such prospects in sight, the brothers approached their company's bank for a loan on a new building. They hired another design engineer and a manager with experience in production control, the first nonfamily manager ever. Sales picked up. In 1986 the company moved.

The move itself, ironically, created as many problems as it solved. Old machines, suddenly transplanted, began breaking down. Employees who knew where everything was in the old shop were lost in the new one, and morale plummeted. (On one ill-fated day, workers filled a trash barrel with freshly manufactured parts and shipped it to a customer. They didn't realize the barrel already had a layer of trash in the bottom.) But most of those problems proved temporary, and the Kennedys forged ahead in their attempt to remake the company.

To visit Kennedy Die Castings at the end of the 1980s was to see a company unrecognizable by old-style standards. It was still a small, family-run business in a thoroughly unglamorous industry. But it was housed in a capacious new building in an industrial park near the Worcester airport; it boasted comfortable offices and a large shop floor. (The shop was still unavoidably hot in the summer, but workers now had access to an air-conditioned lunchroom on their breaks.) Sales—about $9 million—were roughly four times their early-1980s level. The company had some 110 employees, many of them added in the previous few years. In its day-to-day workings, moreover, the company seemed in the last stages of metamorphosis, like a butterfly emerging from its cocoon. The brothers had brought in new technology. They had broadened their manufacturing capabilities to compete in a changed marketplace. They had begun experimenting with new management techniques. Each innovation merits a little explanation, for all were hallmarks of the new, growth-oriented small company.

Bringing in New Technology. "The inherent problem in conventional die casting," chief engineer Terry Trainor explained to me, "is air in the mold. You try to direct the metal in so the air goes out tiny slits while the metal rushes in. But it's really wishful thinking—all the air never goes out. Instead it gets squeezed into the metal. We hope it gets broken up into microscopic bubbles rather than big ones. Even so, there's some porosity in the casting. If a piece needs machining that can be a big problem—you hit air bubbles."

In 1987 Paul Kennedy learned of a German die-caster with an innovative method of addressing this problem: he had developed a vacuum system designed to suck air out as the metal poured in. Without air, the metal would be denser and therefore stronger. Parts could be designed thinner and therefore lighter. Others had thought of this approach before, but none of the available methods seemed as effective and dependable as the German system. Visiting the Bavarian Die Cast Works for a demonstration, Paul decided to spend nearly $50,000 for the rights to the technology.

Like the Japanese when they first licensed American technology, the Kennedys then set about learning how to use it. Machines had to be retrofitted with new equipment, old molds remachined. Workers, accustomed to traditional methods, were now being asked to oversee a more complex process. "We've got to do a marketing job within the company," confided Trainor, shortly after Kennedy had bought the license. "It may be seen by some people as just more things they have to do. But it's not going to work without them." At first, there was some question as to whether it would work at all. Wincing, Bob Kennedy remembered the day a prospective customer, Fairchild Industrial Products, came up to see a part run on the vacuum system. The system had had its first trial on a Tuesday; on Thursday of that same week, the Fairchild representatives arrived for a demonstration.

"They arrived in the morning, and the system wasn't quite ready. We stalled. We told them, 'Right after lunch.' They had to catch a two o'clock flight, so we had no extra time.

"After lunch we tried it. Now, you never want to show a customer the first shot [from a new mold]; it's always bad. But we did a shot anyway. And out comes this spongy-looking black glob. I thought I was going to croak. But then we tried it once more—here goes—and out comes the most gorgeous-looking die casting I've ever seen.

"We did five good shots; on the sixth one the machine seized up. But it didn't matter. They took the samples back and sawed them up. Pretty soon they gave us the job, the first new one in years. They said, 'We want it in vacuum.' " A few months later, a Kennedy manager compared the yield of good parts from a similar mold, run in the past on a non-vacuum machine, with the yield on the new system. The old mold had produced 82 percent good parts; the new one, 98 percent.

By 1990 Kennedy had the vacuum system working for more than 75 percent of its jobs, producing high-quality, lighter parts. New technology was wending its way through other parts of the company as well. One computer system monitored machine operation. Another was being utilized for budgeting, inventory management, job costing, and accounting—all functions that had once resided in the heads of Bob and Paul Kennedy. Elementary steps, to be sure, but steps that small companies in the past seldom took.

Broadening the Company's Capabilities. "In the old days," sighed Bob Kennedy with just a hint of nostalgia, "it was cast, trim, and ship. Cast, trim and ship." The company did no so-called secondary operations, such as drilling or machining a part. That was evidently one of the practices that would have to change in the new environment. Wooing Digital Equipment Corporation back in the early 1980s, Paul rashly promised ready-to-assemble parts. Then he had to scramble to find subcontractors to do everything Kennedy couldn't do.

By 1988, with more customers demanding fully finished parts, Kennedy was doing more secondary operations itself, particularly drilling and tapping. But change in this department was slow. The die-casting machines might be being outfitted with the latest technology, and the quality-assurance staff might be learning the latest techniques in statistical process control, but the secondary department was still utilizing ancient, hand-operated drilling and tapping machinery. Here too, however, new technology was readily available in the marketplace, and in late 1988 Kennedy acquired an $80,000 computer-numerical-control (CNC) machining center, essentially a complex machine tool capable of being programmed to perform any number of operations. When it was installed, the new machine sat next to an Avey hand-operated driller and tapper that looked as if it had been built fifty years before; the Avey's electric motor was linked to the drill mechanism by a big, worn, leather belt. Together, the pair might have been taken from a textbook illustration of the transformation of manufacturing technology.

The CNC machine increased Kennedy's capabilities dramatically. In the past, nearly all of Kennedy's jobs were simple parts. In 1989, by contrast, a typical job was a part known as a board handle, which Kennedy produced for Calcomp, a company that supplied IBM. The board handle was made of an unusual alloy of aluminum; fifteen inches long, it had to be cast and machined to within a few thousandths of an inch. Once cast, each part was drilled, tapped, and punched with one of eighteen possible combinations of holes. The drilling and tapping was a job tailor-made for the CNC machine, which could be programmed to produce all eighteen variations precisely, in the blink of an electronic eye. Kennedy could charge relatively more for such work than it could for simpler parts.

But even simple parts had grown more complex. Instead of making big batches of knife handles, say, and shipping them off to customers such as Stanley, Kennedy was now expected to ship in small batches, almost daily, in direct response to Stanley's production needs. That meant tighter control of production schedules and shipping routines; it also meant that Stanley was willing to pay a higher price per part than in the past, since it had shifted some of the burden of inventory management onto Kennedy. Both the new parts and the new procedures for producing old parts were, as the current managerial buzzword had it, higher in value added. Kennedy, like the auto-parts suppliers, was turning itself from an easily replaceable job-shop manufacturer into a sophisticated specialty producer.

Introducing New Management Techniques. Family-run businesses, in the past, typically exhibited a managerial style that was partly authoritarian, partly paternalistic, and in any event dependent upon the whim of the owner. They could be pleasant places to work if the boss was agreeable, hell if he wasn't, sometimes both at the same time. In the summer of 1964 I worked for a family-owned manufacturer of bathroom vanities and file cabinets in North Philadelphia. It was a good job for a white college kid, partly because the boss's son who ran things treated me pretty well. He treated the other workers, most of whom were black, considerably less well. There was no union. Disciplinary measures, from reprimands to firings, allowed no recourse. Time off during the day—say, for a doctor's appointment—was out of the question. No work, no pay. (I also shudder to think of the potentially toxic chemicals, such as methyl ethyl ketone, all of us were regularly exposed to in those days before OSHA. The chemicals at least were color-blind, and I have no reason to think the company knew any more about their long-term effects than the rest of us.)

Paul and Bob Kennedy didn't seem particularly authoritarian, and even thirty years ago would probably have run their company in benign fashion. But in the marketplace of the late 1980s paternalism wasn't enough, either: higher quality standards and more complex products demanded workers who were engaged in their jobs, who worked with their brains as well as with their hands. So the Kennedys were making a slow-paced but dogged effort to alter some of the traditional relationships between managers and employees. Some of the company's financial records were open for the employees' inspection. A profitable three months would immediately be reflected in profit-sharing bonuses, paid to all. The brothers' long-term plans included establishing an employee stock-ownership plan so the workers would have a stake in the company.

In the meantime, they had begun to involve employees in the day-to-day management of their work. A group that worked solely on Stanley's knife handles, for example, was constituted into the "99 Knife Team" (the 99 was Stanley's model number) and was beginning to take responsibility for its work. The team met regularly to go over production levels and to discuss problems and figure out ways to solve them. The meetings seemed to have a dramatic effect, both on productivity and on morale. The team was formed in February 1988; after only six months the yield (or proportion of "good" products) on Model 99 knife castings had risen from 77 percent to 90 percent. One particular worker, pointed out to me by the foreman, had cast 150 knives an hour for as long as anyone could remember—until the team was formed. Suddenly his productivity picked up, and he was now doing in six hours what used to take him eight.

Participatory experiments of this sort have been common among large companies in recent years, and everyone familiar with them can cite a dozen such anecdotes. But the improvements don't always last. To maintain them, the Kennedys would have to push participation farther and deeper into the company. No doubt they would eventually have to implement their proposed stock-ownership plan. Even so, the fact that they had begun the process set their company apart from the traditional small business. Participatory management is a sophisticated, demanding art, and for most of the twentieth century family-run businesses would have had neither the time nor the inclination to try it out.

What made it possible now, of course, were the changes in the marketplace—symbolized by large companies' long-term reliance on suppliers such as Kennedy. "In the past," said Bob Kennedy, "we'd get orders for 300,000 [Stanley] knives, and we weren't sure we'd get another. Now we're not subject to that uncertainty." That assurance gave Bob and Paul the freedom to invest in new technology, to develop their company's capabilities, and to experiment with new managerial techniques. In effect, it gave them the freedom to transform their company from a traditional small business to a sophisticated, growth-oriented enterprise.

THE INNOVATORS

So part one of the explanation for Birch's growing companies was simply the Kennedy story writ large. Giant corporations—the auto manufacturers, Stanley, and many others—began relying more heavily on smaller suppliers. Suppliers that couldn't adapt to the new demands went out of business. Those that could, like Kennedy, not only grew substantially, but frequently transformed themselves into multifaceted businesses capable of much more complex work than in the past. It wasn't just manufacturing suppliers that were affected. Engineering and consulting firms, business-services companies, even wholesalers and distributors all found themselves doing some of what the Fortune 500 had once done for themselves. New and growing businesses could be found in all these niches.

Part two of the story also turned on big corporations' retrenchment. As the giants drew back and tightened their belts, smaller companies took over the role of innovators and began pushing their way into new markets.

For much of the twentieth century, America's large corporations were the prime source of business innovation. They introduced most of the new products and new services, were first to mechanize and then automate their production processes, and developed the most effective methods of delivering their wares. Indeed, plenty of observers argued that *only* large corporations could effectively bring innovations to market. Their case was strong. Research and development were expensive, so more inventions were likely to emanate from corporate labs than from experimenters in garages. Marketing was expensive, too, so only a large company could persuade consumers (or other businesses) to buy a new product. And only the big corporations could take full advantage of economies of scale in delivering goods and services. That meant they could quickly overpower any smaller company that seemed to be developing a profitable new business. To be sure, a few solitary inventors and entrepreneurs might succeed, despite the odds, in coming up with something new. But those who did seemed to have just two options open to them. They could try to build giant corporations themselves, as Edwin Land did with Polaroid and Kenneth Olsen with Digital Equipment Corporation. Or—much more common—they could sell out to one, as computer entrepreneur Max Palevsky did when he sold Scientific Data Systems to Xerox in 1968 for $900 million.

Gradually, over the past twenty years, this situation reversed itself. Large corporations continued to innovate, but they lost their dominant role. The reasons were those enumerated in the last chapter. The economic environment was fraught with uncertainty and inhabited by strong new competitors—reason enough, so it seemed, for some corporate executives to concentrate on minding the store rather than on broadening the line. Technology was changing rapidly and almost unpredictably, and big companies frequently stumbled as they tried to keep up. (Unlike many industrial technologies, microelectronics could easily be pursued in a lone engineer's garage.) Remember RCA's videodisc and the fretting over how much the damn thing would cost and when, if ever, it should be introduced. With raiders lurking in the bushes, companies were loath to spend millions on R&D, or to take gambles that might backfire.

This corporate caution left elbow room—empty space, so to speak—in the marketplace, and not just for the Japanese. *Suddenly entrepreneurs could innovate, could come out with a new product or service, could try to carve out a niche and build a growing company without bumping into (or being snapped up by) a giant competitor.* Suddenly the marketplace seemed to be rewarding not those with the most capital or marketing muscle, but those who brought out the cleverest product, or those who found a niche first, or those who could follow changing customer tastes fastest. Some big companies were so cautious that they hung back entirely from new markets. Those that did try to compete found they could no longer dominate. In their place, newer and smaller businesses fought with one another for space. Many were successful and grew accordingly.

The prototypical product of the new era, the personal computer, offered the clearest example of this phenomenon. Right from the beginning, the PC industry was a funny business, making little sense by Galbraithian standards. It should have been started by Xerox, which in the late 1960s was huge, rich, and the unchallenged ruler of its marketplace. Xerox bought Scientific Data Systems and set up what was called the Palo Alto Research Center in an effort to compete with IBM in office computing. The researchers at Palo Alto—a team that still enjoys legendary status in computer lore—came up with a startlingly original distributed-computing system they dubbed the Alto. It was close, in concept, to what would soon be called the "personal" computer. (Indeed, similarities between the Alto and Apple computers were the subject of a lawsuit years later.) But Xerox was battered during the 1970s, first by recession and patent litigation, and then by the arrival of high-quality competing copiers, from Kodak on the high end and Japan on the low end. (The Savin 750, the first low-cost copier on the market, was manufactured by Ricoh, a Japanese company.) So it was in no mood to pursue Palo Alto's creations. The field was left wide open for two young men, Steven Jobs and Stephen Wozniak, to create Apple Computer, the first broadly successful personal-computer company.

IBM entered the PC marketplace in 1981, hard on the heels of Apple, and unlike its rival Xerox seemed to do everything right. Like Xerox, it set up a development team freed from the usual constraints of corporate bureaucracy. But IBM's team had the full backing of top management, and unlike Xerox's it knew its mission was to sell computers, not just make them. Xerox's system was costly; IBM's, built largely from off-the-shelf parts, was relatively cheap. Xerox's internal architecture was proprietary; IBM allowed other companies both to copy the hardware and to develop software for the computer, thereby establishing its PC as an industry standard. When it came time to sell the PC, IBM brought the full weight of big-company marketing muscle to bear. It sold the computer through Sears, through its own outlets, and through dozens of other distributors. It blanketed the nation with its famous "Little Tramp" advertisements. As my colleague Joel Kotkin pointed out, IBM's arrival in the market-place generated plenty of knowing pronouncements about the future structure of the industry. *Business Week* opined that personal com-puting would henceforth be utterly dominated by IBM. Esther Dyson, who is probably the industry's best-known analyst, advised would-be personal-computer entrepreneurs to "go into the restaurant busi-ness."

And yet: a decade afterward, IBM's major competitors in the PC industry continued to thrive. They included none of the older, larger companies that, in another era, would have quickly jumped into the market: not Xerox, not General Electric (or RCA!), not even Digital Equipment or Control Data or Honeywell. (Zenith had been a signif-icant player in personal computers, but it sold its operation to the French company Bull.) They included a couple of new companies that had already made the Fortune 500 (Apple and Compaq), and several more, still newer, that sold hundreds of millions of dollars' worth of computers a year (Dell Computer Corporation, Everex Systems, AST Research, Gateway 2000). They also included many smaller manufac-turers such as Cardinal Technologies (founded by RCA veterans), several large foreign firms such as Epson, semiconductor companies such as Intel Corporation, big resellers (who put their own name on somebody else's computer), small, so-called value-added resellers (who customized machines for specific applications), and the ubiqui-tous Tandy/Radio Shack chain. In 1990, according to the research firm Dataquest, IBM had 14 percent of the personal-computer market and Apple close to 11 percent. The next *eight* companies divided up about 30 percent of the market, with the remaining 45 percent shared by companies lumped together by the list makers as "other."

Nor was the rest of the microcomputer business dominated by large companies. Despite the growth of big retailing chains such as Businessland—and despite the attempts of department-store giants such as Sears to sell computers—no single outlet sold more than a tiny fraction of America's PCs. Many different companies made pe-ripheral equipment such as disk drives. No microcomputer software company—not even giant Microsoft—was able to translate success in one market niche into anything approaching market dominance in other niches; on the contrary, tiny software-development shops con-tinued to multiply, while larger ones repeatedly stumbled. To be sure, the industry was still new, and new industries typically undergo a good deal of turmoil. But the PC business showed no signs of settling down. If anything, the trend was in the opposite direction.

Many other technology-oriented businesses resembled the personal-computer industry: a host of companies, large and small, scrambling for turf, with the giants having no clear advantage over newer and smaller enterprises. An example was the unglamorous field of electronic controls for appliances. Historically, dishwashers, washing machines, and the like have been operated by electromechanical controls: you set the knob, then a system of gears drives the sequencing mechanism. The advent of microelectronics enabled engineers to come up with simple and inexpensive electronic controls, and a large corporation, Motorola, soon became the market leader. Then, in 1984, a Motorola executive named Peter Sognefest left to set up his own electronics-control company, Digital Appliance Controls. By 1989 Sognefest had the largest share of the market. In 1986 another Motorola manager, Wallace Leyshon, also left to start his own business. That company, Appliance Control Technology, grew to a profitable $17 million in sales in just two years, shoving Motorola down to third place in the industry.

Why should the traditional structure of an industry be turned so firmly on its head? Motorola, after all, was not a struggling company like RCA; it was a leader in microprocessors, cellular telephones, and a dozen other high-tech fields. But the terms of competition, in the 1980s, were different from what they had been. Motorola's appliance-control operation was part of a much larger division, thus relegated to second-class status. Because starting a company was no longer so difficult (more on this below), the division's key managers had a choice: stay or jump ship. When they chose the latter course, they could focus their new companies' efforts exclusively on appliance controls. In ACT's case, flexible, computer-controlled assembly lines allowed fast, economical production, even on a relatively small scale, and even with all the manufacturing done in the United States. (Motorola had moved its manufacturing operations to Taiwan about the time Leyshon left.) An aggressive marketing strategy put ACT's engineers in touch with its customers' designers early in the product-development cycle. Since Motorola's top managers were necessarily engaged with its larger divisions, the company simply couldn't keep up.

•

Innovation, of course, does not depend on new technology. On the contrary: an innovation in business is simply a new package of goods and services that people will buy. It can be an unfamiliar product (tofuburgers, magnetic-resonance-imaging machines), or a new way of delivering a familiar product or service (automatic teller machines, Mrs. Fields' baked-in-the-store cookies). It can be a service that responds to a change in the marketplace (asbestos removal). Some innovations—automated production lines, new management methods—may be invisible to the buyer, except as they lead to cheaper or better-quality wares. Tumultuous as it was, the past decade called forth innovations of all sorts, some not at all dependent on technology, some only partly so. In the new climate, many provided the bases for growing companies.

One miniconvulsion shaking the marketplace in the late 1970s and early 1980s, for example, was the deregulation of much of the nation's transportation system. The 1978 Airline Deregulation Act phased out the Civil Aeronautics Board and ended government control over airline routes and fares. The Motor Carrier Act of 1980 lifted controls on over-the-road freight hauling. The Staggers Rail Act of 1980 (following the lead of earlier legislation) reduced the Interstate Commerce Commission's authority over the railroads. All three touched off waves of competitive innovations in pricing, internal management, and service delivery—and all three engendered a host of new enterprises.

In air transportation, many of the new companies were short-lived. People Express Airlines pioneered the low-fare, no-frills flight, but was unable to survive the brutal competition it encountered. (The larger airlines' decisive weapons, argued People Express's founder Donald Burr, were computerized reservation systems, which were introduced by two of the industry's biggest players, American and United.) Several other new airlines—and a lot of older, smaller ones—also disappeared, their routes snapped up by bigger competitors. Still, even this industry wasn't completely inimical to entrepreneurship. Regional carriers that established alliances with one of the giants did well. As late as 1991, according to *Business Week,* several groups of investors were trying to launch new, niche-oriented airlines.

Deregulation in other transportation sectors touched off more far-reaching restructuring. Large, old-line trucking companies declined in size or went out of business. New companies sprouted up and grew. Some offered services unheard-of in the past. Greeneville, Tennessee–based Landair Transport, founded in 1981, grew to 525 employees and 250 trucks over the next several years on the basis of what it called "time-definite trucking service." Landair guaranteed delivery during any fifteen-minute period requested by its customer. In the railroad business, companies such as RailTex, in Texas, and Delaware Otsego, in New York, began acquiring short lines unwanted by major railroads. Over a twelve-year period RailTex acquired eleven such lines, building up a profitable $17 million business. More new businesses grew up in the interstices of this newly competitive industry—interstices that hadn't existed in the past. Mark S. Smith, for example, left a career in marketing with Southern Railways to start a company called Hub City Kansas City Terminals, one of several such enterprises loosely linked in a nationwide network. The Hub City terminals negotiated deals with rail lines and trucking companies, offering shippers a door-to-door package of transport services. Before deregulation, a big trucker or railroad would have provided the shipping, and there would have been no "deals" allowed.

Because the large corporations were hanging back, nearly any shift in the marketplace allowed entrepreneurs to move in with one kind of innovation or another. Health care, for instance, witnessed both technological and regulatory change, accompanied by a sort of revolution of rising expectations on the part of consumers. Overall spending on health care rose from 7.4 percent of gross national product in 1970 to 11 percent by the mid-1980s. Yet by no stretch of the imagination was this swelling marketplace dominated by large companies. In health-care delivery, for-profit hospital chains competed—not always successfully—with traditional nonprofits. They, in turn, competed with a variety of newly established service providers, from the general to the highly specialized. (What would a Rip Van Winkle from 1970 make of a company called MediVision, which operated thirty centers that dealt exclusively with eye care? Or a company called New England Critical Care, which specialized in home-based infusion therapy? Both grew explosively during the 1980s.) In medical technology, giants such as General Electric Medical Systems played a major role: GE was the world's largest supplier of diagnostic-imaging technology. But so did midsize companies such as Marquette Electronics, in Wisconsin, and upstarts such as Modular Instruments, in suburban Philadelphia. Modular's niche: signal-processing recorders for medical research. It grew to $2 million in sales in five years.

The most curious part of the medical-care marketplace may have been the medical-insurance industry. Traditionally, it was dominated by the nonprofit Blue Cross/Blue Shield associations, on the one hand, and a handful of big insurance companies on the other. But the past decade took an eggbeater to the industry's structure. The "Blues" in any number of regions saw their share of the market dwindle, and some began running sizable losses. Health maintenance organizations—many of them small, regional enterprises—gained a share, often at the Blues' expense. National companies such as The Travelers developed a variety of innovative but not always successful insurance schemes. (My own employer offered what Travelers called its "preferred" plan. You paid a doctor $5 a visit and Travelers paid the rest—if you could find a doctor who was "on" the plan and who had any vacancies. No gambler would have bet that Travelers, despite its size, would be dominating the market with this plan any time soon.) Amid the turmoil appeared more new openings, again often filled by small, growing companies. An example was the promotionally named WHP, First in Employee Benefits Inc., which was based in St. Petersburg, Florida. WHP was a so-called third-party administration company: it managed health-care benefit plans for companies that chose to self-insure rather than use an insurance company. It grew to $4.5 million in revenues in its first five years.

New companies proliferated in any number of once-staid consumer businesses. "Natural" soft-drink companies nibbled at Coke and Pepsi's market share, just as flourishing regional breweries were nibbling at Miller and Anheuser-Busch. Packaged coffee was still dominated by Procter & Gamble (Folger's) and Kraft General Foods (Maxwell House); but "gourmet" coffee, a niche populated by smaller companies such as Seattle's Starbucks Coffee Company, expanded from 3.6 percent of the market to 10.4 percent between 1983 and 1989. Weyerhaeuser Company failed in its attempt to challenge paper-diaper giants Procter & Gamble and Kimberly-Clark, but plenty of regional and speciality producers were flourishing. (I once wrote an article about three young men, all in their twenties, who had started a diaper company in the Pacific Northwest. It was so successful—and they were so inexperienced—that their investors quickly squeezed them out of the deal. Two of the three promptly went off to Houston and started another wildly successful diaper company.) In broadcasting, cable-television networks (MTV, HBO, ESPN, CNN, etc.) challenged the three national networks, whose share of the viewing audience dropped steadily. In apparel, new clothing and shoe companies (L.A. Gear, Reebok) traded on the latest fashions.

The industry that had to rank highest on the transformation scale—and that provided both one of the most lucrative and one of the most treacherous areas for new-company formation—was, of course, telecommunications, which was shaken both by regulatory changes and by new technologies. Before the mid-1970s it would scarcely have been called an industry at all; it was really just one company, with a few hangers-on in the wings. The American Telephone and Telegraph Company provided virtually all U.S. long-distance service, manufactured virtually all American telephones, and owned the companies that provided virtually all local telephone service. In 1975 AT&T employed 1 million people, making it the nation's largest employer. It had $26 billion in revenues, ranking it just a little below Exxon and General Motors. Its manufacturing arm, Western Electric, ranked number 15 on the Fortune 500 all by itself.

The first chink in AT&T's monopolistic armor was the so-called *Carterfone* decision of 1968. An entrepreneur named Tom Carter had come up with a device that enabled truck dispatchers to hook up two-way radios to the telephone network. In those days, no one connected anything to the telephone network without AT&T's permission, and the company took Carter to court to prevent him from selling his invention. But the Federal Communications Commission ruled in favor of Carter, thereby opening up what was known as the "terminal equipment" market to competition. ("Terminal equipment," observes writer Steve Coll in his history of AT&T's breakup, was the company's favorite euphemism for telephones or telephone equipment.) A year later, the FCC issued another ruling that shocked AT&T. A little company called Microwave Communications Inc. had applied for the right to offer private long-distance lines connecting, say, a company's offices in St. Louis with its offices in Chicago. The FCC approved the application.

Changing technology widened these chinks. MCI (later renamed MCI Communications) could offer long-distance services cheaper than AT&T because it utilized microwave relay towers; it had no costly copper-wire network to maintain. By 1976 it had sales of $17 million and was turning a profit. Meanwhile, the terminal-equipment market, which included private switchboards known as PBXs, was being revolutionized by microelectronics. A Silicon Valley computer company called Rolm Corporation produced a PBX in 1974 that utilized the latest digital technology; Rolm made $6 million on the product in the first year alone. By 1983 the company had installed more than 11,000 such systems.

So the floodgates were waiting to be opened, and the 1982 consent decree issued by Judge Harold H. Greene in the case of *United States v. AT&T* opened them. By the middle 1980s about the only thing a telecommunications entrepreneur couldn't do was establish a regional company offering local telephone service. Long-distance services of various sorts, public and private, were offered by several different companies. Telephones and telephone equipment were manufactured all over. Technology continued its march: cellular phones appeared in cars, and pocket telephones were said to lie just around the corner. Many of the new products and services were being offered by huge corporations, both American and foreign; even MCI itself had grown into a multibillion-dollar enterprise. But many sophisticated smaller companies had begun to carve out niches for themselves as well, giving the industry as a whole a decidedly non-Galbraithian appearance. Some examples:

• The Big Three of long-distance communication were, of course, AT&T, MCI, and US Sprint. But plenty of second-tier long-distance companies prospered by servicing specific markets, often with technology unequaled by their larger competitors. "Most such providers have aggressively been laying their own fiber-optic cabling and establishing digital switching facilities in the last year or two," observed *Computerworld* in 1989. "Having all-digital facilities enabled the second-tier carriers to provide better reliability, greater manageability and the band-width flexibility associated with digital media—often ahead of AT&T, MCI, and Sprint. . . ." LiTel Communications, based in Worthington, Ohio, set up a digital fiber-optic network linking several midwestern cities. In 1989, only six years after its founding, the company employed nearly 700 people and boasted revenues of close to $200 million. Meanwhile, so-called aggregators such as Mid-Com Inc. were carving out profitable niches of their own. The aggregators signed up smaller companies as telephone customers, channeled their calls into one of the big long-distance companies, and thereby enabled customers to qualify for volume discounts. The aggregation business began only in 1988, but by 1990 it covered 3 percent of the $50 billion long-distance market. Aggregators depended on the giants to do the billing for calls. Rebillers and resellers (other new companies entering the long-distance market) bought long-distance capacity wholesale from AT&T, then took care of all telephone billing to their customers.

• The biggest players in cellular telephone networks included some of the regional Bell companies and a company called McCaw Cellular Communications, built up by an entrepreneur named Craig McCaw from a small cable-TV company in Washington State. Pocket telephones, under development by the end of the decade, were being pursued by several large companies, including Motorola and AT&T. But the *New York Times* reported in 1990 that a small New York communications company called Millicom Inc. was first out of the gate. "Last week it won experimental licenses from the Federal Communications Commission to build pilot systems in Houston and Orlando, Fla., that would use the tiny phones beginning in 1992."

• The computerization of telephone answering and call routing opened up dozens of niches for new businesses. A company called InterVoice Inc. pioneered the automated answering systems that were already becoming familiar by the end of the decade ("To talk to a salesperson, press 1. For an operator, press 2"). Voice-messaging equipment was being offered by companies such as Genesis Electronics, VMX, Octel Communications, and Tigon. Several other new companies offered equipment that could add automated-attendant and voice-messaging capabilities to existing PBXs, removing the need for businesses to buy a whole new system. With all these choices available, of course, the telecommunications market had grown too complex for some customers to manage—which opened up yet another niche, this one for so-called telemanagement companies such as Centex Telemanagement. Telemanagers maintained a small business's phone system, programmed it to provide specific information (such as the time a lawyer spent talking to each of several clients), and routed calls over shared lines to achieve the most economical rates.

THE ENTREPRENEURIAL MARKETPLACE

The story so far: Like takeovers, the wave of enterpreneurship owed its existence to the marketplace tumult of the previous two decades. Large manufacturers, facing stiff new competition, restructured their operations, relying more on small suppliers such as Kennedy Die Castings. And as markets of all sorts shifted, big companies typically retrenched rather than expanded. That left space for innovative entrepreneurs, who proceeded to build sophisticated, growth-oriented new companies, both high- and low-tech. One businessperson's problem, it turned out, was another's opportunity. As younger, smaller companies sprouted up amid the older, larger ones, the business landscape as a whole began to look different.

Then, too, just as takeovers developed a logic and momentum of their own, so did company building. In fact, a kind of snowball effect was at work here: the more enterpreneurial companies there were, the easier it was to start one. The reason could be found in the logic of entrepreneurship.

Any new company needs prospective customers, buyers who are willing to try out the goods or services it's offering. It also needs what economists call inputs: skilled people, money, and the expertise necessary to put them to work. For a growth-oriented company, the requirements are more exacting. The prospective market must itself be growing, or at least changing fast enough to give new entrants a toehold. The people and money must be more plentiful, the expertise more sophisticated. Many of us could assemble the resources and marshal the skills necessary to start a small restaurant or gas station. Not many of us could do the same for a state-of-the-art manufacturing company or a telecommunications business.

So long as the Fortune 500 dominated the business landscape, would-be entrepreneurs faced a bleak prospect. Large companies swooped into growing markets. They snapped up the best people: college graduates for the front office and dependable blue-collar workers for the shop floor. They were rich—with retained earnings, with access to the stock and bond markets, with lines of credit at the big banks. Other companies were correspondingly poor, both in resources and in prospects. Entrepreneurs typically limited their aspirations to small, local markets. They rarely expected to make a lot of money, let alone generate any for investors or employees. Small business, even of the traditional variety, could have its rewards, notably a feeling of independence, and plenty of sole practitioners and family-run businesses did well enough. But the economic action—the money, the power, the security—lay mostly with the giants.

But when the giants' fortunes turned—and when entrepreneurs began filling the gaps they had left in the marketplace—many different trend lines reversed themselves; now it was small-scale business that was gathering momentum. The new flow of resources could be seen in any number of areas.

Markets. In the past, a company that sold its wares to other businesses faced a choice: it could sell to the giants, with all the uncertainties that entailed, or it could rely on the slow-moving small-business market. As industry after industry began spawning smaller, growing companies, however, the marketplace offered dozens of new opportunities. New companies—in manufacturing, health care, computer services, whatever—needed accounting, legal advice, advertising services, printing, travel-agent services, consulting help, janitorial services. Few could afford to hire full-time help in any of these areas, so they contracted with other companies to provide the services.

This secondary entrepreneurial boom could be seen in the decade's economic statistics. Employment in what the government calls business services more than doubled between 1980 and 1987, even though service-sector employment as a whole grew only about 25 percent. It could also be seen in the experience of individual companies. A Detroit advertising agency called CTS Associates, started by a Young & Rubicam refugee named Tom Scholl, grew to $1.6 million in revenues by focusing on companies Scholl felt Y&R was overlooking. The health-insurance firm WHP, First in Employee Benefits sold its services to businesses that were growing but that weren't big enough to have their own insurance staff.

The change was visible in other business marketplaces as well. A graphic example was the office-supplies business. Historically, the industry was as bifurcated as any. Big companies bought directly from office-supplies manufacturers, thereby getting big breaks on price. Everyone else bought from stationery stores and office-supplies dealers, perpetuating companies that had been around for decades. In the new, Birch-like economy, however, there was an opening for another kind of enterprise entirely: large office-supplies discount houses that catered to companies too small for direct deals but big enough to worry about office costs. In the Northeast, the new market entrant was Staples. In the Southeast, it was Office Depot; in California, Office Club. "Staples would buy directly from the manufacturers, cut out the wholesalers, and pass on the savings to its customers," wrote Stephen D. Solomon in *Inc.* "That's how 12 yellow pads for $11.55 at an office-supply dealer go for $3.99 at Staples." In its third year of operation, Staples had thirty-nine stores and $120 million in revenues. Office Depot, with fifty-five stores and $132 million, was even larger. Sprinkled among the fast-moving businesses that *Inc.* tracked every year were many such enterprises, their growth piggybacked onto the growth of new companies in other parts of the economy.

People. As the Fortune 500 cut their work forces, people with extensive experience in the business world were thrown out of work. Others, seeing opportunities for corporate advancement closed, chose to leave. Both phenomena created a pool of talented, seasoned managers, the kind that simply hadn't been available to small companies in the past, who were now ready to go out on their own. Phil Pachulski, of Prime Technology, was trained at General Motors. Wallace Leyshon, of Appliance Control Technology, came from Motorola. James Hanahan, who founded WHP, First in Employee Benefits, spent twenty-three years at Connecticut General Life Insurance Company, now part of Cigna, the insurance giant. At one point, *Inc.* surveyed the chief executive officers of every company that had ever been on its annual list of the 500 fastest-growing privately held companies in the United States; nearly one-third had spent most of their prior careers with a large corporation. For the 100 fastest-growing small public companies—somewhat larger, on average, than their privately held counterparts—the comparable figure in 1988 was about two-thirds.

Infusions of such talent frequently had a dramatic effect on existing companies, as well as on new ones. In 1985, for example, an Ohio company called Yellow Springs Instruments was a sleepy manufacturer of scientific and industrial measuring devices. Its two founders, ready to retire, approached a forty-year-old executive of NCR Corporation named Malte von Matthiessen about taking over the company. Von Matthiessen, a sixteen-year veteran of giant NCR, agreed. Five years later the newly renamed YSI Inc. was a booming growth-oriented business, its managerial ranks populated not only by other NCR alumni but by talented young people such as Fayre Crossley-McKinney, a Yale School of Organization and Management graduate who had tried out life in Fortune 500 companies and found it not to her liking. YSI's sales were up nearly 50 percent over their 1985 level; the company had moved aggressively into several new technologically sophisticated product lines; and it was setting up joint ventures in both Europe and Japan, the better to position itself for competition in worldwide markets.

Money. Venture capital—money put into risky new companies in hopes of a big payoff—has always been an essential ingredient of American enterprise. William Ogden, a former mayor of Chicago, put up $25,000 for a half-interest in Cyrus McCormick's reaper factory. Gardiner G. Hubbard and Thomas Sanders financed the inventions of a young man named Alexander Graham Bell. But not until after World War II did investors begin looking for high-risk, high-return ventures in any systematic way. Laurance S. Rockefeller, fresh from early-stage investments in Eastern Air Lines and McDonnell Aircraft Corporation, set out to find (in the words of *Business Week*'s John W. Wilson) "science-based or socially-useful projects that had the potential for substantial growth and profit." A group of wealthy Bostonians established a fund to support local scientist-entrepreneurs and recruited General Georges Doriot to serve as its president; it was called American Research & Development, and by most accounts it was the first organized venture-capital pool in modern times. Among the investments: $70,000 for 78 percent of a young company called Digital Equipment Corporation. By 1972 the stock was worth $350 million.

Organized venture investing flourished in the 1960s, petered out in the 1970s, then—as might be expected—took off in the 1980s. It both reflected and fed the boom in entrepreneurship, particularly the creation of fast-growing new high-tech companies. Investments by venture-capital firms increased about tenfold during the decade, totaling some $32 billion by the end of 1988. The most visible entrepreneurial companies, those that grew quickly and then offered their stock to the public, created hundreds of instant millionaires, not only among company founders and executives but among astute venture investors. Benjamin M. Rosen, who left a vice-presidency with a big New York investment bank in 1980 to set up his own business, was involved in some forty-five venture investments during the decade. They included Compaq Computer, Lotus Development (creators of the best-selling 1-2-3 spreadsheet program), and such other highfliers as Cypress Semiconductor and Silicon Graphics.

To be sure, most new companies were never—could not have been—candidates for investment by organized venture-capital funds. "Formal" venture capitalists were looking for companies entering large markets with explosive growth potential. They were also looking for companies that could be taken public. (A public offering of stock gave them a sure way to "exit," or sell out their holdings, and thus realize their profits.) Most new companies, even those oriented toward growth, fit neither bill. Even so, large quantities of investment capital were available to new companies with good ideas and modest growth potential. A study by Robert J. Gaston for the Small Business Administration put the total of informal venture capital or "angel" investing at $27 billion annually, or nearly ten times what organized venture-capital firms ordinarily invested each year. Angels, of course, were simply well-heeled individuals who made a practice of putting up capital for new ventures. Many—such as Sophia Collier, founder of the company that manufactured Soho Natural Soda, and John William Poduska, founder of three computer companies—were themselves successful entrepreneurs. Poduska invested in some twenty small companies during the decade, with deals typically running between $100,000 and $200,000 apiece.

Expertise. Accountants, consultants, and lawyers, as we'll see below, began paying new attention to small, growth-oriented companies during the 1980s. That was hardly surprising, given the number of new companies looking for (and able to pay for) their services. More surprising was the fact that large companies themselves began offering both money and expertise to start-up firms. Corporations such as General Electric established internal venture-capital funds. Others set up what they liked to call strategic alliances. McKesson Corporation, a $7 billion distributor of pharmaceuticals and other merchandise, sought out and invested in new companies that somehow tied in with its own lines of business (for example, a software developer that had come up with a new computerized warehousing system). Compaq Computer invested $12 million in a new disk-drive manufacturer called Conner Peripherals, thereby providing itself with a reliable source of disk drives.

In years past, wrote my colleague Joel Kotkin, large companies might have invested in smaller ones, but they generally treated the acquisition either as a subsidiary or as a passive investment. The new kind of alliance, by contrast, was "based on the assumption that each partner had a strong interest in the other's ability to be an established, successful, independent company"—and that the two companies would remain allies even as each of them pursued independent ventures. In the case of Compaq and Conner, for instance, Conner gradually reduced its dependence on the computer giant. By the time it was three years old it was selling sizable amounts of computer equipment to Compaq competitors such as NEC and Zenith.

•

Stories that illustrate any one of these trends abound; a few, like the story of Thrislington Cubicles, seem to illustrate them all. A more unlikely enterprise than Thrislington could scarcely have been imagined. Its founder was a middle-aged itinerant Hollywood actor who had once flunked out of business college. Its management team, as we like to say in the business press, consisted of the founder's friends. Its product was described as "bathroom partitions," which was a euphemism for toilet stalls. The company started on a shoestring.

And yet only a couple of years after its founding, Thrislington had begun to establish a national market; it had a $3 million investment from a well-established, old-line Fortune 500 company; and its founder was worth—on paper—close to $4 million. All this had happened because the climate for entrepreneurs had changed—drastically.

I came on the story of Thrislington Cubicles purely by chance. As a child in the 1950s, my wife had known a boy named Gregory Braendel (pronounced *Bren-DELL*), one of five brothers who lived down the road from her in suburban Philadelphia. Greg was a friendly, outgoing kid who nevertheless faced some uphill battles. He was dyslexic. He suffered from hyperactivity. He did poorly in school. After high school, he attended a military college. When that didn't work out, he transferred to Bryant College, a business college in Providence, Rhode Island. There, too, he lasted only a short time before being asked to leave.

Braendel's first love was acting, and he set out for Los Angeles, hoping to study the craft and eventually find work. He and my wife kept in sporadic touch thereafter; occasionally he would call her up, or drop a postcard, to let her know of a bit part he had landed in a television show or commercial. In 1984, on a family trip to California, she and I and our two children visited him in Hollywood. He took us on an insider's tour of the studios and arranged for my older son, then thirteen, to have a mock screen test. He showed us a tape of his brief role in the made-for-television movie *The Grace Kelly Story*. (He played Jimmy Stewart, and he got to kiss Cheryl Ladd, who played Grace Kelly.) He told us about the precarious life of an aspiring actor. When he wasn't acting or auditioning—which was to say most of the time—he pursued odd jobs and business ventures. He hawked floor mops at county fairs and home shows. He fixed up houses. He once started a company to market lithographs, but it lasted only a few months. He worked as a salesman for a company that sold solar energy systems for apartment buildings.

In 1987 Braendel came to Boston, where we lived, and asked if we could put him up. Now, however, he had matters on his mind other than acting. "Look at this," he said, pulling out a small traveling case. "This is a model of the bathroom partitions I'm selling."

Frankly, it took a few minutes for us to understand what we were looking at. Bathroom partitions? Right—the metal stalls that grace the rest rooms in schools, offices, airports, hotels, and every other public building in America. The traveling case folded out into a little scale-model stall, complete with working door and latch. But it bore no resemblance to any bathroom partition we'd ever seen. The model—and the glossy brochures Braendel got out next—depicted high-design stalls that seemed to belong in the pages of a glossy architectural magazine. The walls were stark-white laminate or else brightly colored; the fittings and hardware were flat-black nylon. Walls and doors extended nearly from floor to ceiling, with no cracks between. They could be built, explained Braendel, from almost anything: fiberglass or plastic laminate, marblelike materials such as Du Pont's Corian, even frosted glass. The stalls were virtually indestructible (no bent panels and busted hinges when a teenager decided to swing on a door) and most of the materials could be washed off with solvent, thereby eliminating graffiti.

Well, sure, here was a new product that a good salesman might have some success with. But pretty soon it dawned on us that Braendel wasn't just selling these cubicles. On the contrary: he had started a company and was proposing to manufacture and market them all across America.

The story unfolded. The bathroom partitions had so far been made in England, by a small company with the elegantly British name of Thrislington Cubicles Ltd. An English cousin of Braendel's worked with the man who had designed them and had come to America to look for ways to market them here. Braendel had agreed to help his cousin out, figuring maybe he could make a little money on the deal. He flew to Hollywood, where he visited a company called Bobrick Washroom Equipment. Starting his own business was not on his agenda then; he was just trying to learn about the industry, and eventually he hoped to set up a U.S. production arrangement for

Thrislington. "My idea was to find a manufacturer and sit back and collect royalties," he later told me. "Then I could pursue my acting career."

Bobrick wasn't interested in the fancy English stalls. But a wholesale distributor Braendel talked to was very interested; so was a small sales company that represented manufacturers in the industry. Intrigued, Braendel went to England and met with Brian Moore, the managing director of Thrislington. Moore took a liking to the American and came back to the States with him to visit other manufacturers. But none seemed just right.

Finally—it was now late 1986—Braendel and Moore were sitting on the patio outside Braendel's Hollywood home. Brian, said Braendel, why don't I just manufacture the damn things myself? Bloody 'ell, said Moore, why not? Braendel formed a company, and in January 1987 he flew to England to negotiate an agreement. The British Thrislington—which had more work than it could handle and little interest in exploring alternative arrangements—leapt at the opportunity. Braendel came back with North American manufacturing and marketing rights, with a modest royalty to be paid the parent company on every unit sold.

Greg Braendel the friendly kid had turned into an upbeat kind of man, with an optimistic outlook and a salesman's natural gregariousness. But even he must have been daunted, at times, by what he had committed himself to do. He was setting out to build a company—something he had never done successfully—in an industry he knew virtually nothing about. He would be making a low-tech product that, while distinctive, could easily be copied. To succeed he'd have to line up sales representatives and distributors all over the country, set up and operate at least one factory and ultimately several more, persuade architects and interior designers to specify the products of a new and untested enterprise—and do all this before competitors moved in on his turf. Braendel figured that he could count on his parents back in Pennsylvania for some seed capital. But he had little money of his own and no notion how to raise more.

As for the start-up team he assembled, you would have to say that they didn't have much in common with the seasoned corporate executives that were joining a lot of other new companies. Braendel's friend Jack Dunsmoor, then forty years old, gave up a middle-level marketing job at Republic Pictures to become Thrislington's vice-president. Dunsmoor's half-brother, Tim Haase, only twenty-four, became manager of production, and a twenty-five-year-old actor named Bo Rostrom took the title of marketing coordinator. Jo Strate, a sixty-year-old friend who was training director for a company called General Nutrition Centers, managed the office and kept track of the cash.

Things went smoothly enough at first. Working out of Braendel's home, the friends lined up vendors for parts and supplies, found a subcontractor to build the partitions, and began an intensive selling effort utilizing marketing materials from England. By July 1987 they had their first order: seven cubicles for a Palm Springs, California, convention center, owned at the time by Hilton Hotels Corporation.

Then, predictably, things started to come unglued. Monitoring the quality of the subcontractor's work, Braendel began noticing flaws. Edges didn't fit right. Screws protruded. His cubicles were supposed to be a top-of-the-line item, with prices to match, and Braendel knew he couldn't afford sloppy workmanship. But when he complained to the subcontractor he was given an ultimatum: give us a contract for *all* your manufacturing or get your stuff out of here in twenty-four hours. Not one to be bullied, Braendel had a truck there the next morning. But he had no time to track down another subcontractor, so he quickly bought $1,500 worth of tools and put in a desperate call to England for someone to come over and help him fill the order. Sorry, was the reply, we're too busy. You'll have to assemble them yourself.

After a few twelve-hour days the incipient panic subsided; making the cubicles wasn't as hard as it had seemed. You cut the laminated panels to size. You edged them with a custom-designed aluminum extrusion, then fit them into a patented foot, or floor support, obtained from England. You added the stylish door latches, complete with red-and-green "occupied/vacant" indicators. Tim Haase and Bo Rostrum found they had a flair for the work, and at the end of a week the group had all seven finished. They were shipped out to Palm Springs only a day behind schedule.

But that, of course, was only the beginning—and Braendel was slowly realizing how little he knew. A natural salesman, he was comfortable winging it on the marketing front. But he knew nothing about managing a factory, and nothing about financing a business. He had no business plan; indeed, he had no idea what a business plan looked like. In another era, someone setting out to start a toilet-partition company might have been content to make a few partitions, sell them, and make a few more. But this was the 1980s, and Braendel, for all his inexperience, had big ambitions. He wanted to create a national company, one capable of dominating its niche in the market and growing accordingly. For that he would need help.

Fortunately, Braendel discovered that his interests as an entrepreneur coincided with a lot of other companies' interests. By the late 1980s much of the business marketplace had undergone a kind of sea change—a change directly beneficial to would-be company builders such as Braendel.

Consider, for example, the company KPMG Peat Marwick, better known in this country as Peat Marwick Main & Company.

Peat Marwick is a huge accounting firm. In 1989 it had 135 offices, 1,930 partners, and $1.64 billion in revenues in the United States alone. That placed it number 2 among what was then known as the Big Eight. (Only Arthur Andersen was larger. Since that time, mergers have left the profession with a Big Six rather than a Big Eight.) In the past, all of the large accounting firms concentrated almost exclusively on providing tax and audit services to the giant corporations. Their smaller clients were sort of an afterthought. "The same guy who handled Nabisco," one accountant confessed, "would also work with a small textile company. In that situation large accounts would often get more attention than the smaller accounts."

But like everything else in the business world, the accounting profession began to undergo a transformation in the late 1970s. The pressures for change were hard to ignore. The Big Eight's traditional clients were retrenching. Newer, smaller companies were beginning to grow. Deregulation was in the air. Under pressure from the government, the American Institute of Certified Public Accountants changed the rules that had restricted competition in the profession; henceforth, accountants could advertise and actively solicit business from nonclients, practices that until then had been considered unethical. "Rather than wait for the big companies to come calling," explained Joel Koenig, the national director of what was then Touche Ross & Company's Enterprise Group, "the Big Eight began aggressively going after new business. A big chunk of the business they were courting was small-company owners."

Peat Marwick's own turning point came in 1977. Prodded by a consulting study that pointed to small companies as future sources of growth, the firm decided to set up separate divisions to solicit—and handle—their business. Not surprisingly, the corporate culture changed slowly. "At first," said Robert A. Swan, "all we did was take our existing clients that fit the description and put them into this new 'middle market' category."

A newly minted M.B.A. who had previously worked for a plumbing-supply business, Swan had joined one of Peat's Los Angeles offices in 1976, and was toiling in the vineyards of the Fortune 500. But he wasn't happy there, and when the opportunity arose to move into the newly created middle-market practice, he jumped at it. It was the right time. Stimulated by the booming growth in small companies, Peat's Los Angeles middle-market division grew from three partners in 1980 to ten by 1988. When Swan heard from a mutual friend about Greg Braendel, his ears pricked up. He went out to see Braendel, saw some cubicles under construction, heard the story of the company.

"I had never seen anything like it," he remembered later. "And I thought, if [the cubicle] appeals to me it would appeal to others." No company of Peat Marwick's size would have wanted to do business with a tiny bathroom-partition manufacturer. But this could become a growing national company, and that was a different story. To Swan, Thrislington's niche-oriented approach seemed smart, and Braendel a man worth betting on. "Greg didn't have the experience. But he had the capacity to make things happen. I figured we had a reasonable chance of a winner here."

Over the next several months, Peat Marwick effectively transformed Thrislington Cubicles from a seat-of-the-pants start-up into a young but well-thought-out business capable of attracting serious investment. First, Swan conducted a Business 101 seminar for Braendel and his group, explaining the basics of corporate finance. He sent in a team to examine the company's books, and agreed to do annual audits and tax work at a discount. He called his colleague Robert H. Van der Linde, a consultant and senior manager in Peat's downtown L.A. office. Van der Linde came out and met with Braendel; then he, too, agreed to take the company on, in this case as a consulting client. Van der Linde sent in an associate to tear apart the company's finances and projections and to prepare a full-fledged business plan.

As it happened, the assistance Braendel got from Peat Marwick was only the tip of an iceberg; between 1988 and 1990 several more big companies got involved in helping him along.

• A prestigious downtown law firm named White & Case (no relation to the author) took Thrislington on as a client early in 1988, vetting a memorandum offering stock for sale and doing some trademark and logo work. The firm's interest wasn't accidental. Originally based in New York City, White & Case had branched out; in the newly competitive economy of the 1980s, it had opened offices in Tokyo, Singapore, and Los Angeles. Branching out geographically meant searching out new, growth-oriented companies. "In Los Angeles we came to a market that was [already] well served by other firms," explained Harold Reichwald, the partner who originally suggested taking on Thrislington. "We had to begin to build a practice. And part of that process is to identify clients who will be significant players down the road."

• E.I. du Pont de Nemours and Company, the chemical giant, manufactured a marblelike material called Corian, which could be used in Thrislington's partitions. Once, a company like Du Pont would have been only a supplier to Thrislington, and even then might have been less than eager to do business. Now it was a potential marketing partner, and so eager that Braendel didn't even have to ask. Don Duffey, the West Coast regional accounts manager for Corian, called Braendel as soon as he heard about Thrislington. Listen, said Duffey, why don't you use Corian in your partitions? And, by the way, why doesn't Thrislington buy national advertising in architectural magazines under Du Pont's corporate umbrella, thereby getting the big company's volume discount? Since Braendel had planned an extensive ad campaign, the offer would save him as much as $30,000 a year. Later, Du Pont invited Braendel to its Wilmington, Delaware, headquarters to discuss further joint-marketing plans.

That such moves would be made at all reflected a dramatic change in the big company's view of the marketplace. "Ten years ago we weren't doing any ventures at all with small companies," said Peter Walmsley, Du Pont's manager of acquisitions and divestitures, "because the ones we had done before hadn't worked out that well. But in 1984 we decided to give it another shot." By 1989, said Walmsley, Du Pont held part ownership in at least fifteen smaller companies and had "many, many" contractual relationships with others. This change in the corporate culture, in turn, gave regional managers such as Duffey a freer hand in setting up *ad hoc* deals. "I don't know that we'd routinely do this," he said of the arrangement with Thrislington. "But we thought they had some potential in a part of the marketplace we weren't doing much with. So we're trying to help."

• Formica Corporation, which made the plastic laminates often used in Thrislington's partitions, mapped out even more extensive joint-marketing arrangements. Kevin Nicusanti, who at the time was the West Coast regional marketing representative for the company, met with Braendel early on and developed a cooperative literature-distribution program. Then he introduced Braendel to Formica's head of marketing and other top executives. "We have sixteen or eighteen professional spec people around the country," explained Nicusanti, "and if we can put Thrislington material into their hands that's pretty powerful."

Formica, as it happened, was itself symbolic of 1980s trends. Until 1985 the company was a sleepy division of American Cyanamid; since it contributed only a small fraction of the big company's profits, it didn't get much attention and didn't make many waves. Then its managers purchased Formica through a leveraged buyout, and sold stock to the public two years later. That, said Nicusanti, turned it into a more aggressive, entrepreneurial company. "We went public, raised money, reduced our debt. We got whole new marketing teams." Nicusanti himself went on to a new job as product manager for new ventures: "I've been around the country talking to lots of guys just like Braendel—younger, smaller companies with decent potential that can use our packaging, marketing, name, our spec effort, maybe some engineering help." In effect, the search for relationships with smaller customers became one more point of competition in the marketplace. "I know Du Pont did some nice things for Braendel," acknowledged Nicusanti, "and Du Pont is a head-on competitor with us."

By 1989 Braendel had his little factory humming; helped out by the likes of Du Pont and Formica, he was making inroads into the marketplace; and he had a carefully drawn-up business plan with Peat Marwick's blue-chip name on the cover. What he didn't have, yet, was money. Despite Peat Marwick's help, and despite Thrislington's growing sales, the only substantial investor so far was Braendel's father, and his pockets weren't deep enough to fund more than the company's start-up phase.

Capital, of course, is the essential ingredient of capitalism, and all the assistance in the world is useless without the money to finance a company's growth. The organized venture-capital industry was of no help to Braendel; most venture capitalists preferred technology-based companies, and all expected more management experience in the chief executive alone than Braendel had in his entire company. Banks were no help, either. Naively, Braendel had applied to a series of banks for a line of credit; only one had responded positively, and then only because Braendel's father had personally guaranteed the loan. Changing economy or no, banks didn't provide unsecured loans to small start-up businesses. Even private investors had been scared off by Braendel's lack of experience. Visiting Los Angeles in 1988, I attended an "Entrepreneur's Forum," sponsored by the local Stanford Business School alumni club, with Braendel presenting his plans to a dozen or so potential investors. "We took a poll of five or six people after the meeting," one confided later. "It was unanimous: [Thrislington] wouldn't get the money they needed, and they wouldn't succeed if they did."

So much for skepticism. In 1988, while at a trade show, Braendel met a man named Brian Jellison. Jellison was head of a lock manufacturer called Von Duprin Incorporated, which itself was a subsidiary of giant Ingersoll-Rand Corporation, the construction-equipment manufacturer. Reportedly, Jellison was being groomed for a higher slot at Ingersoll-Rand, and he had the ear of the vice-chairman, Clyde Folley. Jellison seemed to think Braendel's company might be a profitable investment for Ingersoll-Rand.

In the past, Jellison might have made an offer to buy Thrislington, and Braendel, who, after all, wanted to be an actor, not an entrepreneur, might have accepted it. But in the 1980s corporations such as Ingersoll-Rand were beginning to realize the value of entrepreneurial management; and Braendel, who still wanted to build Thrislington into a national player, wasn't about to give up control. Sure, he told Jellison, I'll sell you part of the company—up to 30 percent. But it will cost you $3 million, and you won't have the right to buy any more of the business unless I consent. You can appoint two people to our five-person board. I will name the other three. Ingersoll-Rand, number 134 on the Fortune 500, $3.4 billion in 1989 sales, agreed. When the deal was consummated, in 1990, Thrislington Cubicles was thereby valued at $10 million. Braendel, who owned 39 percent of the stock, saw his own net worth jump to $3.9 million. To be sure, it was only a paper valuation; it wasn't as if he could go out and sell his stock on the open market. Even so, for an actor, it wasn't bad.

•

The last time I visited Braendel was in the spring of 1990. Before, Thrislington's little plant had been tucked away behind a plastics-molding company, on an industrial strip in suburban Los Angeles. Now, it had moved to another suburb, into a modern 25,000-square-foot building with the name THRISLINGTON CUBICLES in big black letters across the top. Inside were white walls with oak trim, and wall-to-wall carpeting that led into well-appointed offices. Out back was a huge shop space, two stories high, with floor-to-ceiling windows.

What struck me wasn't Thrislington's success, which, despite the physical trappings, was still in doubt. The company had made inroads into the marketplace, selling cubicles by the dozen to the big Kaiser-Permanente health maintenance organization, to Brunswick bowling centers, and to other big customers. It had created what was in effect a new product, adapting its cubicles for use as modular prefabricated dressing rooms in trendy new clothing stores such as Wet Seal. And there were still-bigger marketing plans on the drawing boards that were aimed at chains such as Wendy's. But Thrislington wasn't yet profitable, and even then Braendel was grousing about the financial controls Ingersoll-Rand was trying to force on him. It would be many months, maybe years, before anyone knew whether—or to what extent—Thrislington would succeed as an enterprise.

The most striking aspect of Thrislington Cubicles was what it symbolized about the change in our economy. In the past, anyone setting out to start a toilet-partition company would have begun small and probably stayed small, serving a local market with products pretty much like anyone else's. Such a company would have fit comfortably into the Galbraithian world of small businesses, big businesses, and not much in between. By the end of the 1980s, by contrast, even a business neophyte such as Braendel could perceive the possibilities for rapid growth based on an innovative product. And he could begin to realize some of those possibilities, thanks to a network of support from the same big companies that once would have ignored or squashed him.

So it was, in fact, in industry after industry—in old-line manufacturing businesses, where growing companies such as Kennedy Die Castings were doing more of the work, and in technology and service businesses, where new companies were opening up new markets. Birch could see it in his economic microscope: thousands and thousands of not-quite-small businesses scrambling to grow, and in the process creating millions of new jobs. In effect, the economy was being restructured from the ground up—meaning, as we'll see in the chapters that follow, that the texture of economic life was undergoing a dramatic transformation.

4

The New Economy: Chips

For most of the 1980s the entrepreneurial revolution enjoyed a pretty good press. Scholars and policymakers repeated as a catechism David Birch's figures about small business and job creation. Newspapers and magazines—*Inc.* among them—told stories of fabulously successful company builders, and business-school students flocked to newly created courses on entrepreneurship. In the corporate world, consultants advised managers to think small. Trim the staff. Sell off divisions. Set up independent, autonomous business units. Anything less, they warned, and a large corporation might not be able to compete with more entrepreneurial companies. *Business Week*'s 1989 cover story "Is Your Company Too Big?" contrasted several struggling giants with smaller, nimbler, and more successful competitors.

As the decade wore on, however, there were antagonistic rumblings in at least one industry's wings. The industry was semiconductors; the rumblers suggested that entrepreneurship was more bane than blessing. "A small but growing number of influential scholars and business executives," reported the *New York Times* in a 1988 front-page article, were "reassessing" the desirability of new-company creation. "In particular, they point to the notable decline of the American semiconductor industry and argue that the ideal of the entrepreneur has been taken to excess. Rather than propelling the economy to new creative heights, the constant spawning of new companies actually may be sapping America's economic might, they assert."

"Semiconductors," of course, is shorthand for integrated circuits, the silicon-based microchips that make possible desktop computers and a hundred other miracles of modern technology. Though the semiconductor industry is an arcane world of acronyms and jargon (an insider doesn't flinch at neologisms such as MIPS or CMOS [pronounced *see-moss*]), no one doubts its economic importance. "What steel was to the American economy for the 30 years after World War II," wrote economics columnist David Warsh, "semiconductors are today." The industry was created largely by U.S. companies, who, along the way, licensed much of their technology to the Japanese. Then, in the 1980s, Japanese producers began to take big bites out of their American mentors' markets. They even drove some U.S. producers out of certain segments of the business. In tones reminiscent of the earlier auto-industry debacle, observers began to write about the "crisis" in the U.S. chip industry.

Who was to blame for this crisis? When Detroit lost customers to Toyota and Honda, Americans generally acknowledged that the Big Three had blown it, and that the Japanese simply outdid their U.S. competitors on quality, price, and design. In semiconductors, however, policy analysts and industry leaders blamed entrepreneurship. Older, larger companies in the U.S. industry, they charged, were constantly being weakened by the departure of engineers and executives to start businesses of their own. The new companies themselves were too small to compete with huge, integrated corporations from Japan and other Asian countries. Entrepreneurship may once have been America's pride, wrote Clyde V. Prestowitz, a high Commerce Department official during the Reagan years. Now it seemed likely to be America's burden.

The most articulate—and most vociferous—proponent of this view was a young political scientist named Charles H. Ferguson. Ferguson had worked as an analyst for IBM, and he had been a consultant to various semiconductor companies. Now, based at the Massachusetts Institute of Technology, he was making his case in speeches and in op-ed articles, in congressional testimony and in the *Harvard Business Review*. Though he was only thirty-three in 1988, his extensive research and his experience in the industry lent weight to his opinions.

The Japanese semiconductor industry, Ferguson pointed out,

was "a stable, concentrated, government-protected" oligopoly. It was dominated by six huge companies—the same companies that controlled "80% of Japanese computer production, 80% of telecommunications equipment production, and about half of Japanese consumer electronics production." Competing against these megaliths were smaller, less diversified U.S. enterprises. A few of the biggest, such as Motorola and Texas Instruments, might at least hope to play in the same league as the Japanese. Most were too small to have a chance.

Worse, the largest U.S. companies kept being undermined by that incorrigible American tendency to start new ventures. "Half of U.S. semiconductor and related capital equipment production occurs in companies that did not even exist 25 years ago," Ferguson complained, "and industry leadership rises and falls with technological generations." Because existing companies were always in danger of losing key people, they avoided long-term research and development, planning, and training of personnel. They were "unable to sustain the large, long-term investments required for continued U.S. competitiveness." The new companies, meanwhile, might succeed for a couple of years—but only until the Japanese giants decided to move in and take over their markets. Then they'd be out on their ear.

Ferguson's views had plenty of support in the semiconductor industry itself, particularly among the chief executives of older companies. W. J. "Jerry" Sanders, the flamboyant founder of a billion-dollar corporation called Advanced Micro Devices, said in a speech, "It is simply unlikely that more than 800 relatively small U.S. manufacturers can survive against 15 or 20 giants in Japan." The leaders of Intel Corporation, probably the industry's best-known company, were equally vocal. Andrew S. Grove, Intel's president, argued that too many new companies were "based on theft,"—i.e., were started by people who took a project from an existing company to a new one. Gordon Moore, Intel's chairman, began referring to the venture capitalists that funded start-ups as "vulture capitalists." (Both men ignored the fact that Intel itself had been founded by Moore and the late Robert Noyce, who had quit one company to start another with the backing of venture capitalists.)

Yet entrepreneurship in the semiconductor business had its proponents. Executives of newer companies, not surprisingly, leaped to their own defense. "Cypress [Semiconductor] and a few other start-ups are the only U.S. companies still able to compete in the

Japanese-dominated high-technology market," said the president of Cypress. And scholars such as Michael Borrus, deputy director of the University of California's Berkeley Roundtable on the International Economy, argued that Ferguson was dreaming if he thought most U.S. companies would ever look like the big, integrated Japanese giants. "We don't do I.B.M.s very well in this country," he told the *New York Times,* "I.B.M. being the major exception."

The strongest advocate for the benefits of entrepreneurship was George Gilder. Gilder had transformed himself, in the 1980s, from an iconoclastic apostle of traditional sex roles (*Sexual Suicide* [1973] was his best-known book in this vein) into a widely read philosopher of free-market economics; his best-selling 1981 tome *Wealth and Poverty* helped set the ideological tone in Washington during the early years of the Reagan administration. In the middle of the decade Gilder turned his considerable talents to a study of semiconductors, ultimately producing a book called *Microcosm* (1989). Along the way he, too, wrote an influential article for the *Harvard Business Review,* this one attacking the assault on entrepreneurship.

To Gilder, Japanese companies' success in semiconductors stemmed mainly from Americans' managerial blunders. But unlike Ferguson and his allies, Gilder wasn't particularly worried about it. For one thing, he observed, the conventional measures of Japanese versus U.S. market share in semiconductors omitted companies such as IBM, which produced chips only for their own use. But it didn't really matter if the United States was losing chip markets to the Japanese, anyway. Large-scale manufacture of commodity products such as memory chips was something the Japanese were good at, and they should be allowed to do it.

What Americans excelled at, said Gilder, was innovation: designing new chips, building new computer systems based on the new chips, writing new software. And it was these activities that accounted for most of the value in a semiconductor. So what if the Japanese had the best chip production facilities? The value of a book lies not in its paper and ink but in the information it contains, and so it was with silicon. "To say that huge [Japanese] conglomerates will take over the world information industry because they have the most efficient chip factories or the purest silicon is like saying Canadians will dominate world literature because they have the tallest trees." Chip design, system design, software—these were activities done best not by giant corporations but by nimble new companies.

And Gilder had plenty of successful smaller companies to point to. Cypress Semiconductor, founded in 1982, had annual revenues fast approaching $200 million. So did a company called Chips and Technologies, founded in 1984.

Gilder clearly knew his stuff: even his critics acknowledged that he had researched the industry thoroughly, and his book was studded with fascinating anecdotes from the history of the silicon chip. But his style of argument left friends and enemies alike almost equally uneasy. Whatever his subject, Gilder had always been a true believer, an ideologue whose fact-gathering and exposition were geared toward hammering home larger philosophical points. His writings about semiconductors were no exception. In Gilder's interpretation, one man—a visionary Caltech engineer named Carver Mead—understood the overriding importance of ever-faster chip design, as opposed to chip manufacture. One group of businesspeople—American entrepreneurs—were implementing Mead's vision, constructing a new microcosmic technology that would transform industry, business, even society itself. The Japanese, pursuing printing presses rather than information, were largely irrelevant. The only obstacle the heroic Americans faced were the bureaucrats, socialists, and Democrats who would increase the power of government. ("The central conflict in the global economy pits the forces of statism against entrepreneurs using the new microcosmic technology to integrate world commerce.")

Ultimately, good would triumph over evil. The "microcosm" would liberate human beings from mindless work, would curtail the arms race, and would replace the economics of scarcity and fear with the economics of hope and faith. "These are not mere prophecies," insisted Gilder. "They are imperious facts of life. Any nation, corporation, or government that ignores them will begin to fade away. The new technologies—themselves largely the creation of Promethean individuals—completely transform the balance of power between the entrepreneur and the state. Inventive individuals have burst every link in the chain of constraints that once bound the entrepreneur and made him a servant of parliaments and kings."

For readers—even friendly ones—it was all a bit much. Gilder's "optimism verges on the fanatical," said Business Week in a generally favorable review. "Will the microchip really prevent nuclear war, topple totalitarian regimes, and restore traditional family values?" "Mr. Gilder . . . is fond of overstatement," chided the Wall Street

Journal's also-friendly reviewer. Less charitable critics nearly gagged. "His conclusions are so grandiose, deductive and lacking in evidence that one is left disbelieving the entire text," wrote Robert Kuttner in the *Washington Post*. "Pop-spiritual, pseudo-scientific doctrine," sneered the *New Republic*.

Entrepreneurship—Gilder's case for the economic value of new businesses—got lost in the shuffle. That may not have mattered much; any reader acquainted with Gilder's previous writings wouldn't have expected him to come to any other conclusion. (Gilder's "ideological zeal keeps intruding on his story line," cracked Kuttner.) Even so, Gilder had pointed to plenty of companies, particularly in California's Silicon Valley, that had done well in the 1980s, despite the Japanese competition. And, yes, for the most part, these companies were both newer and considerably smaller than the industry leaders who were watching their markets disappear. Those who saw entrepreneurship as a curse had to wonder—as time went on and new enterprises not only proliferated but thrived—why all their dire predictions weren't coming true.

The trouble with the debate, at any rate, wasn't just the quality of the argument. It was that both sides were missing much of what was happening in the semiconductor industry. The business had indeed changed in the 1980s enormously. But the changes did not depend purely on technology, still less on ideology. And it really wasn't a matter of big companies versus small, or established corporations versus entrepreneurial ones, or even American companies versus Japanese. What was emerging, rather, was an entirely new kind of industry, in which the most successful enterprises looked and acted differently from successful companies of the past. Many of these companies were American, and many of them happened to be both relatively new and relatively small. But their success depended on their unusual approach to business, not just on new technology or an entrepreneurial style.

The changes in semiconductors, in turn, were emblematic of shifts taking place all over the industrial world in the 1970s and 1980s, shifts that contributed mightily to the restructuring of the business landscape. To understand them, it helped to know a little about the pioneering research of two scholars at MIT: an economist named Michael J. Piore and a political scientist named Charles F. Sabel.

TWO PARADIGMS OF PRODUCTION

Chuck Sabel got an inkling that some kind of historic change might be afoot way back in the 1970s, in Italy. What he was hearing from workers and managers in the factories he was visiting didn't jibe with the way he understood the economic universe.

Sabel had graduated from Harvard in 1969 and had gone on to graduate work in the university's government department. (Everywhere else the discipline is called political science; at Harvard it's government.) He had, of course, read Galbraith. He had also read the economists who were beginning to develop a more sophisticated theory of the corporation-dominated economy—a portrait in line with Galbraith's thinking but one step more refined.

The theory was called dualism. Modern industrial capitalism, said the dualist theorists, would inevitably be dominated by large corporations. They could afford to make huge investments in mass-production machinery, thereby lowering their costs. They were big and powerful enough to take whatever steps were necessary to stabilize and manage their respective marketplaces. They provided steady, high-wage work for "regular" workers—full-time, year-round employees. In the United States, these regular workers were overwhelmingly white and overwhelmingly male.

Alongside these giant corporations was another sector of the economy, populated by smaller companies. These companies weren't found only in marginal businesses such as hairstyling or handicrafts, as Galbraith had implied. Some small companies could be found in nearly every manufacturing industry. A few industries, such as women's clothing, were composed almost entirely of small firms. Nor were the small companies just historical leftovers. Some manufactured the machinery on which mass production depended. Others survived on the fringes of the marketplace: filling smaller niches, responding to short-term changes in demand, in general acting as buffers for the large, stable corporations.

The dualists agreed with Galbraith, however, that these small companies played a subordinate role. They weren't as profitable as the large companies. They rarely utilized the latest technology (they couldn't afford it), and they weren't particularly innovative. When a large corporation chose to expand it could put dozens of smaller ones out of business. Because of their marginality and lack of stability, small companies couldn't compete with larger ones for "prime" workers. They drew instead on women, on minorities, on the young and on the elderly. They paid lower wages, provided fewer benefits, and offered less job security than the large corporations.

Sabel, fresh from his doctoral work at Harvard, had gone to Europe in the early seventies, originally to Germany. His idea was to study the sociology of work: how different social groups wound up playing these different roles in an industrial society's division of labor. But Western Europe in the late 1960s and early 1970s was the scene of a good deal of unrest that was difficult for a curious young social scientist to ignore. In the United States, protests and rebellions focused on racial grievances and on the war in Vietnam. In Europe, they were likely to focus on industrial issues. Sabel traveled to Italy, where the industrial conflicts were most acute, and began nosing around factories, interviewing plant managers and union officials. (He spoke Italian as well as German—and French, Polish, and Spanish. "Everyone has a trick," he told me. "Mine is to learn languages.") For a while he conducted his research alone. Later he was joined by Michael Piore, an MIT economist who had helped to originate the dualist model and who became interested in what Sabel was finding. They would continue the work, off and on, for several years, because they were surprised by what they were discovering.

One fact was clear: overwhelmed by the labor unrest of the 1960s, large Italian companies had closed factories and farmed out production to new, smaller companies. Formed specifically to avoid unions, the new enterprises were often little more than sweatshops. "The new shops used rudimentary technologies; evaded taxes and payments to the social-security system; ignored health-and-safety regulations; and, when the market demanded it, insisted on brutally long working hours," the two researchers later wrote. It seemed as if the Italian economy might be evolving into a caricature of dualism, with the small-company sector a throwback to the harsh conditions of the nineteenth century.

Over time, though, a funny thing happened. Some of these small companies began to federate and to undertake joint research-and-development projects. More new companies came into being, both drawing on and contributing to newly thriving regional economies. They began to utilize computer-controlled machinery and other new technology. Small steel mills in Brescia experimented with the innovative production method known as continuous casting. Ceramic makers in Sassuolo, Piore and Sabel observed, had "devised new clay mixtures, tunnel ovens, and microprocessor-based devices for sorting output by subtle differences in the hue of each tile." As the companies grew, they began paying their workers more. Slowly, wage levels in regions such as Emilia-Romagna (where nearly all of the businesses were small) drew even with those in northern Italy's traditional industrial regions. The two researchers wrote: "A dramatic sign of the prosperity in the new small-firm sector was the rise of Modena—the capital of the decentralized economy—in the rank list of provincial wealth: in 1970 it had only the seventeenth per-capita income of the Italian provinces, but in 1979 it had the second highest."

The companies generating this prosperity no longer fit comfortably into the dualist model. They were relatively small, yet they were innovative, technologically sophisticated, and prosperous. They seemed in some ways on the cutting edge of economic change: they were faster than their bigger competitors to experiment with new machinery, and were quicker to bring new products to market. Piore and Sabel found themselves wondering what they were looking at. It might be that these enterprises were somehow unique, called into being by the peculiar circumstances of the Italian economy. It might also be that they had some precedents, either in history or in other countries. Repairing to the library, the two scholars began reexamining earlier periods in industrial capitalism. They studied what the Victorian-era economist Alfred Marshall had called industrial districts, such as the concentration of silk producers around Lyons, France, and cotton-goods producers in and around Philadelphia. They also looked at the origins of the mass-production corporation and how it had come, during the twentieth century, to dominate most Western economies. Finally, they began gathering data on what was happening to the large corporation in the 1970s, both in the United States and elsewhere.

The book that resulted from all this work appeared in 1984, and was called *The Second Industrial Divide*. Piore and Sabel wrote with clarity but not with the biting wit of a Galbraith, and their book was dense with historical detail and statistics. So *The Second Industrial Divide* never made the best-seller list. Even so, it was a book that few academics or thoughtful observers of business could afford to ignore. Lester C. Thurow, the prolific writer and economist who subsequently became dean of MIT's Sloan School of Management, declared it "must reading for those who want to understand the changes that are occurring and will occur in the structure of the American and world economy." The *Harvard Business Review* pronounced it a *tour de force*. "What makes this book remarkable is the authors' ability to sustain their argument, to support it with examples drawn from around the world and across time, and ultimately to win their points. It is a book that could become a landmark."

Essentially, argued Piore and Sabel, you could interpret the history of industrial capitalism as the history of competing paradigms of production. One was the familiar one: mass production, incarnated in the giant corporation. The large manufacturing corporation thrived by installing huge, special-purpose machinery (continuous-process machines, or assembly lines and the various specially designed machine tools that feed them), then cranking out ever-larger quantities of standard-model goods. Well before Henry Ford, companies such as Quaker Oats and American Tobacco Company had discovered the economic virtues of mass production, and had created large plants to turn out immense quantities of product. (By the late 1880s, James Bonsack's new cigarette-making machines were turning out 120,000 cigarettes per ten-hour day, compared with the 3,000 or so that the most highly skilled workers could produce by hand.) Ford and other pioneers adapted mechanization to the production of complex products. The mass-production factory typically didn't ask much of its workers, only that they show up and do what the foreman told them. Production skills, in effect, were designed into the machinery itself, and into the carefully engineered sequence of steps by which the workers assembled the products.

The other paradigm of production, said Piore and Sabel, was quite different. They called it craft production, a term that meant not handicrafts but a method of manufacturing that used skilled workers and general-purpose machinery to turn out a range of different products. If autos were typical of mass production, then furniture building might be typical of craft production. In a furniture factory, skilled employees use essentially the same woodworking machinery to turn out many different models of chairs, tables, dressers, and credenzas. Their expert knowledge of jigs and fixtures enables them to tool up for efficient production of each job.

Piore and Sabel's research turned up a multitude of examples of craft production: in the industrial districts of the nineteenth century; in industries such as machine tools, where no mass market existed; women's clothing, where rapidly changing fashions made mass production difficult; and, increasingly, in pockets of the modern world such as the Emilia-Romagna region of Italy. Craft-oriented companies were typically smaller than mass-production companies, the two researchers observed, because they weren't based on the same economies of scale; ten lathes in ten different factories often proved as productive as ten lathes in one factory. They frequently clustered together, with several companies each tending to specialize in a particular product, or in one step in the production process. Craft-based companies were most successful when they were innovative—that is, when they continually came out with new or improved wares. When they grew fat and lazy, they were likely to be driven out of business by the mass producers. The clusters worked best as a group, moreover, when they were complemented by a variety of noneconomic institutions—trade associations, unions, and joint research-and-development institutes which provided services (such as training) that no small company could provide for itself. The creation of these institutions was often facilitated by prior ethnic, religious, or political ties. In New York City's garment district, for example, ethnic ties (first among Jews and Italians, later among Chinese and Hispanics) were supplemented by organizations such as the International Ladies Garment Workers Union and the Fashion Institute of Technology ("a public school that trains designers for the multitude of small firms").

Thus far, the two scholars' work might have been no more than a reinterpretation of modern economic history, which would have been of interest to their colleagues and not many others. What gave the book its timeliness—and its interest to the readers of the *Harvard Business Review*, for example—was its examination of present-day trends. Piore and Sabel described what had happened to the economic environment in the 1970s: upheavals in the macroeconomy, growing international competition, changes in the technology of production. Mass-production corporations, they pointed out, couldn't easily prosper amid that kind of uncertainty. The logic of mass production presupposed stable markets and long production runs, which allowed companies to amortize the huge cost of their elaborate machinery. In the 1970s those stable markets were in turmoil. Craft-based companies, by contrast, could more quickly adapt to new opportunities and new conditions. The smaller enterprises were aided by the advent of computer technology. When a product needed modification, for example, some of the fabrication machinery could now be reprogrammed instead of being rebuilt or replaced.

In short, the conditions of the 1970s had altered the balance of advantages between mass production and craft production. That was one reason so many large corporations were struggling and so many smaller ones were prospering. The change was most visible in what Piore and Sabel termed "exceptional successes"—that is, companies pursuing different strategies in the same industries. Small specialty-steel mills proliferated and thrived, while large, integrated producers floundered. In the United States, the so-called minimills increased their share of the market from 3 percent in 1960 to 18 percent in 1982. (Chapter 6 examines this phenomenon in detail.) In textiles, new competition from the Far East drove many large-scale producers in the developed countries out of business. Yet the textile district of Prato, in Italy, flourished, partly because the many small companies in the region prided themselves on adopting the latest in textile-making technology. Other industrial districts began to flourish as well: machinery producers and metalworking companies in the Baden-Württemberg region of West Germany, plastic injection molders around Lyons, a concentration of machine shops in the Japanese village of Sakaki.

What seemed to be emerging was not just a new generation of companies but a different kind of industrial system. "There is something arresting about the proliferation in such different industries and locations of [such] an industrial system, novel for this century, and able to hold its own against the world's most powerful enterprises," wrote Sabel. He and Piore called the system flexible specialization, and argued that it was likely to spread. In many ways it was the diametric opposite of the mass-production world. An industry or region marked by flexible specialization would be populated by many companies of varying sizes. These companies would compete not by trying to dominate the marketplace but by rapidly adapting to it. They would push the market's limits not so much by reducing costs, like Henry Ford, but by constantly introducing new products. No single company could assure long-term, stable employment, but the system as a whole could. As in the garment district of New York City, companies would come and go, but a population of workers, entrepreneurs, salespeople, designers—everyone needed to make the industry thrive—would endure.

If Piore and Sabel were right, the business landscape would, over time, look more and more different in more and more places. Large, mass-production companies would find themselves struggling to compete. Smaller, more innovative craft-based producers would flourish, as would the industrial districts they inhabited. Employees would move easily from company to company rather than spending most of their careers with a single organization. The training and retraining once done within the confines of the large industrial corporation might be picked up by public or private regional institutions.

Enterprises would look different from the inside as well, and they would behave differently. Fewer companies would be willing to invest in big, special-purpose factories. More would focus their resources on flexibility and innovation: on staying on top of a perpetually changing and highly competitive marketplace. Large corporations would be forced to divest themselves of marginal business units and to concentrate on what they did best. To encourage innovation, they would have to decentralize. Smaller, flexible companies would focus on particular market niches. To extend their competitive reach they might establish alliances with other specialist enterprises.

To be sure, all this upcoming change wasn't the kind that lent itself to easy measurement. But someone familiar with the new system's characteristics might recognize it when he or she saw it.

SAXENIAN'S SURPRISE

Where semiconductors were concerned, that someone proved to be AnnaLee Saxenian, a young academic and student of Sabel's who had devoted ten years of her life to studying Silicon Valley.

Saxenian graduated from Williams College, in Massachusetts, in 1976, with a B.A. in economics and an interest in third-world economic development. Teaching English in Hong Kong, she found herself learning about the local electronics industry, in which many of her students worked. In 1978 she returned to school and enrolled in a master's-degree program in city and regional planning at the University of California at Berkeley; she told her adviser she wanted to write a thesis on the internationalization of electronics manufacturing. That, he replied, would be a bit ambitious for a master's thesis. Why didn't she write about Silicon Valley instead?

Once called the Santa Clara Valley, Silicon Valley encompasses a handful of cities and towns at the foot of San Francisco Bay. The largest is San Jose, which grew from a population of roughly 200,000 in 1960 to more than 750,000 at the end of the 1980s. By the late 1970s the region had become the center of America's electronics industry, the home of giants such as Hewlett-Packard and upstarts such as Apple Computer. Valley companies made all kinds of electronic systems, from sophisticated military hardware to video games. But the heart of the business was the semiconductor industry itself. Nobody kept exact statistics on the geography of production, but for a while it was safe to say that more microchips were designed, developed, and manufactured in the valley than in any other region in the world.

As a student in the planning department, Saxenian began asking the kind of questions planners ask about such regions. How and why did companies decide to locate there? How was the industry changing, and what effects would the changes have on the area's economy? "The notion was that regions and cities grow because of the decisions industry makes," she explained later. "So you needed to understand industrial location and industrial organization to understand regional dynamics. At that time, the valley was one of the fastest-growing regions in the country, so it was a logical thing for a planner to study."

Starting her research in 1979, Saxenian interviewed public officials, union leaders, executives of semiconductor companies. She read the local newspapers and the trade press, as well as the few existing academic studies on the region. What she learned, however, made her think that the valley's heyday had already passed. The semiconductor industry seemed to be maturing: that is, consolidating into a few big companies that might keep their central offices in the valley but were likely to move their production facilities to lower-cost regions. New companies were unlikely to enter the business. The increasing complexity of chips meant that the costs of entry were simply too high. Smaller companies, in any event, were unlikely to prosper. "As a consequence of the technological leadership and price advantage gained by . . . large, integrated operations," observed a Commerce Department study in 1979, "many small producers are being relegated to the less competitive, low-volume sectors of the market." In effect, a classic dualist economy was being created out of what had been a freewheeling entrepreneurial industry. Since that seemed to be how most industries in America had evolved, no one, including Saxenian, found the prospect surprising.

Master's in hand, Saxenian set off for a job in New York City; later, in 1983, she enrolled in MIT. She began her doctoral work in planning, but soon transferred to political science, Sabel's department. Maintaining her interest in high-technology regions, she studied Boston's Route 128 and the area around Cambridge, England. She also visited Silicon Valley regularly over the next several years.

The more time she spent there, however, the more puzzled she grew. Battered by the Japanese, the semiconductor industry's biggest companies—the very companies her earlier respondents had expected to dominate the industry—were finding themselves in trouble. By the mid-1980s they were laying off thousands of workers and losing millions of dollars. (A 1985 cover story in *Business Week* was bluntly titled, "America's High Tech Crisis: Why Silicon Valley Is Losing Its Edge.") But in other respects things seemed much brighter than she or anyone else had anticipated. Despite the layoffs (and despite reports such as *Business Week*'s), the valley itself wasn't an economic basket case, nor had it become purely a center for corporate headquarters. On the contrary, manufacturing employment was up. New businesses were being formed and were growing at a blistering pace. "More than 85 new semiconductor firms were started during the 1980s," Saxenian wrote later. "This new wave of chip makers . . . has generated some 25,000 jobs and more than $2 billion in annual sales. While the region's established producers struggle to stay in the black, several of these start-ups boast growth rates of 45-50% a year, and only a handful have failed."

It was an astonishing development, almost as if the auto industry of the 1940s, rather than consolidating into the Big Three, had suddenly spawned dozens of profitable new companies. All this had happened, moreover, as competition from the Japanese intensified. Saxenian, who was then studying directly with Sabel, didn't take long to connect what she was learning about Silicon Valley with the notion of an industrial divide, and with Piore and Sabel's concept of flexible specialization. Maybe something in their ideas could help her solve the puzzle of why the valley was evolving in so unexpected a fashion. In any event, the question itself was a ready-made subject for a doctoral dissertation. Embarking upon a new and more extensive round of interviews and reading (this one lasting a couple of years), Saxenian came up with a radical reinterpretation of Silicon Valley's recent history and future prospects.

•

The chief characteristic of Silicon Valley's evolution, she argued—a characteristic replicated nowhere else, at least not to the same extent—had always been its astonishing fluidity. Companies were born, grew, contracted, split up, combined, and collapsed with amazing rapidity. Many almost seemed to give birth to offspring, so frequently did engineers and executives leave to start their own ventures. Any new industry, of course, tends to be entrepreneurial. Even so, large semiconductor companies elsewhere were able to hold on to their key people and thereby to establish dominant positions in their regions. Texas Instruments, in Dallas, and Motorola, in Phoenix, generally "discouraged spin-off activity and encouraged the internalization of product and process innovations." In Silicon Valley the opposite was the case: even the leading companies struggled, and at various times most had been decimated by departures. Forty of the forty-five independent semiconductor companies formed between 1959 and 1976, Saxenian pointed out, were located in the valley.

By the 1970s all this entrepreneurship had created a distinctive culture: a culture in which even high-level employees felt more loyalty to their industry than to any particular company, and in which it was taken for granted that companies themselves would come and go. Job hopping was pervasive. One estimate put annual employee turnover at 35 percent, higher at small companies. Networks of personal relationships evolved, nurtured by the new combinations of people working at any given company. "We all know each other," one industry veteran said. "It's an industry where everybody knows everybody because at one time or another everyone worked together." The networks extended into venture-capital firms, which were often staffed by industry veterans, and into industrywide associations such as the American Electronics Association, which itself encouraged start-ups. "The AEA's focus during the 1960s and early 1970s was on building the local electronics community by providing services to assist the management of emerging firms rather than on lobbying for established corporations," wrote Saxenian.

Did the valley's chronic entrepreneurialism weaken the industry? On the contrary, Saxenian argued. The fluid environment—with people and ideas flowing freely across corporate borders, and new companies emerging easily—was responsible for Silicon Valley's explosive growth and extraordinary level of innovation. "While most major technological breakthroughs in the semiconductor industry during this period occurred in large, non-Silicon Valley firms, the region's flexible new enterprises excelled at exploiting these technical advances rapidly and generating incremental innovations and product engineering improvements." Thanks to the networks, the smaller companies had rapid access to information about changing technologies and customer needs. They could count on support, not only from the growing number of specialized suppliers locating in the valley but even from competitors. "When the gas line stopped at 2 A.M.," one industry veteran told Saxenian, "you just called your buddies at the company across the street and shared their gas. Or if the epi-reactor was down, your friend did your chips on his second shift and you helped him out next week with his ion implants." People shared ideas as well as hands-on help. An executive said, "I have people call me frequently and say, 'Hey, did you ever run into this one?' and you say, 'Yeah, seven or eight years ago. Why don't you try this, that, or the other thing?' We all get calls like that."

By 1980 there were nearly 2,700 manufacturing enterprises in the valley, including ninety-two companies in the semiconductor industry alone. Nearly 90 percent of the region's manufacturing establishments employed fewer than 100 workers. Paradoxically, it was right about then that valley executives began to anticipate a turning point. They began to talk about a "maturing" of the semiconductor industry and how they expected it to consolidate into a few large corporations. They expected entrepreneurship to die out. This was the view Saxenian had heard in her earlier, master's-thesis round of interviews.

And, in fact, plenty of evidence supported it. For one thing, five big companies (Texas Instruments, Motorola, Intel, Advanced Micro Devices, and National Semiconductor) already seemed to be establishing dominant positions. For another, chip designs and manufacturing were growing more and more complex, and the investment required for production facilities was growing by leaps and bounds. ("This technology completely stops startups . . . unless they are backed by someone like Exxon," said a semiconductor executive in 1977.) Finally, competition from big Japanese companies was already heating up. How could a small enterprise hope to compete with the likes of Toshiba or Fujitsu? "In the 1980s," predicted an industry veteran in 1979, "there may be only about ten firms worldwide that remain as major suppliers of microcircuits."

To most valley executives, maturity meant large-scale mass production. The task for the 1980s, said Intel president Andrew Grove in 1979, was to "market pre-fabricated mass-produced solutions to [chip] users." The five apparently dominant companies had reached their lofty status by mass-producing chips; now, facing Japanese competition and costly new technology, they and other big firms decided to redouble their efforts. "The top seven [commercial producers] spent over $1 billion on plant and equipment in 1980," wrote Saxenian. "That represented a 51% increase over 1979, which in turn was 63% higher than 1978." Most of the new high-volume facilities were built outside of Silicon Valley, often in low-wage Far East countries; they were thus separated from engineering and design centers, which remained in California. In hopes of lowering costs— and in fear that someone would steal their production secrets—chip companies took an adversarial attitude toward their equipment suppliers, sometimes not even letting them into the plant where their equipment would be used. Customers, too, were kept at arm's length. Like Henry Ford, the manufacturers figured the customer would buy anything so long as the price was right.

The big companies thus left behind the networks that had nourished Silicon Valley's innovation. Ideas and advice were no longer flowing quite so freely from customer to supplier, or among competitors, or among design engineers and manufacturing specialists. Lawsuits were launched against apparent imitators and against employees who left to start their own companies. The industry's traditional practice of "second sourcing"—that is, one company licensing its technology to another, so that customers would have two sources for the same product—began to crack. "Even though you're in a [second-source] partnership," admitted one industry veteran, "you do everything you can to prevent the other company from being successful."

Gone was the constant exchange of information, the perpetual small-scale tinkering with products and manufacturing processes. In the new environment, the large companies' success depended on just one thing: the ability to manufacture high-quality, low-cost, standard-model chips. But that was exactly what the Japanese were doing. And taking on the Japanese in mass production was like taking on the French in wine making, as Detroit's automakers had already discovered. A 1980 study by Hewlett-Packard showed that Japanese chips contained fewer defects. The chairman of Advanced Micro Devices, Jerry Sanders, admitted, "The brutal truth is that they manufacture better and with more productivity than we do." The crisis of the middle 1980s was not long in coming. The large companies cranked out plenty of chips from their new factories, but with so much competition from Japan they couldn't sell the chips at a profit. Japanese companies kept gaining market share, and eventually most U.S. producers pulled out entirely from some of the biggest chip markets.

Beaten in the marketplace, the large companies turned to politics. An organization called the Semiconductor Industry Association, dominated by the biggest chip producers, began lobbying in Washington for protection from the Japanese. The charge was dumping, or selling products in the United States below their manufacturing cost. Advanced Micro Devices, Intel, and National even advocated embargoes on the importation of certain chips. Eventually, in 1986, the United States and Japan signed an agreement setting price floors for several kinds of chips. Still, for the rest of the decade, the press echoed with the complaints of the big semiconductor manufacturers against the Japanese, and portrayed Silicon Valley as faltering before the intense foreign competition. "The trenches dug in America to slow Japan's drive to dominate the world's semiconductor business seem to be collapsing," reported the *Economist*. *Fortune* quoted Sanders: "Without the U.S.-Japan trade agreement, the U.S. [semiconductor] industry would be essentially dead."

As Saxenian had discovered, however, the valley wasn't faltering at all. It was booming. And the entrepreneurship that had always characterized business in the valley hadn't died out, as so many people had expected. On the contrary, a host of newer, smaller semiconductor companies were coming up with new products, taking market share from the older companies, even selling their wares *in Japan*. These new companies, acknowledged the always quotable Sanders, "have been eating the older guys' lunch." Unfortunately, he admitted, Advanced Micro Devices was "now one of the older guys."

How could this be? Focusing her interviewing on the new chip companies, Saxenian now began to piece together an explanation of their surprising success.

The new companies had been founded, by and large, in the first half of the 1980s: thirty-four in 1983, twenty-four each in 1984 and 1985, a pace that far outstripped earlier (or later) start-up rates. As usual, the founders were enterprising engineers with experience in the industry. For example: T. J. Rodgers, a graduate of Dartmouth (B.A.) and Stanford (Ph.D.) had spent several years in a Stanford lab, several more with a company called American Microsystems, and three years with Advanced Micro Devices. In 1982 he started his own chip company, Cypress Semiconductor. Another example: Gordon Campbell, an entrepreneur who had left Intel to form a company called SEEQ, was fired by the venture capitalists on SEEQ's board of directors. No matter: in 1984 he started yet another new company, this one with the almost-frivolous name of Chips and Technologies Inc. Both Cypress and Chips took off like rockets. By the end of the decade each was recording more than $200 million in annual sales, with after-tax profits in the 15 percent range.

Few other companies grew so big so quickly; nevertheless, many of the new ventures rapidly forged themselves into solid, profitable enterprises. Weitek Corporation, a specialist in chips for math-intensive operations, did nearly $50 million in sales in 1989, with profits of $7 million. Altera Corporation, which designed special chips known as programmable logic devices, was up near $60 million, with $11 million in profits. The list went on: Cirrus Logic, Adaptec, Orbit Semiconductor, Performance Semiconductor, Maxim Integrated Products. Silicon Valley was once more dotted with a host of money-making new chip companies—at the very time that things were hardest for the older, larger producers that observers once thought would dominate the industry.

This success couldn't be ascribed to the restrictions on imports, since few of the new companies made products covered by the agreement. Nor could it be ascribed solely to the development of new technologies, as Gilder had suggested. The new companies were technologically innovative, without a doubt. But few had access to patents or expertise not available—at least in principle—to the older, larger companies.

What was truly different about the new companies—and what Saxenian saw as the real key to their success—was their approach to business. Although these were substantial, fast-growing enterprises (each of them employing hundreds of people and generating many millions in sales), *they didn't seek to become big, integrated manufacturers*. Instead of aiming at the large semiconductor markets, they focused on niches: a particular kind of memory chip, say, or a specialized processor chip such as Weitek's. Cypress built a sizable business out of such niches: its $199 million in 1989 revenues reflected sales of 159 different chips. And they avoided anything that could be construed as mass production. Most of the new companies didn't even have their own manufacturing facilities ("fabs," as they are known in the industry); they preferred to contract out their production. Those that had fabs, such as Cypress, took pride in their fast, flexible equipment. An automated assembly line at Cypress's San Jose facility could "mount chips in 40 or so different packages," according to a report in the trade press, and could "perform such assembly in 3½ days, versus 8 to 10 weeks for many competitors." Cypress's vice-president of marketing, Lowell Turiff, told Saxenian, "We don't want to be a high-volume, low-cost producer, cranking out millions of standard parts on rigid, capital-intensive fab lines."

In an industry as competitive as semiconductors, Saxenian argued, these companies' specialization gave them immense advantages. Chip technology was changing so fast that no engineer could hope to be an expert in more than a few areas. A specialist company could attract the best and the brightest people in its area, thereby gaining an edge in the marketplace. ("We get the cream of the programmable-logic crop," an executive at Altera said to me, a claim undisputed by anyone else I talked to.) The companies specialized not only in particular products, but in particular parts of the production process. Weitek and Altera engineers could concentrate on design, testing, and marketing. Cypress and other manufacturers, such as Orbit Semiconductor, could pour resources into the latest manufacturing technologies.

It was a powerful logic. The industry's ever-increasing complexity made it difficult for a company to stay at more than one technological leading edge. "Manufacturers *can't* design special products," said the chief executive of Weitek, Art Collmeyer, with only a little overstatement. "They have this hundred-million-dollar plant that they have to keep working efficiently. If they have an extra dollar they *always* must spend it on process technologies." As another industry watcher put it, specialization means "you don't have to be brilliant in design and marketing and manufacturing all at the same time. That is a dramatic advantage for the small firms. . . ."

But the most interesting aspect of the new companies was not so much their own specialization as the intricate web of relationships that bound them one to another. Design-oriented companies such as Altera had long-term relationships with the manufacturers who actually made their chips. Custom-chip specialists such as Weitek developed similar relationships, not only with their own manufacturers but with their customers. Every business, of course, has contracts and agreements with the companies that sell it parts and materials, and with those that distribute or use its finished products. But most intercompany relationships in America are at arm's length—that is, they define exactly what each company can expect from the other, and they make no commitment beyond a set of specific, agreed-upon transactions. As a matter of business strategy, moreover, most companies prefer to rely as little as possible on these relationships. They do as much of the production process as they can under their own corporate roof. When they must depend on outsiders, they want the mutual obligations clearly spelled out.

The new relationships in Silicon Valley, by contrast, seemed almost intimate, the corporate equivalent of setting up housekeeping together. The chip companies depended on customers, on suppliers, even on competitors for critically important operations and for help in developing new products. They shared people, equipment, and information—again, even with competitors—across corporate borders, in ways that would have appalled managers in most businesses. At times it could be hard to tell where one company ended and another began. The network of relationships extended each company's economic reach, giving it a larger presence in the marketplace than its size would otherwise have permitted. It also allowed the companies to share the risks of developing new products in a complex and fast-changing business. "They share both the risk and [the] cost of chip design, development, and production across design firms, process specialists, silicon foundries [and so on]," Saxenian wrote, "so that no one firm bears the entire burden of this increasingly complex and capital intensive process. These highly focused firms are in turn both more innovative and more flexible than the traditional integrated producers."

In effect, concluded Saxenian, the new companies had rediscovered—and rebuilt—the networks of relationships that had always been Silicon Valley's strength. Only now they were stronger than ever before. Companies traded not just on personal relationships among their employees but on long-term, contractual alliances among themselves. They sought to grow by leveraging their own specialties, not by trying to incorporate more and more under their own roofs. The valley as a whole, she realized, had become in some respects a perfect example of Piore and Sabel's second industrial divide. Companies that pursued mass-production strategies had foundered on the rocks of a newly competitive marketplace. Companies that pursued specialized niches—and were able to navigate through the market's shifting currents—were doing well. In the course of a decade, flexible specialization had replaced mass production as the valley's, and the industry's, dominant paradigm of successful production.

BUSINESS IN THE VALLEY

By the time I arrived in Silicon Valley, in 1990, I was familiar with these arguments: I had read Saxenian's doctoral thesis, as well as the flurry of academic papers that she had spun off from it. (This reading was no great chore; unlike a lot of scholarly studies in the social sciences, Saxenian's were free of both jargon and mathematics and were heavily laced with compelling real-world examples.) I had also talked with Saxenian herself. A woman with a mild, earnest manner, she had recently settled into a house in San Francisco's Noe Valley district. Some day soon, she told me, she would be writing her own book about Silicon Valley. In the meantime, she was happy to point me in the direction of what she thought were the most interesting new companies.

I was curious about how this transition to flexible specialization had felt, so to speak, from the inside. It is one thing for scholars to look back over a period of time and analyze the advantages of one production system over another. It is another matter for business managers to grope their way, day by difficult day, toward a new way of doing business. It isn't always clear that there's a new system at the end of one's groping. Particularly for a new company, business strategy is usually more a matter of experimentation than of careful planning.

Yet a lot of new companies seemed to be experimenting in similar directions, and it seemed unlikely that their chief executives had all become devotees of Piore and Sabel. So what were the competitive pressures forcing them in these directions? What opportunities and problems, what perceptions of strength and weakness, guided them? I also hoped that a business analysis of the trend toward flexible specialization would provide a sense of its durability. Was this simply one generation of chip companies improving on the strategies of their struggling predecessors? Or were we seeing the evolution of a system that would stay with us for a while?

To me, an Easterner, Silicon Valley had something of the surreal about it. The region looked less like a valley than like a plain, a flat expanse of land bordered on one side by the Coastal Range mountains (which run up the peninsula toward San Francisco) and on the other by the Diablo Range (which runs along the east side of San Francisco Bay). Broad avenues, dotted with flat-roofed plants and offices, crisscrossed this plain, while curving drives in the middle of each huge block led to well-landscaped industrial parks. I drove through an industrial park in Sunnyvale, one of several towns in the valley, and recorded, in the course of a mile or two, the following companies: Stardent Computer, BTI Computer Systems, Saratoga Semiconductor, Indesys Inc., Epson, IBM, HLS Duplication, Sunnyvale Auto Body, Applied Technology, Lockheed, Unison Software, Strategic Simulations Inc., ST Microwave, California Microwave, Oki Semiconductor, Quest Technologies, Exar Corporation, Modulus Medical Data Systems, Resonex, Hoechst-Celanese Electronic Systems, ADI Systems, CVIS, UVXS Inc., Mark Products Inc., Identix Inc., Northern California Graphics, Peregrine Inc., VICTS Technology, Poquet Computer Corporation, HIQ Computer, and SC Systems Control. This was only one of many, many such parks; most were pure high tech, without even an admixture of companies such as Sunnyvale Auto Body. Oddly, despite the density of companies, despite the traffic congestion that density generated, there was still vacant land in Silicon Valley, acreage that simply wouldn't exist in built-up regions around Eastern cities. Available, the signs read. Weeds grew in the dirt that was once the Santa Clara Valley's rich farmland. Here, the weeds were a sign of an economic boom. No one wanted to grow anything on land that might shortly be sold for thousands of dollars an acre.

In search of the business story behind flexible specialization, I had set up appointments at a half-dozen companies. I should note that interviewing in Silicon Valley presents a major obstacle. Most of the journalists who cover the companies there work for the trade press, or work regular beats for the national press. They have learned the language and can at least nod knowingly when an interviewee begins talking about *megaflops* or *CMOS PROMs*. I had boned up, like a foreign correspondent traveling to a country with an unfamiliar language; even so, the avalanche of techno-terminology regularly left me with a spinning head. When someone like marketing manager Stan Kopec, of Altera Corporation, took me aside before the formal interviewing began and defined the technological terms I was likely to encounter, I was grateful to a point that bordered on the pathetic.

Altera, founded in 1983, inhabited 145,000 square feet of newly leased space in Orchard Technology Park, just off Trimble Road in San Jose. According to its annual report, the company was "the inventor and a leading manufacturer of high-density CMOS programmable logic chips." These chips were usually called PLDs, for programmable logic devices. Kopec explained what they were. If you went inside a personal computer, for example, you would find the microprocessor and the chips that served as the computer's memory. You would also find a number of other chips, logic chips, that glued the system together and helped it exchange information ("interface") with the outside world. The older logic technology was known as transistor-transistor logic, or TTL. PLDs were gradually taking over from TTL. Altera was number three in the PLD market overall, but a leader in the particular kind of PLD known as CMOS.

PLDs were called programmable because of a unique feature. Typically, chips came either in standard models or made-to-order. The customer used them as they arrived from the factory. PLDs, however, could be configured for specific applications—programmed—after manufacture, by the customers themselves. Altera sold its customers programming equipment along with the chips. It was a high-tech version of the business world's time-honored strategy of "give them the razor, sell them the blades."

Before long, Kopec and I were joined by Rodney Smith, Altera's chief executive; Paul Newhagen, one of the company's founders; and several other employees. Smith was a fifty-year-old Englishman who spoke without audible trace of an accent. He had a passion for restoring English sports cars, and at the time we met had six, including a 1931 Riley Brooklands, which had finished first in its class at Le Mans in 1933. Newhagen, then forty, was a small, talkative man with thinning hair and a neat mustache. For the next several hours they told me about the company's seven-year history and the unusual approach to business that had evolved out of it.

The idea for the company's products had come from Newhagen and two partners. They were running an engineering consulting firm called Source III, but they weren't happy. "Like a lot of consulting firms we were spending one-third time selling, one-third providing service, and one-third on overhead—taxes, paperwork, whatever," said Newhagen. "We were undercapitalized, so we were scared to add people. And there was this problem, which was that every time you did a design, you put your best effort into it, and then you handed it off to the manufacturer, who made it for the customer. You never saw it again, and the money stopped coming in. We said, We need a product."

After one false start, Newhagen's group hit on the idea of erasable programmable logic devices, made with the technology known as CMOS (complementary metal-oxide-semiconductor). They developed a business plan, and sent it around to some friends in the industry. Eventually it found its way to a venture-capital firm. Not bad, responded the venture capitalists ("I've seen a lot of plans worse than this one," Newhagen remembered one saying). But they pointed out that neither Newhagen nor his partners had ever run a company of any size, and so were unlikely to get any money. Mounting a search, the three tracked down Smith, a former boss of Newhagen's at Fairchild Semiconductor, and convinced him to accept the job of chief executive. With Smith signed up, they got two checks from the venture capitalists: one for $500,000, one for $800,000. Soon thereafter, they attracted another $9 million in financing.

What they didn't have—what they had no hope of getting, so it seemed—was the $30 million to $50 million it would take to build a fab of their own. "We decided up front we wouldn't be able to manufacture wafers," said Smith, referring to the fabricated pieces of silicon from which chips are cut. "We would have to buy them." They approached Intel, one of the few companies with the capability of manufacturing what Altera wanted to sell. Intel agreed to make the chips—provided Altera licensed Intel to make and sell Altera's products under its own name as well. Altera agreed.

Back then (this was 1984) Altera's strategy seemed at best chancy, at worst foolish, like a farmer asking the fox to oversee his egg production. "People said they'd take all the business," observed Smith. They had the well-known name, the big sales force, the economic muscle. An industry analyst told the press at the time, "Intel can put the parts on the market a lot faster than Altera can."

In an ordinary marketplace, Intel might have driven Altera out of business, or maybe bought it up, much the way General Motors and Ford once scarfed up most of the smaller companies that brought innovations to the automotive marketplace. Alternatively, one of Intel's giant rivals could have done the same thing, thereby readying itself to confront Intel in a growing new market. In this situation, however, Smith hatched a plan to remain independent. Altera was a pioneer in its field, and other companies, he figured, might be interested in a deal much like Intel's. Sure enough, in 1986 he found another partner, a company called WaferScale Integration, which in turn had a manufacturing deal with Sharp, the Japanese company. WSI and Sharp agreed to produce a slightly improved version of the product Intel had. Like Intel they got the right to make and sell products for their own account. But now Altera wasn't quite as dependent on Intel as it once had been.

When Altera was first getting under way, cofounder Robert Hartmann had gathered up published papers on the technology that Altera's products would be based on. Then he called the authors of the papers and offered them not only jobs but equity—stock ownership—in the young company. He hired twenty people this way in three months. As the years went by, Altera became an employer of choice for bright young programmable-logic engineers; it was where some of the best work was being done. So new products followed quickly. In 1988 the company came out with a second-generation product dubbed MAX, with many more electronic elements crammed onto a single chip. MAX was farmed out through a manufacturing-and-licensing agreement to Cypress Semiconductor, just down the street. A year later, again not wanting to be too dependent upon any one supplier, Smith signed a similar agreement with Texas Instruments. TI, too, would produce MAX, and would get the right to make and sell the product for its own account.

By conventional standards, Smith was still on shaky ground. Maybe he was no longer solely dependent upon Intel. But his small company, Altera, was still getting *all* its products manufactured by considerably larger and better established companies. They, as a group, had rights to sell *all* of Altera's devices under their own names. Cofounder Hartmann had once admitted to a reporter that the lack of a fab was his single biggest worry. "We had agreements with silicon foundries," he said, using the valley's term for a chip manufacturer, "but they seemed tenuous. Our fear was that because we were not a big company, we could get shunted aside by a foundry if its business increased and it got overcommitted. That was a constant fear." Altera looked like what *Business Week* had once dubbed a hollow corporation: a company like RCA in the VCR industry that marketed products manufactured by someone else and was thus vulnerable.

But this was the semiconductor industry—and it was Altera that was coming up with the new technologies. That changed the terms of the equation right away, and as time went on it changed them still more. When it struck its first deal, with Intel, Altera's products were new and untested, so Intel held all the cards. In return for its manufacturing capability, it got the right to sell everything Altera had. Once the products began selling, Altera held a few cards of its own. WaferScale Integration obtained rights to fewer products than Intel had. Cypress got only a few products from the MAX line, and none of the software that went with them. Texas Instruments also got only a few products—and Altera was to receive a royalty on everything TI sold under its own name.

Such were the advantages of specialization. Altera had expertise that the others didn't, and so the relationships between the small company and its larger partners became relationships more or less of equals. Each company depended on the other: Altera needed its partners for manufacturing; the manufacturers relied on Altera for the new products it could provide. The relationships among the companies reflected this interdependence. They lasted for a long time, typically seven years. Because the technology was so complex, they were not so much contracts, in the conventional sense, as agreements to develop products together. "We put runs through their fab," said Smith, referring to Texas Instruments. "We generate test programs and software to support [a new product]. Within the year we'll be figuring out the process technology and which fab it'll be manufactured in." Engineers from both companies worked jointly on such issues. By the time the new product appeared on the market, they would have spent thousands of hours in direct collaboration.

Plenty of companies—in semiconductors and other industries—contract out their manufacturing when they're young, then build a plant of their own once they get big enough. Altera, however, became more rather than less intertwined with its manufacturing partners. By 1990 Smith had enough money—and enough of a track record—to consider building his own fab. He would have sacrificed only two things: flexibility (because now he would have a massive investment in plant and equipment) and specialization (because he would have had to hire manufacturing specialists as well as programmable-logic specialists). But his and his partners' experience with alliances had worked so well that he chose to extend and deepen them rather than set out on his own. Instead of building his own fab, he agreed in 1990 to pay up to $15 million, over time, for an ownership interest in a *Cypress* fab.

It was a deal with remarkable potential benefits for both sides. Altera was to get a guaranteed fraction of the fab's output at cost-plus, along with full access to the fab's financial data (so it would know what costs really were). It also was to get early access to Cypress's next-generation manufacturing technology. Best of all, it didn't have to spend $30 million on its own fab, wait a couple of years for the fab to get up and running, and then hope it could keep the fab busy. Cypress, in turn, got a sizable cash investment; it was also able to run its fab closer to its capacity, thereby lowering costs. And it would get first crack at whatever next-generation products Altera developed.

"Climbing into bed together" was how Silicon Valley wags had dubbed the new relationships in the semiconductor industry. Now Altera and Cypress had effectively gotten married—provided you thought of it as an open marriage, with each partner involved in plenty of other relationships as well.

The new model of production, Saxenian had told me, wasn't limited to chip companies. It was spreading throughout the valley: into the peripheral-equipment industry (disk drives, for example); into the semiconductor-equipment industry (machines for making chips); into computer-systems companies themselves. It was even beginning to affect the valley's largest corporations, such as Hewlett-Packard. If you could plot corporate relationships on a map, the valley would look like a spider's web of networks.

This pattern suggested that there were many more reasons for the arrival of flexible specialization than one chip company's inability to afford a fab. And so there were: reasons that varied from industry to industry, yet had a common thread.

The thread was the intensity of the competition. Virtually every company in virtually every high-tech industry took it for granted that today's products would be obsolete in a few years. They took it for granted that companies from Japan and other nations would be scrambling into their markets—and that their domestic competitors could include anyone from deep-pocketed giants (Texas Instruments, IBM) to the latest high-glamor, venture-capital-funded start-up. The executives I spoke with felt a pressing need to keep their companies as small and lean—and flexible—as possible, yet at the same time to establish as large a presence as possible in the marketplace. A strategy based on relationships with other companies was the only way to do that. Immediate problems and opportunities naturally differed from company to company. But the common theme, as the following three examples should suggest, was hard to miss.

A New Computer Maker. Big computer companies once behaved pretty much like big companies of all sorts: they made most of the important parts that went into their machines. (IBM's development of the PC, in which it bought a lot of off-the-shelf components, was a radical departure for the giant company.) But a new generation of computer-systems companies, Saxenian had pointed out, were avoiding this kind of do-it-all-yourself strategy in favor of relationship-based enterprise. A prime illustration was Sun Microsystems, which had grown from a start-up in the early 1980s to $1.8 billion in sales by the end of the decade (ranking number 232 on 1990's Fortune 500). Saxenian wrote:

> When Sun Microsystems was established in 1982 . . . its founders chose to focus on designing hardware and software for workstations and to limit manufacturing to prototypes, final assembly, and testing. Sun purchases application-specific [integrated circuits] (ASICs), disk drives, and power supplies, as well as standard memory chips, boxes, keyboards, mice, cables, printers, and monitors from suppliers. Even the CPU [central processing unit] at the heart of its workstations is assembled by contract manufacturers.
>
> Why, asks Sun's vice-president of manufacturing Jim Bean, should Sun vertically integrate when hundreds of specialty shops in Silicon Valley invest heavily in staying at the leading edge in the design and manufacture of microprocessors, disk drives, printed circuit boards (PCBs), and most other computer components and subsystems? Relying on outside suppliers reduces Sun's overhead and insures that the firm's workstations use state-of-the-art technology.

So it was with other systems companies: Tandem Computers (which made its own printed circuit boards but bought nearly everything else); Mips Computer Systems (which "set out to manufacture the microprocessors and PCBs for its workstations, but quickly sold its chipmaking and board assembly operations in order to focus on design and development"); and Apple Computer (whose chief executive, John Sculley, wrote in his autobiography: "The lifeblood of the network is the free flow of information and mutual support. Any single entity is only as strong as the other parts make it"). The growing sophistication of the final product demanded sophisticated technology and management throughout the network. "As they are increasingly treated as equals in a joint process of designing, developing, and manufacturing innovative systems," Saxenian concluded, "the suppliers themselves become innovative and capital-intensive producers of differentiated products."

MasPar, a new computer company that I visited, could have been lifted from a textbook on this phenomenon. "Relationships were fundamental to our entire business strategy at MasPar," said William A. Hogan, the vice-president of marketing, shortly after I walked in the door. "That was why we started the company here in Silicon Valley."

MasPar's name came from the words *massively parallel,* which referred to a computer architecture that was thought by many to be the next great wave of technological advance in the field. There weren't many massively parallel machines on the market by 1990, and the few that were available were expensive. The goal of MasPar's founder, Jeffrey Kalb (a veteran of National Semiconductor, Data General, and Digital Equipment), was to build a less costly computer using this architecture, and to bring it to market in less than two years. This was not a modest goal. Unlike a PC, which could be built from readily available components, Kalb's machine was to be a high-performance computer that required state-of-the-art design work and custom manufacturing. Even so, Kalb and the team he assembled pulled it off. He formed the company in March 1988. By January 1990 MasPar had designed its product, built it, tested it, and sold it. This was eight years less than it took Gillette Company to develop its latest advance in shaving, the Sensor razor.

The secret, Hogan told me, was that MasPar limited itself to a few key steps in the design and production process; everything else was done in close collaboration with other companies. The design software came from a company called Cadence Design Systems Inc.; the two companies worked together to make sure the software performed as it was supposed to. The chips were manufactured to MasPar's design by Sierra Semiconductor. Digital Equipment Corporation (DEC) provided workstations—smaller, conventional computers—to serve as a kind of connection between the user and MasPar's high-performance processing unit. Small companies called ParcPlace and Compass provided custom-designed software.

As in the case of the chip companies, MasPar's ties to these suppliers were much closer than traditional contractual relationships; they involved extensive sharing of information and resources. DEC agreed to release confidential internal plans of its next-generation workstations to MasPar. It loaned the young company a dozen computers to help it get started. It agreed to cooperate in various joint-marketing efforts. Compass and MasPar set up a joint team of engineers that regularly traveled back and forth between the two companies' headquarters. Vendors were incorporated into MasPar's electronic-mail system, with daily messages being sent back and forth about product development. Some of the vendors (Hogan declined to reveal which ones) had accepted stock in the computer company in lieu of cash.

As the Gillette example suggests, large, market-dominating corporations innovate slowly. There's a lot at stake, and they can ill afford a mistake. Small companies can innovate quickly, but they can't afford to undertake products of substantial size by themselves. MasPar, like the other computer-systems companies, was walking a middle path, tackling sizable objectives yet keeping the business itself small and highly focused. A network of relationships with other companies made that middle path possible—and made it possible for MasPar to construct and sell a complex, dramatically new computer in just two years.

A Semiconductor-Equipment Company. Robert Graham, chief executive of Novellus Systems Inc., chuckled at my bewilderment. I was on a tour of Graham's company, which made sophisticated equipment used in chip manufacture, and was looking through a glass window onto the factory floor. It was the middle of the afternoon, and I could see no more than seven people working there. There were no robots and no hidden operations. Yet the company was then manufacturing more than $50 million worth of equipment a year.

Graham answered the obvious question. "How do we do it? Simple. We buy completed, tested modules from our vendors. We don't allow major items even to come in here until one week before they're ready to be used. Our machine sells for between $800,000 and $900,000, but it can be assembled in a week and a half. And it only takes seven people."

The semiconductor-equipment industry, like any capital-goods business, goes through severe boom-and-bust cycles. When the outlook for semiconductors looks bleak, the chip companies stop buying. Novellus's approach to business—depending heavily on suppliers—kept its fixed costs low. The company had a small payroll. There were few expensive machines on the shop floor. Its inventory costs were minimal. Novellus specialized in design of the machinery, final assembly, and a couple of other key steps. Everything else was contracted out.

Such a production system blurred the boundaries between Novellus and its suppliers almost beyond recognition; Graham, in effect, had to manage other people's businesses as well as his own. "If our vendors have a little problem," said Graham, "we want some special test performed, say, and they don't have the capital to buy the test equipment, we'll buy them the tester to use on our product. If they have a problem putting enough inventory in place to ensure delivery, we'll buy the inventory and sell it to them. That way, they don't have to pay for it until they deliver it back to us as finished product." Graham told not only of helping vendors financially but of training them. The "shower head" through which gas diffused onto the silicon needed a laser weld, which never seemed to come out right. Novellus engineers visited the supplier's shop, diagnosed the problem, and bought $10,000 worth of tooling to modify the production process. The gas-containment chambers were plagued with leakages, because the company producing them didn't have the equipment to test them in a vacuum. "We bought them a vacuum tester and showed them how to use it," said Graham.

Because so little was done under its own corporate roof, Novellus recorded some truly startling sales-per-employee figures: roughly $375,000 in 1989 (compared, for example, with the $166,000 in sales per employee recorded by IBM). Conventional measures of corporate health were pretty startling as well. The company recorded its first sales—$3.2 million worth—in 1987. By 1989 it was up to $51 million. Its after-tax profits were in the neighborhood of 22 percent, and it expected to do some 30 percent of its 1990 business in Japan. To be sure, the test of Graham's strategy would come during the next cyclical downturn: he would have to cut back his purchases from suppliers, and he would have to hope that none of them had allowed themselves to become too dependent on Novellus's business. Even so, he was better positioned to weather the inevitable storm than a company with a big plant and payroll.

A Specialty-Chip Company. Weitek Corporation (the name is pronounced *Way-tek,* and means "microtech" in Chinese) was started in 1980 to produce chips for math-intensive computing (computer graphics, for example, which requires rapid, extensive calculations). Like Altera the company had no fab of its own and relied on larger companies for its manufacturing. Unlike Altera, which sold its chips to hundreds of different customers all over the world, Weitek had a small number of key customers, and had also developed long-term relationships with them. Its biggest single customer, for example, was Sun Microsystems. When Sun wanted a new math chip for its SPARCstation 1 computer, it asked Weitek to develop it—then sent over two engineers and two sizable computers to help in the development.

At times, these relationships overlapped and blurred, to the point where an outsider might wonder exactly where Weitek ended and the corporations with which it was allied began. Hewlett-Packard, for example, was a customer; it had been building computers using Weitek chips. But it was nervous about Weitek's capabilities. Could Weitek deliver the chips on time, in sufficient quantity, and with sufficiently high levels of quality? Art Collmeyer, the president of Weitek, chuckled as he recalled the exchange. "They said, 'We like your technology, but you're a teeny-weeny little company and your part is going to be a critical part of our system.' " The solution the two companies arrived at: H-P would become a supplier as well as a customer. It would build Weitek's chips in its own fab, then put them in its own computers. Weitek developed the chip designs, a job it did better than anyone else; Hewlett-Packard served simultaneously as the manufacturer and the consumer.

Weitek's story illustrated a fundamental characteristic of the new relationship-based strategies in Silicon Valley. Plenty of technology-intensive companies, notably in the biotechnology industry, had established alliances with larger corporations; the giants provided capital, manufacturing capacity, or marketing muscle. But the relationship was typically one small company to one large company, which made the smaller venture wholly dependent upon its partner. Companies such as Altera or Weitek, by contrast, maintained their independence by not relying too heavily on any one partner. Agreeing to make H-P's chips in H-P's fab, Collmeyer added a proviso to the deal: H-P would also make chips *for other Weitek customers* in the fab. Since some of those customers competed with H-P, Hewlett-Packard thus found itself in the peculiar position of manufacturing Weitek chips for competitive computers in its own facility. Weitek took a similarly independent stance toward its customers. When Sun's workstations took off—with Weitek's chip aboard—Sun soon accounted for a sizable fraction of Weitek's total revenue. Collmeyer redoubled his efforts to court Hewlett-Packard and other big customers. He also agreed to sell chips to Toshiba, the Japanese company, which was making plans to compete directly with Sun. (Those chips were to be made—where else?—in Toshiba's fab.)

I don't mean to minimize the difficulties, either in making alliances work or in building a company on the basis of this kind of strategy. Relationships themselves can be hard to establish, if only because companies are political organizations. "There was a faction at Sun that didn't want Weitek's chip-development project to succeed," said Collmeyer. That faction had worked on a competing set of chips that would have gone into the computer if Weitek's hadn't performed properly. Then, too, relationships can be hard to perpetuate. For a while after Cypress Semiconductor and Altera signed their first production deal, the bugs in the production system were still being worked out, and the output of usable silicon wafers varied considerably from one time period to the next. During one quarter things went better than expected, and Altera got more wafers than the agreement between them had called for.

The next quarter? "Sure enough," said Cypress president T. J. Rodgers, "one of my bright young men decided, well, we'll have to cut you below the contract so we'll be even again. From a legalistic point of view that might be reasonable. But with the extra wafers we'd given them, Altera had gone out and built up a business. Now we wipe them out? We make them go to their customers and say they can't deliver?

"I got a phone call from Rodney [Smith] and he told me the problem. I said, Don't worry, it's not going to happen. I'll just go kick somebody in the ass. The next day the problem was solved." Rodgers added, however, that orders from the president couldn't substitute for a bottom-up understanding of the relationship between the two companies: that was why it was so important for Cypress to get a significant product line from the deal, not just cash. "Now if they have to stay late, or whatever, they're working on our product, not just the other guy's."

What was striking about the relationship-based strategy, however, was how well it seemed to work in spite of such problems. It allowed companies to focus on a core expertise, and thereby to stay ahead of the competition—even the Japanese. It encouraged innovation and rapid adaptation to changing conditions. It extended their reach into the marketplace. Not incidentally, it provided the basis for the resurgence of Silicon Valley—which grew substantially by virtually every measure during the 1980s.

Seen as a whole, it was simply the replacement of one system, mass production, by another, flexible specialization. "In short," wrote AnnaLee Saxenian in 1990, "while the region's established producers sought to mass-produce general-purpose, commodity devices, the new Silicon Valley chipmakers compete by getting to market first with a continuing flow of specialized products. These start-ups are organized to develop state-of-the-art products and processes, and to target technological 'windows of opportunity,' rather than to pursue the high volumes required to move down the 'learning curve' and reduce unit costs on standardized parts."

To an observer familiar with flexible specialization, the noisy debate about entrepreneurship in the semiconductor industry—about whether new companies were good or bad for America's competitive position—missed several marks.

On one side, Charles Ferguson and his allies measured the health of the industry purely on the basis of the health of its largest companies. That was a myopia so pronounced as to undermine the credibility of their Chicken Little stance. If the U.S. semiconductor industry was crumbling before the Japanese onslaught, why were so many smaller companies doing so well? Why were they selling their wares in Japan? (In 1990 Weitek did 6 percent of its business in Japan, Altera 15 percent, and both companies were expanding their presence there.) Without a doubt, the market was being reshaped, and aggressive Japanese companies were elbowing their way into an industry that had once been dominated by the United States. But now American companies were coming back, and in ways that the slow-moving Japanese giants found difficult to combat.

Unlike Ferguson, George Gilder spotted the up-and-coming companies and trumpeted their success. His own myopia lay in his technological determinism. In Gilder's telling, young American companies were succeeding because and only because they were riding the technological wave of the future, emphasizing the design of custom chips rather than their manufacture.

But technology was at best only a part of the story. Not all of the successful new companies focused on custom chips; Altera, for one, emphasized the fact that its chips were general-purpose devices, to be customized only after purchase. Not all of them even emphasized design. Orbit Semiconductor (a division of an only slightly larger company called Orbit Instrument Corporation) jumped from $10 million in 1987 sales to more than $21 million in 1989, purely by manufacturing chips to customers' specifications. More generally, Gilder's analysis left a host of economic questions unanswered. Why were the smaller companies able to get a technological edge on the larger ones? How were they able to establish a presence in the marketplace? The problem for an entrepreneurial company in a high-tech industry isn't getting started; that's pretty easy, as Ferguson had pointed out. Rather, the problem is how to stay the course and take on deep-pocketed competitors. Gilder's determinism offered no reason why the larger companies, Japanese or American, wouldn't eventually snap up their smaller competitors or drive them out of business.

The Japanese, he had said, were like printers, while the American design-oriented companies were like authors, providing the information in the chips. It was a clever simile, but it was ultimately unsatisfying. If book publishing were the entire economy, no one would want the United States to be populated only by writers. So it was with semiconductors. A healthy chip industry needed design specialists, manufacturers, marketers, equipment builders, and so on. Gilder downplayed the importance of everything but design—yet it was just such a multifaceted system that was evolving in Silicon Valley.

Like lawyers, Ferguson and Gilder each seemed to be arguing a brief. One held forth on the benefits of large corporate enterprise, the other on the benefits of entrepreneurship, as if the two were mutually exclusive. Yet the situation was too complex for such courtroom-style debate. The emerging system of flexible specialization in Silicon Valley was indeed heavily dependent on entrepreneurship. But it married the strengths of big companies such as Hewlett-Packard and Texas Instruments with the strengths of smaller, newer ones, such as Weitek and Altera. A series of networks linked companies with each other, the linkages often blurring the boundaries between them. Indeed, the alliances even blurred the notion of large and small. MasPar was by any measure a small company when I visited. But its alliances with Digital Equipment Corporation and a half-dozen other companies gave it a presence in the marketplace much larger than its size alone would suggest.

In such a situation, it made little sense to argue for the advantages of big companies over smaller ones, or for entrepreneurship as opposed to existing businesses. What mattered to the semiconductor industry's health was the strength of companies' alliances with partners—in particular, partners with complementary assets. (Some of the new companies even had partners in Japan. So long as the Americans brought plenty of strength to the table, there was no reason to think these relationships would weaken U.S. competitiveness.) The business world had changed, in Silicon Valley as elsewhere. It was time to forget much of what we had learned about what made an industry, or an economy, prosper.

This was a lesson that also seemed relevant halfway across the country, in Akron, Ohio.

5

The New Economy:
Rust Belt

O F ALL the gloomy economic news in the early 1980s, the gloomiest was the seemingly endless procession of mills and factories shutting down. "Between January 1979 and December 1980," wrote Barry Bluestone and Bennett Harrison in their 1982 book *The Deindustrialization of America,* "domestic automobile manufacturers closed or announced the imminent shutdown of twenty facilities employing over 50,000 workers." On Thanksgiving Day 1979—an interesting choice of holidays—U.S. Steel announced the closing of fourteen plants, throwing 13,000 people out of work. Some companies were quitting the North for the Sun Belt: on a single day, the *Newark Record* announced three such moves, which together idled nearly 1,500 New Jersey workers. But even the South and West had their troubles. In California, "at least 150 major plants closed their doors permanently [in 1980], displacing more than 37,000 workers." In 1981 and 1982, with the recession deepening, the pace intensified; now the so-called Rust Belt was hit the hardest. Cleveland lost tens of thousands of manufacturing jobs as General Electric, Westinghouse, and a host of other companies closed plants. Michigan lost some 200,000 factory jobs in the auto industry alone. Unemployment in Michigan that year hit a Depression-level 17 percent.

You didn't need to be a blue-collar worker, in other words, to begin worrying about the decline of American industry.

Politicians were making speeches on the subject, balladeers writing songs about it (Billy Joel: "Well, we're living here in Allentown/ And they're closing all the factories down. . . ."). Newspapers and TV newscasts developed a generic death-of-American-manufacturing story: a report on the latest closing, interviews with bitter, newly laid-off workers, alarmed comments from economists or public officials. In time, best-selling books such as David Halberstam's *The Reckoning* (1986) impressed on the reading public just how far America's manufacturers had fallen. "By 1982, the sheer magnitude of this crisis had become evident to many," wrote Halberstam, reciting the familiar litany of shutdowns and joblessness. "This was not some minor cyclical downturn but in fact might mark the beginning of the end of a historical era."

As the decade progressed, however, there were signs that the Apocalypse hadn't yet arrived, not even in the Rust Belt. Paradoxically, there were also signs that Halberstam was right about the end of an era.

The item that first caught my eye was a 1988 newspaper article on, in fact, Allentown, Pennsylvania. Yes, it said, the twin cities of Allentown and Bethlehem had lost 22,000 manufacturing jobs during the previous decade, 14,000 from Bethlehem Steel alone. But, it added, all those jobs had been replaced, and more besides. Now this Lehigh Valley region was doing just fine, thanks. "Once the subject of a Billy Joel dirge, the valley now has rising per-capita income, soaring real-estate values, and a jobless rate of 4.6 percent."

Indeed, most of the states and cities of the Rust Belt did quite nicely during the 1980s. Cleveland recovered and Pittsburgh boomed. The unemployment rate in Michigan plummeted ten percentage points, and Detroit suburbs such as Troy found themselves in the midst of rapid economic growth. Milwaukee, as I discovered when I visited Sam White, was thriving. Even in 1990, when the Northeast was hurting and the rest of the country tightening its belt in anticipation of a downturn, the Midwest was still humming.

To be sure, America as a whole prospered after the recession of 1981 and 1982. Inflation and unemployment in most places were low. The economy was once more growing. Industries such as automobiles and steel, given a pleasant boost by restrictions on Japanese imports, returned to profitability, and big manufacturers such as Caterpillar bounced back from their doldrums. Even so, the Rust Belt's recovery was in many respects mystifying. For in this recovery (unlike in every previous one), the biggest plants and mills stayed shut. And the giant manufacturers, for the first time since the Depression, didn't call back their laid-off employees.

You could see the end of an era in the industrial landscape itself: Milwaukee's ill-fated Allis-Chalmers plant, the shuttered General Motors factories in Flint, the moribund steel mills sprinkled throughout Ohio and western Pennsylvania. You could also see it in the statistics. Maybe the auto industry was recovering, but in Michigan it employed 190,000 *fewer* workers in 1987 than in 1978. And maybe Cleveland was coming back, but manufacturing employment at the end of 1987 was lower than it had been in the depths of the recession several years earlier. As for Pittsburgh, the city might be thriving, but not because of steel: employment in what the government's statistics call "primary metals" fell by two-thirds between 1979 and 1986. The Rust Belt as a whole lost close to a million factory jobs between 1977 and 1987.

So where was the recovery? It wasn't as if some dramatic source of new jobs had miraculously turned up in the Rust Belt; the insurance industry, for example, hadn't suddenly moved from Hartford to Cincinnati. And the biggest concentrations of new, high-tech industries—computers, software, biotech, and so on—had remained where they had always been, on both coasts. Somehow, the Rust Belt was prospering even without the kind of industrial base it had once had, and without any obvious replacement. It made me wonder what people in the region's puzzling new economy did for a living—and what the business landscape looked like without its familiar reference points.

So I found it pretty intriguing when, on a trip to Akron, Ohio, I ran across two men who might as well have been constructing the new economy piece by piece, not only in the heart of the Rust Belt but in a vast complex of buildings that looked as if they represented everything American industry used to be.

RUBBER CITY

In Akron, symbols of economic change abound. The most fashionable hotel, smack in the middle of downtown, is a complex of upright cylinders that look like giant paper-towel tubes. These cylinders were the bins, or silos, once used by F. Schumacher Milling

Company (later Quaker Oats Company) to store grain ready for processing. They now house circular hotel rooms. In the newly developed minimall adjacent to the hotel, shoppers pause to take in historical exhibits, such as the one that explains how grain was once blown under the street from the silos to the mills. Across the parking lot, families eat lasagna in a converted Railway Express depot.

I had my eye out for such symbols, because I had figured Akron to be a compelling example of the Rust Belt's conundrum. Not so long ago the city had been home to four of the world's largest tire makers, its factories churning out a sizable proportion of American tires. (In the business press, *Akron* was shorthand for the tire industry, the way *Detroit* is shorthand for autos.) Its work force was large, unionized, and well paid, typical in many ways of the Rust Belt's prosperous blue-collar labor. During the 1980s, however, the tire business essentially vanished from Akron. Though some tire companies still had their headquarters there at the end of the decade, the production lines had been moved out or shut down.

Yet Akron, I knew, was doing OK, even without tires. Hence its symbolic value. Understanding how this city had come back from so classic a case of deindustrialization should shed some light on how the Rust Belt as a whole had recovered from its morass of shutdowns. Learning what Akron's companies and workers now did for a living might indicate something about the shape of the next decade's economy.

Akron's career as Rubber Capital of the World lasted most of a century. The city stands on land once known as the Connecticut, or Western, Reserve, a tract allocated to the state of Connecticut as part of the Treaty of Paris that ended the Revolutionary War. In the early 1820s the young state of Ohio established a commission to plan a canal that would link the Ohio River with Lake Erie, and two well-connected landowners laid out a town at a strategic point near the summit of the canal route. ("Akron" was derived from *akros,* which is Greek for "highest.") The choice location fed a booming nineteenth-century industry, first in grain milling (it was the German-born Schumacher who introduced oatmeal to Americans) and later in farm machinery. The city's healthy commerce, in turn, appealed to one Benjamin Franklin Goodrich, a medical doctor who owned a small rubber factory in Melrose, New York, and was looking to relocate. When Akron businessmen pledged $14,000 to assist in the move, Goodrich made his decision. By the end of the nineteenth century, with the farm-machinery business fading, B.F. Goodrich Company was the city's largest employer, turning out hose, bicycle tires, and other rubber goods.

Goodrich also made tires for some of the earliest automobiles, including those made by Cleveland's Alexander Winton, who was said to be the first to offer a car for sale in the United States. Soon the company was taking advantage of this booming new market, and thereby attracting the attention of would-be competitors. A group of local businessmen set up the Diamond Rubber Company right next door to Goodrich. Two brothers named Seiberling—Frank and Charles—established Goodyear Tire and Rubber Company, naming their enterprise for the originator of vulcanization. A young man named Harvey S. Firestone, "attracted by the large profits being made by B.F. Goodrich" (as one historian put it), moved from Chicago to set up shop in Akron. Akron had good rail transportation by then, and it wasn't far from Detroit, which was already emerging as the center of auto production. It also had plenty of low-rent factory buildings, left by the now-departed farm-machinery companies, and a pool of laborers who would work for lower wages than their counterparts back East. Presto: Rubber Capital of the World.

Tire companies and city grew up together, a boom industry shaping a boomtown. Goodrich bought out Diamond Rubber in 1912, boosting its sales and consolidating its position as market leader. Department-store heir William O'Neil founded General Tire and Rubber Company in 1915, and within two years was doing more than $1 million in revenues (the equivalent of maybe $25 million today). A booklet commemorating Firestone's first quarter-century, published in 1925, shows the company's sales jumping from $460,000 (13,000 tires produced) in 1904 to $86 million (6.7 million tires) two decades later. Goodyear, too, grew rapidly. Eventually it would pass Goodrich in size, and would retain title as the world's largest tire maker until the end of the 1980s.

Young workers, primarily men, poured into Akron, most of them coming from rural and mining communities in southern Ohio, Kentucky, Tennessee, and West Virginia. Homes and cheap board-inghouses proliferated, as did saloons, barbershops, movie theaters, and brothels. Goodyear and Firestone, in particular, became little cities unto themselves. Both companies developed extensive housing tracts for their employees and sought to organize most of their social life as well.

I learned much of this from George Knepper, an enthusiastic man who was a professor of history and university historian at the University of Akron, a sprawling, 28,000-student institution. Born in the city in 1926, the son of a minister, Knepper remembered some of the local history that he had made his professional specialty.

"People talked about working at 'the' Goodyear, 'the' Firestone, almost as if it were part of the landscape," said Knepper. "For a generation or more, people worked for the company and lived in the residential areas those companies built, Goodyear Heights and Firestone Park. Goodyear and Firestone went out of their way to provide parks, theaters, gymnasiums, athletic teams. They sponsored scout organizations, women's clubs, bake sales, sporting clubs. Goodyear or Firestone could embrace most of your life."

The paternalism came to an end in the Depression. The companies cut wages, laid off employees, and speeded up production. "Factory hands are now sweating for $10 to $12 a week," the Akron *Beacon Journal* editorialized in 1933. "They can't continue taking it forever." A fledgling union called the United Rubber Workers of America, spawned in 1935 from a dozen different craft unions, responded to the wage cuts with organizing drives and a couple of bitter strikes; by 1941 the URW had signed contracts with all the major rubber companies. The tire-dominated city prospered with America's postwar boom, and because of the union the wealth was widely shared. "We had tens of thousands of high-pay, high-benefit jobs, among the best in the industrial world," said Knepper.

High pay indeed. In 1969 a *Fortune* writer named Peter M. Swerdloff was sent to Akron to find out what young blue-collar workers were thinking; he returned with a report emphasizing their affluence. "Married rubber workers no more than twenty-two or twenty-three years of age live in large apartments filled with new furniture, and garnished with expensive television sets and phonographs. They drive late-model cars and often own more than one. As one twenty-two-year-old tire builder pointed out, 'A guy right out of high school can take home $250 a week if he can get the overtime and is willing to put in the hours.'" That $250 comes to about $860 a week in 1990 dollars, or more than $40,000 a year. As for the companies, they had grown into huge multinationals with diverse interests. All four were among the nation's 100 largest manufacturing concerns; Goodyear ranked among the top 25. Few cities of Akron's size could boast such a concentration of industrial wealth.

•

The undoing of this prosperity seemed for a while like a labor-management morality play, in which you could choose your villain according to your political sympathies. Certainly the United Rubber Workers guarded its members' interests vigilantly. In 1967 the union won a 6 percent annual wage increase for each of the following three years, along with generous benefits in case of layoffs. By 1972 Akron's tire workers were making straight-time cash wages of $5 an hour (about $15 in 1990 dollars), well above tire workers in other cities. Strike-influenced contracts signed in 1973 and 1976 helped the rubber workers to keep up even with spiraling inflation. (The 1976 settlement, for example, provided $1.40 an hour extra over the following three years in addition to a cost-of-living adjustment.) The union maintained a host of restrictive work rules, governing matters such as job classification and seniority rights (a veteran worker could bump another with less seniority, even without knowing the bumpee's job). There were other employment issues as well, including what one news report euphemistically called "lunch and quitting time 'irregularities.'" (Asked about that, one former B.F. Goodrich employee in Akron chuckled: "Guys would come into work, work half a day, then leave and go home. The company knew about it, but the union would make some excuse and get 'em back in again.") Partly because of such problems Akron's tire plants were estimated to be only 50 percent to 75 percent as productive as nonunion plants elsewhere.

For their part, the tire companies had decided earlier that it didn't pay to expand in Akron. "Even in the 1950s and 1960s, when Akron was an affluent society, there was a dry rot," explained Knepper. "The movement outward of production facilities was already well under way." Some of the earliest departures, pointed out to me by Knepper's colleague Daniel Nelson, a specialist in labor history, came right after the organizing drives of the 1930s. "Firestone took a strike in 1937—a calm, almost quiet strike, not like the conflict with Goodyear. But the company then cut employment [in Akron] 50 percent between 1936 and 1939. There was a sharp recession then, so the layoffs camouflaged the move. But they never brought the jobs back. They went to Memphis, and Noblesville, Indiana, instead."

Over the next three decades the number of tire-factory jobs in Akron declined—slowly. "It just wasn't dramatic enough to be noticed," Knepper observed. "Occasionally a plant would close down, but there were still plenty of good jobs around. Even knowledgeable people failed to see what was happening." By the 1970s, however, this emigration was becoming a bone of labor-management contention, which only worsened the process. Firestone told the union in 1971 it would need wage-rate and work-rule concessions if it were to start a new truck-tire operation in Akron. When the union balked, Firestone built the facility in Tennessee. A year later the union did vote to change work rules, both at Firestone and at Goodrich. But mistrust persisted. By 1977 a union official was telling a reporter that the URW had worked out a compromise on work rules at Goodyear, but "they moved the jobs out at the end of the year anyway. So next time they come to us with a plan to keep a plant open, we're going to be skeptical."

In retrospect, it's hard to avoid the feeling that union and management were playing out their accustomed roles while the stage was crumbling around them. In 1948 the French tire maker then known as Michelin & Cie. introduced the first radial tire, called the Michelin X. The durable, longer-lived radials caught on quickly in Europe, but were virtually unknown in the United States. Then, in 1965, Sears, Roebuck & Company put a question to Michelin: Would the company care to sell radial tires through Sears? "We had to convince Michelin to develop an American-sized tire," a Sears official remembered later. "They were reluctant. But we saw the market developing, and we wanted the best." To Michelin, Sears offered a way of testing American waters. When the trial succeeded, the company built plants in Greenville and Anderson, South Carolina, and began selling under its own name.

Ironically, B.F. Goodrich had announced U.S. production of radials in 1964. But Goodrich didn't push them hard, and by the early 1970s, even before it built its plants here, Michelin held a sizable fraction of the American market for radials. For the most part, as a report on the tire business noted, "The U.S. tire fraternity resisted the radial trend fiercely." Industry leader Goodyear placed its bets on polyester- and glass-belted tires, variations on the popular bias-belted tire introduced in 1967; its chairman, Russell DeYoung, prophesied that radials would be a third-choice tire for many years to come. There were good reasons, of course, for the stalling. Unlike Michelin, which had converted to radials right after World War II, American manufacturers had huge investments in conventional tire-making equipment that would have to be sacrificed. Besides, the tire-makers' biggest customers, in Detroit, were waffling. Radials, it was said, caused a harder ride on cars built with American suspensions. And U.S. consumers might not want to spend the extra money.

In time, of course, fighting against the longer-lived radials proved fruitless. Consumers bought more and more of them as replacement tires, and Detroit eventually began ordering them as original equipment. The tire companies made the changeover, grudgingly and with difficulty. In 1976 Goodyear quietly dropped its fifty-year-old guarantee to replace tires that failed before a certain number of miles; it also announced a $69 million retooling of its Gadsden, Alabama, plant. Both moves were sure evidence, said a *Forbes* article, "that it is having trouble building radials satisfactorily in existing plants." Firestone, in 1978, recalled hundreds of thousands of apparently defective "Firestone Radial 500" tires, one of the biggest product recalls to date, and in the process recorded a $148 million loss. But the tire makers' longer-term problems dwarfed even these difficulties. Every radial sold lasted at least twice as long as a bias-ply tire, ultimately reducing demand. International competition was heating up, not only from Michelin and other European companies but from Japan (the many thousands of Japanese cars finding their way into the United States all came equipped with Japanese tires). And Americans were driving less anyway, because of high gasoline prices. Themselves hit by rising raw-materials costs, the tire makers weren't making money. Some didn't see how they would in the future.

The steps they took over the next several years were predictably drastic.

Between 1978 and 1981 the tire industry cut its production capacity 20 percent, closing nineteen plants while opening only one. The first to go were the older, unionized factories, many of them in Akron. Goodyear closed its Plant No. 2 in Akron, idling 730 workers, in January 1978. Firestone shut down its own Plant No. 2 in June. Closings continued throughout the next few years. By the time Firestone's Akron Plant No. 1 shut down in April 1981, eliminating 1,345 jobs, General Tire was the only company left with full-scale production facilities in the onetime rubber capital. A year later General, too, was gone. Between 1979 and 1983 Akron lost roughly 10,000 jobs in the tire industry.

The industry itself—contrary to the trend in most businesses—began a period of worldwide consolidation, with big companies getting bigger and others dropping out entirely. B.F. Goodrich abandoned the new-car tire market in the early 1980s; then, in 1986, it set up a joint venture with Uniroyal to take over both companies' tire-making operations. Uniroyal Goodrich Tire Company, as the new business was named, operated independently for a short while, then was bought out by New York investors, who eventually sold it to Michelin. Firestone, under new chairman John Nevin (the same John Nevin who had spent the 1970s trying to fight off the Japanese on behalf of Zenith Radio Corporation) sold off many of its nontire businesses, closed ten of its seventeen tire plants, cut employment from 107,000 to 55,000, and focused its efforts on the new-car radial market. Nevin took home a $5.6 million bonus for his "rescue" of Firestone, then proceeded to negotiate a sale of the company (for what later turned out to be an absurdly high price) to the giant Japanese tire maker Bridgestone. General Tire and Rubber, renaming itself GenCorp, sold its own tire-making operations to the German company Continental AG. The only big American company left making tires was Goodyear, and in 1986 it had to fight off a takeover attempt by the British financier Sir James Goldsmith.

Throughout this consolidation, the tire industry improved both its products and its productivity. Radial tires made in 1990 lasted about 60,000 miles. At $60 apiece, that was 1,000 miles per dollar, as compared with 450 miles per inflation-adjusted dollar twenty years earlier. Thanks to automation, output per worker-hour increased 32 percent between 1981 and 1988. By 1991 all this productivity had created worldwide overcapacity, and with a recession on, several of the giants were gasping for financial breath. Goodyear, the American contender in the industry, was barely holding its own in the newly competitive marketplace. It had dropped to number three in sales revenue, and even though its plants in Lawton, Oklahoma, and Tyler, Texas, were among the most sophisticated anywhere, it experienced its worst operating results ever in the first three months of 1991.

But little of this drama was being played out in Akron. There, curiously, it was the mergers and takeover attempts (not the last tire-factory closings of a few years earlier) that symbolized the end of an industrial era. People I spoke with told me over and over of their anger at John Nevin, who before he sold Firestone had moved its headquarters to Chicago. "Harvey would never have done it if he were alive," groused one irate businessman. (Bridgestone later moved the headquarters back to Akron.) Akronites also told me how the town had "united" behind Goodyear chairman Robert Mercer, who was leading the fight against would-be acquirer Goldsmith. Dozens had put Save Goodyear signs in their front yards. Thousands had signed petitions of support at a University of Akron football game. Somehow the fact that Goodyear, too, had moved all its tire production out of Akron was lost in the shuffle. When Goodyear "won" the fight (by buying back Goldsmith's stock, purchasing portions of other shareowners' holdings, and thereby incurring a multibillion-dollar debt), the company had to sell off most of its nontire operations. One of the first to go was Goodyear Aerospace, which by then was its only big manufacturing division in Akron. It was sold for $588 million to Loral Corporation (though Loral was headquartered in New York City, it kept the aerospace facility in Akron).

One day in 1989 I asked two business journalists from the Akron *Beacon Journal,* Peter Geiger and Larry Pantages, to list the city's biggest employers of local blue-collar labor. "Other than Loral, there just aren't many," said Geiger. "There's a Babcock & Wilcox plant out in Barberton [a few miles away] and a Chrysler plant in Twinsburg [fifteen miles], and a few others. Goodyear still has a few hundred production workers, maybe 200 in the air-springs plant and 200 in the mold plant. Otherwise, not much. General is down to fifteen hourly employees, Firestone has 200, mostly in maintenance. Uniroyal Goodrich has none."

"When Firestone brought its headquarters back from Chicago," added Pantages, "it was big news. Anytime a big company creates new jobs it's big news. But how many jobs was it? Only a hundred or so."

Nevertheless, Akron's labor force—70,000-plus manufacturing workers and close to 200,000 in other private-sector employment, for a total that was roughly what it had been in 1979—was holding down jobs somewhere. The question still was, where?

GAMBLING ON RECOVERY

One of the people whose life was most affected by this deindustrialization was a man named Dennis K. Oleksuk, an Akron resident who turned forty in 1988. Not realizing I was about to stumble on the most striking symbol of economic change in Akron that I had yet seen, I arranged to meet Oleksuk at the old B.F. Goodrich plants on South Main Street.

As it happened, "plants" wasn't quite an adequate description of these astonishing buildings. Scarcely a mile from the heart of downtown, surrounded largely by open land, the sprawling complex of factories covered nearly forty acres. The twenty-seven buildings, aging red brick, stretched massively upward, five or six or seven stories each. I had driven around the complex early one morning, on an earlier trip to Akron, and had had the eerie feeling of trespassing in an abandoned city. A sign facing the street said B.F. Goodrich Engineered Systems Division, Gate 1; the adjacent drive led into a cracked and weed-filled parking lot. Out back, huge bays stood open, rusting machinery still visible within. From that perspective the buildings had looked ready for industrial archaelogists, or else the wrecking ball.

Oleksuk (as he later told me) had come to work in these buildings in 1971. It wasn't his first factory job out of high school; that was at Goodyear Aerospace, where he worked as a spray painter. ("I met this guy outside the factory gates. He said, 'Tell 'em you're a painter. They're hiring painters.' ") He stayed at Goodyear for a couple of years, was laid off, worked for a while in construction. He then applied for a job at Goodrich and was hired as a maintenance mechanic.

Hardworking and capable (he had finished third in his class in high school and had taken some courses at the University of Akron), Oleksuk moved up the ladder. He was made a maintenance supervisor after only two years. Later, he was put in charge of Goodrich's construction shop, overseeing equipment installation and building renovations. He became facilities manager for the office buildings in the group. Finally, in 1985, the company made him facilities manager for the whole complex. From his corner office on the first floor of building 25, the headquarters building, Oleksuk oversaw the maintenance and operations of B.F. Goodrich's world headquarters.

B.F. Goodrich was always the odd company out among Akron's giant tire makers. First in the business, it was passed in size by Goodyear. When the others reacted to unionization by moving production away from Akron, Goodrich, beset by a series of management crises, did nothing. "B.F. Goodrich became the largest employer in town almost by default," explained Daniel Nelson, the labor historian. "They weren't aggressive in addressing the union situation. In fact, they were on the verge of failure throughout the 1930s." The company always maintained a diversity of product lines, reflecting its

origins as a maker of many different rubber products. It made industrial products such as conveyor belts, and consumer products such as
golf balls. It manufactured space suits for the National Aeronautics
and Space Administration, and exit slides for aircraft manufacturers.
It had a large chemicals division.

For a while, particularly during the 1970s, Goodrich's mix of
products served it well. A 1974 report for investors in *Barron's,* the
financial journal, acknowledged this fact: "Less dependent than its
industry fellows on tire volume, Goodrich, thanks to a better than
50% sales and profit contribution from chemicals, is headed for its
fourth earnings gain in a row." But in the late 1970s and early 1980s,
with the tire business in the doldrums, the company invested a whopping $600 million in the production of a plastic called polyvinyl
chloride (PVC). The move turned out to be an equally whopping
blunder. PVC, made partly from petrochemicals, was priced high
during the oil-scarce 1970s, and Goodrich thought it would remain
so. When oil fell, so did PVC—and Goodrich was left with a mammoth money-loser. By 1984 the company was barely breaking even.

At this point, John Ong, a longtime Goodrich executive who had
taken over as chief executive officer five years earlier, began to re-
structure the company. Like many other Fortune 500 CEOs of the
time, he sold off some of his organization's divisions and closed
others. He shut down a $200 million PCV plant in Louisiana. He set
up the joint venture with Uniroyal to take over Goodrich's tire operations. Revenues fell, from $3.3 billion in 1984 to a low of just over $2
billion in 1987. But profits rose. "I always knew that inside this bad,
fat company was a great, thin company just dying to get out," Ong
told a reporter from the *New York Times.* As part of the restructuring, Ong had to figure out what to do with the company's huge, aging
complex of buildings on South Main Street, in Akron.

This was, to put it mildly, no small matter, either financially or
logistically. No wonder I had thought of a city: back in the 1920s, the
Goodrich plants had accommodated 28,000 workers. They had had
their own water, electric, and telephone systems; police and fire
departments; medical and dental clinics. Even in the 1970s, with the
work force reduced to several thousand, the South Main Street complex had been the heart of the big company's operations. Offices there
were rebuilt and modernized. The huge conveyor-belt plant was
renovated at a cost of $6 million. Then, however, came Ong's restruc-
turing, and now there was no question of staying; the trimmed-down

company would move its headquarters to more efficient space on the outskirts of Akron and shut down or sell off the manufacturing units housed on South Main Street. The logical thing to do with the buildings—for who would want a set of factories so big and so old, particularly in Akron?—was to raze them.

The man responsible: Denny Oleksuk. "I was charged with the wind-down of the complex. I was involved in moving people out, moving businesses out, dealing with the layoffs, physically getting the equipment out, severing utility services, you name it. They called it Operation Greengrass. We were preparing the complex for demolition—ultimately for green grass." This was Ong's restructuring seen from the inside out: divisions and business units were closed, moved, or sold off, emptying the premises. Goodrich was at last going the way of the rest of Akron, eliminating blue-collar jobs by the thousands. Resentment and resignation pervaded the place, and Oleksuk was not immune. "There were 8,000 people working here when I hired in. It steadily diminished over the course of my employment. By the end I was one of only five B.F. Goodrich employees.

"We'd done so much renovation, brought in so much new equipment. We'd spent hundreds of thousands of dollars—$550,000 on a new corporate medical center alone. And now this stuff was going under the burners' torches, being cut apart, carried out in pieces. It was going out in the scrap dealer's trucks."

And the buildings that Oleksuk had worked in for most of his adult life, that he had been in charge of, were slated for destruction. "I felt maybe the people who got out early were the lucky ones. They didn't have to watch the place being put to sleep."

Unbeknownst to Oleksuk, however, a young man named Michael Owen, the manager of Goodrich's real-estate division, was working exactly at cross-purposes to his.

Owen, born in 1954, had graduated from Ohio State University in 1976. He had studied real estate in college, worked in his father's real-estate brokerage after college, and had even gone to law school, at age twenty-eight, not to join the bar but to ensure that no lawyer could outsmart him in real-estate negotiations. He had supervised the real-estate division for the city of Akron's law department, and he had coordinated a land-banking and development company set up by some of the city's leading businesspeople to rescue underutilized property. He joined Goodrich in 1985—just as the company was making plans to raze its headquarters.

The plan didn't sit well with Owen. "I'd always been fascinated with rehabilitation projects," he told me. "I traveled all around the country for Goodrich. By days I'd be out looking at new sites. In the evenings I'd wander around the city looking at old buildings that were being fixed up." On a trip to Pittsburgh to see a Pirates game he stopped off in Youngstown, Ohio, where part of an old steel mill had been renovated for industrial use. Up in Cleveland he could see that the industrial Flats district near the river was being brought back.

Maybe it could happen in Akron. "Goodrich's plan seemed ridiculous to me; they never stopped to think what was different about this property. It was on the doorstep of the central business district. It was in the middle of a wonderful transportation configuration. It was only a stone's throw from the university. Besides, look at the quality of construction! Afternoons, sometimes, I'd grab a folder so I looked busy and just wander around. The buildings are beautiful, architecturally. It seemed like such a shame to tear it down."

Owen sent a memo to his boss suggesting that the buildings be "recycled" into mixed-use development. His boss told him he was crazy. Undaunted, Owen asked for a meeting with his boss's superior. He got his meeting—and it was there that he met Denny Oleksuk.

"I had seen Denny around, but I didn't really know him," Owen recalled. "At the meeting, they said, 'This is Denny Oleksuk. He's in charge of Operation Greengrass.' Operation Greengrass! I didn't even know there *was* an Operation Greengrass. I thought it was still at the talking stage. But Denny had drawings, data sheets, a book of plans two inches thick. All I had was this idea."

Oleksuk remembered the meeting well, because it changed his life. "In that meeting, Mike was overwhelmed with how far along we were. But we got to talking. The buildings had potential—I knew that. But I didn't know what the potential was until I began talking with Mike. It didn't take him long to convince me."

Goodrich's management had put the two men on a collision course. Oleksuk's wrecking ball was scheduled to fall nine months later, in early 1988; Owen had only until then to figure out some way to save the buildings. But as they talked over what could happen to the buildings, the pair gradually became friends—and began working more in tandem than in opposition. Owen started contacting developers. Oleksuk began taking steps to cut costs and preserve anything that could be preserved. "They were losing a million and a half dollars a month on these buildings. Being able to minimize these costs, or reduce them—that bought us some time."

Before long, Owen's search led him to a New York real-estate partnership called Covington Capital Corporation, which specialized in redeveloping old commercial and industrial buildings. The partnership's first project had been an American Can Company factory in Hillside, New Jersey, which it had remodeled for industrial use. It had gone on to buy and renovate other properties—in Indiana, New York State, and elsewhere. Covington expressed interest, but both Goodrich and the city of Akron were skeptical: Covington had never taken on a project anywhere near as large, and the last thing either party wanted was a developer taking on the property and going broke in the process. "Goodrich really would have preferred to tear the place down, rather than take a chance," said Owen. Negotiations, nevertheless, proved fruitful. Covington persuaded Goodrich of its capabilities. They agreed on a nominal price, and the city encouraged the transaction. The deal was closed at the end of June 1988.

Still employed by Goodrich, Owen and Oleksuk entered the negotiations as representatives of the seller. But midway through the discussions, Covington partner Stuart Lichter asked Goodrich if it could make an offer to Oleksuk. Goodrich agreed, and Lichter offered Oleksuk a job managing the new facility when the sale was complete. Oleksuk accepted. As soon as the deal was done, Covington offered Owen a job as well, in the partnership's New York office. He, too, accepted.

On July 1, 1988, Covington Capital Corporation—with Owen and Oleksuk now on the payroll—became the proud owner of twenty-seven well-used factory buildings, some of them crumbling, which it promptly rechristened Canal Place, in honor of the still-visible Ohio Canal out behind the complex. Now all the two men had to do was fill them up with tenants.

On the face of it, this was one of the farther-fetched propositions to come along in some time. Covington's plans called for mixed-use redevelopment of the complex, with most of it dedicated to industrial and commercial space. But this wasn't a property that could easily be

converted to offices and trendy shops, like some Rust Belt version of
Baltimore's Inner Harbor or Boston's Faneuil Hall Marketplace. It
was as big as eight or ten Faneuil Hall marketplaces and considerably
less quaint. It was in a metropolitan area of only a few hundred
thousand, with a downtown district that was not exactly blooming.
Nor were there any large industrial employers on the horizon ready
to move in, as computer companies had moved into the old textile
mills of eastern Massachusetts. By necessity, the developers' hopes
hinged on finding a lot of little companies oriented toward growth
and hoping that their expansion would ultimately fill up the space.
Their hopes were much the same as Akron's and the Rust Belt's in
general: that the kind of economy Birch was describing would somehow grow up to replace the declining Galbraithian one.

The outlook wasn't wholly bleak. Rather than turning into the
industrial graveyard that a prophet of 1982 might have foreseen,
Akron had in fact been edging back to prosperity. According to
figures complied by James L. Shanahan of the University of Akron's
Center for Urban Studies, the region's employment rose nearly 10
percent between 1983 and 1987, even though none of the tire factories
had reopened. Manufacturing employment had increased a little,
with the biggest jump occurring in plastics products. Service-sector
employment was up considerably more: 8,000 new jobs in retail
trade, close to 7,000 in such categories as health services and business
services.

So maybe there were some growing companies around. Still,
Shanahan's figures raised as many questions as they answered. Where
was this employment coming from? How, indeed, could companies
be growing? Manufacturing in the region, like manufacturing in most
of America, had always depended on large corporations, with small
ones existing mainly to supply the giants. Services had typically followed manufacturing, growing only when the factories were thriving.
It was only common sense, most people figured, that a region couldn't
prosper if its residents were doing nothing but taking in each other's
laundry. Why should anything be different now? Shanahan, who was
probably the city's foremost expert on local economic trends, was
himself cautious in his prognostications. "The growth of service
sector jobs and new manufacturing enterprises has only stabilized the
Akron economy," he and a colleague wrote. "It has not stimulated a
phase of rapid growth. . . ." The same could be said of the rest of the
Rust Belt as well.

But Oleksuk and Owen, in effect, were betting their careers, along with millions of dollars in Covington Capital's money, that there *was* something different about this new economy—that it could spawn a new kind of growth in the region, even a new kind of company, and in the process turn Canal Place from a rusting collection of tire factories into a bustling center of industry.

By the time of my last visit to Akron, several months after my initial meeting with Oleksuk, I could see just how far they had gotten.

THE NEW COMPANIES

"We'll build PCs over there. Over here, this is electronic assembly." The speaker was Allen Ross, a young man with dark hair, a mustache, and a manner bordering on the manic. He was waving his hand in the direction of some 14,000 square feet of industrial space, some of it still being renovated at the time of my visit in early 1990. Ross was running an electronics manufacturing company called Minor Assembly & Design, which had recently relocated to the fifth floor of building 17 at Canal Place. I was on a tour of the complex with Oleksuk, and I was stopping to talk with as many business owners in the complex as I could.

In the meantime, the thought crossed my mind that heaven ought to help the ordinary mortal who tried to keep up with Oleksuk, a fast-moving, energetic man, lean as a rail, with chiseled features and tightly curled brown hair. He strode through the buildings and alleyways like a doctor on rounds: greeting every tenant by name, promising to look into problems, checking out the new walls going up, now and then talking softly into the sputtering walkie-talkie on his belt, all the while keeping up a rapid monologue about the history of the buildings where he had worked for nearly twenty years. We had just come, for example, from a huge factory space where heavy machinery was being manufactured. Oleksuk recited the space's provenance:

"This is the old conveyor-belt plant. This six-story part here was built in 1910, the rest in 1949. When I first came here, this portion of the building was where they manufactured V-belts. They moved that to South Carolina, put it in an old Elgin Watch plant. In the mid-1970s there was a big conveyor-belt expansion here in Akron, and Goodrich put $6 million into the plant. They tore out a couple of floors, put in a new steel structure and new equipment, specifically for the conveyor-belt operation."

As we walked past two workers building a cement-block wall, Oleksuk continued his exposition. "The mining industry was going good—they bought a lot of conveyor belts—and I venture to guess Goodrich didn't see an end to it at the time. Then in the early eighties the bottom dropped out of the conveyor-belt business. When the facility shut down, we were told that conveyor belts were a material-intensive product—that even if you took all the labor costs out, it would still cost more to produce than you could sell it for.

"So they shut it down. And until we got this building, there was still a lot of equipment in place. This was one of the buildings you'd walk into and it was almost like they shut it down for the weekend. It looked like somebody could come in Monday morning, turn the lights on, and start it up."

As we took a creaky freight elevator up to Allen Ross's electronics-assembly space, Oleksuk explained that he tried to match up tenants, where possible, with the kind of space they needed. "This was Goodrich's old machine-development space. They'd build a piece of equipment here and try it out before they'd go into production. The last few years, it was a prototype area for evacuation systems, deicer systems, airplane chutes, and so on. They needed high levels of lighting—that's why all the windows. It lends itself perfectly to an assembly operation."

What was happening in these buildings, of course, was not simply a transition from B.F. Goodrich to Canal Place, or from one set of tenants to another. (Some of the tenants, as we'll see, stayed put.) The transition was from one kind of business to another. That change, in turn, raised interesting questions about what kinds of companies had taken over from the displaced giant; about what they did and who owned them; and about whether they could be expected to last. In particular, if the notion of filling up Canal Place—and Akron—with small companies was more than a pipe dream, the businesses already there had better have good prospects for growth.

Not surprisingly, many had no such prospects. They were expansions or start-ups or relocations of everyday small companies, part of the ordinary ebb and flow of the marketplace. Oleksuk pointed out to me an electrical-supply distributor that was headquartered in Cleveland but was opening up an outlet here in Akron. We walked through the warehouse of a novelty wholesaler, the shelves piled high with school supplies and cheap plastic toys for distribution to drugstores. We ate at a stylish new restaurant called Satchmo's, its industrial decor an attempt to capitalize on its surroundings. No reader of John Kenneth Galbraith in 1970 would have been surprised by such small enterprises. As for other tenants, the only thing new about some of them was their ownership, which might or might not make a difference in their futures. The headquarters of Uniroyal Goodrich Tire Company, located in a modern building adjacent to Canal Place, overflowed into Canal Place itself. A company called RJF International, its corporate offices located on the fourth floor of Canal Place's main building, was the residue of Goodrich's fabricated-polymers division; it made products ranging from commercial wall coverings to the little magnets that stick on refrigerators. Some of its employees had remained in the same offices throughout the change, but the company itself was now wholly owned by the division's former head, Richard J. Fasenmyer. In Oleksuk's office I met three electricians named Craig Fleet (ten years with Goodrich), Keith Tatum (eleven years), and Harold Mingo (seventeen years). Fleet and Tatum were now partners, and Mingo an employee, in a tiny new business called Fleet Electric, which had been doing much of the electrical-contracting work on Canal Place.

Then, alongside the everyday companies, were some that made you sit up and take notice precisely because of their prospects for growth. It was these companies—entrepreneurial businesses that were well adapted to the new marketplace—that lent credence to what Canal Place's new owners were trying to accomplish. They fit into two categories: craft manufacturers and service providers.

Craft Manufacturers. In the past, the prototypical American manufacturing facility was exactly what Akron's tire makers ran: a large, integrated operation, focused on high-volume output and utilizing special-purpose machinery. Not for nothing was the twentieth century called the century of mass production. Akron was one of many cities that prospered by sending huge quantities of mass-produced goods out into the world. But mass production, as Michael J. Piore and Charles F. Sabel argued in their book *The Second Industrial Divide,* wasn't well suited to the unstable environment of the 1970s and 1980s. More and more production was being done by craft manufacturers, smaller companies that typically used sophisticated general-purpose machinery to turn out a wide variety of specialty products. As in Silicon Valley, these manufacturers frequently clustered together, cooperating as well as competing. Though each company might specialize in one set of products or another, the companies as a group were highly flexible, and thus easily able to adapt to changes in the marketplace.

Whether or not they were familiar with Piore and Sabel or their term flexible specialization, Akronites had come to think of that concept as a model for the city's future. State and regional economic-development specialists were pushing the notion of "Polymer Valley," hoping to boost the already-sizable number of plastics suppliers and fabricators located in the area. The University of Akron's polymer-science and polymer-engineering faculty was being beefed up, and joint research-and-development projects established between the university and industry. A state-sponsored organization called Edison Polymer Innovation Corporation (EPIC) encouraged and helped to fund other applied-research projects. Several companies, acting without benefit of public subsidy or encouragement, were already planning to help along—and trade on—the emerging cluster of plastics companies. An ambitious enterprise called Akron Storage and Warehouse ran a large warehouse, as its name suggested. But, at the same time, it sold raw plastics to fabricators; had set up a plastics injection-molding plant to do contract manufacturing; and was undertaking to develop an industrial park for plastics-related businesses.

Clusters of companies in other manufacturing fields were appearing as well. Before visiting Canal Place, for example, I met a man named Lee Combs, who took me on a tour of his well-equipped machine shop on the outskirts of the city. Incredibly, Combs had started his business in 1979; asked about the intense recession that had hit almost immediately thereafter, he laughed and said, "I didn't know it happened." The reason: cutbacks in large, integrated manufacturing operations opened up opportunities for companies like Combs's. He now had seventy employees and sales of close to $5 million, much of it work that would once have been done in-house by large corporations.

But Combs rarely worked alone. On the contrary, he frequently accepted a job making complex metal parts, performed the specific operations for which he had the most appropriate equipment, and farmed out the rest to other machine shops in the area. They returned the favor with jobs of their own. Each shop, in effect, could invest in a few state-of-the-art machine tools, knowing that it didn't need to buy costly equipment for every possible step of a job. The machine-shop owners had even gotten together to start a school for training new employees.

It was craft manufacturers such as these that had begun to locate in Canal Place. Some of them could be considered part of a cluster; others were working alone. But nearly all occupied specialized—and growing—market niches.

The best established of these companies was a forty-year-old enterprise called Rogers Industrial Products, which had bought Goodrich's old conveyor-belt building from Covington and was just completing its move when I visited. Rogers got its start as a rebuilder of tire-making equipment, specifically tire-curing presses; back then, most new equipment was manufactured either by the tire companies themselves or by larger enterprises such as NRM Corporation. But the same trends that had transformed other American industries overturned the status quo in this one, too. U.S. manufacturers had licensed their technologies to overseas competitors, thereby losing their technical advantage. Japanese companies such as Mitsubishi Heavy Industries and Kobe Steel had entered the market. Meanwhile, Rogers was learning to improve on the designs of the presses it was rebuilding. Seeing a newly turbulent marketplace, the company leaped into it.

"First we went into subassemblies," explained owner John Cole, a longtime Rogers employee who bought the company in 1984. "Now we're beginning to manufacture complete machines; in fact, we sold a million dollars' worth of new equipment this week. Our customers are the major tire companies—Goodyear, General—plus several smaller foreign companies. About 30 percent of our sales are overseas, and that's growing rapidly." Because it was able to innovate quickly and thus keep up with marketplace demands, said Cole, his company had no trouble competing with the likes of Mitsubishi. And, though small, it was expanding. It already had seventy employees when I was visiting, and Cole expected to add fifty more in the following twelve months.

Cole's company and the other manufacturers in and around Canal Place seemed to me like incubators of innovation. In building 7 was a fledgling company called Plastic Lumber Company, which made decking and other products wholly from recycled scrap plastic. Down at the end of the parking lot, near the restaurant, was a new business with the grandiose name Akron Polymer Container Corporation. Its product was a rubber-sleeve mechanism designed to re-place the pressurized (and ozone-destroying) gas in ordinary aerosol cans. As the can was filled up, the sleeve would expand. Its natural tendency to contract would then squeeze the product out.

Risky ventures, no doubt. But both businesses were serious, innovative manufacturing enterprises capable of substantial growth. Robert Winer, the slim, middle-aged man who had developed the rubber-sleeve mechanism, was still answering his own phone the last time I talked with him. But he had already had inquiries from some of the biggest consumer-products marketers in the country, and was about to close a deal with a larger partner that would provide him with some $10 million in capital. His prospects, of course, were greatly enhanced by the new level of environmental concern over aerosols.

At any rate, not every innovative young manufacturer in Canal Place was so chancy. A company called Beta Medical Products, slated to move into the complex in late 1990, had begun its corporate life a few years earlier by developing a new kind of trauma bed, the hydrau-lic stretcher used in hospital emergency rooms. Two years after its founding the company was selling the trauma beds around the coun-try; it also had a deal with Siemens, the German industrial giant, to market them in Europe. The company's second product was an ad-justable X-ray imaging bed, developed in conjunction with a radiolo-gist at the Cleveland Clinic. The third product, developed under contract for Siemens, was an imaginative trolley-and-stretcher system allowing seriously ill patients to be wheeled into a hospital's CT-scanning room and put directly into the CT-scan machine without being moved from one bed to another. Though it was to be marketed under the Siemens name, Beta had exclusive manufacturing rights to the product. The company's estimated sales for 1990 were $4 million, up from about $500,000 in 1988.

Another new company at Canal Place, called Signs and Blanks Inc., was entering the aluminum street-sign manufacturing business, and planned to compete on the basis of a custom-designed, computer-controlled production line. "Our line should be able to do twenty to thirty times what a normal plant can do," said Dan Lang, the com-pany's president. "We start with an aluminum coil, level it, clean it, apply a coating, then cut and shape to a finished product. All these steps are usually done separately. We'll automate them all." What differentiated such a process from mass production was its flexibility. Here, reprogramming the computer allowed the machinery to turn out products of different size, shape, and design.

Even the manufacture of microelectronics products can lend itself to craft methods. Listen to Allen Ross, the owner of Minor Assembly & Design (up in Goodrich's machine-development space), as he described his five-year-old company. "Our basic business is electronic assembly. All kinds of contract manufacturing: cable assemblies, printed-circuit-board assemblies. We bought a mold machine to do molds for computer-cable assemblies." Minor Assembly was on the verge of what Ross hoped would be a Great Leap Forward into personal computers, and he pointed out the area where they would soon be assembled. "We have our own brand, Michada Computers. It's my father's trademark; he owns R&R Electronics, out in Las Vegas. They sell 500 computers a month, mainly to computer stores across the country." Michada, Ross explained, was an amalgam of Michigan and Nevada, the two states in which R&R had facilities. When I called him back a couple of months later to find out how things were going, he had already begun assembling the machines, thirty in the first month and 100 in the second. His work force was up to twenty-five, with another fifteen to be added in the following sixty days. Ross planned to equip his computers with easy-to-use software for small businesses, thus targeting the small-company owner buying his or her first computer.

The companies at Canal Place, it should be noted, weren't unique. Indeed, the same vitality among small-scale manufacturers was visible in the annual survey of manufacturing conducted by the Akron Regional Development Board. About twenty new plants opened up in Akron in both 1988 and 1989, while about 350 in each year made significant investments in new facilities or equipment. All but a half-dozen or so were small and midsize companies. The vitality was also visible in the labor-force figures gathered by James Shanahan of the University of Akron. No big manufacturers had recently moved into Akron, and manufacturing employment overall was substantially less in 1987 than in 1979. Yet several industries actually gained employment over the period, with the "miscellaneous plastic parts" business (as the government classified it) rising by nearly 2,000 jobs.

Services. Alongside Canal Place's (and Akron's) craft manufacturers were companies in service-providing industries. Services as a whole had grown substantially during the middle 1980s. Construction employment in the Akron region was up 34 percent; retail trade, 15 percent; and other services, 11 percent.

That growth presented the conundrum mentioned earlier. To oversimplify only a little, Akron prospered in the past because its factories "exported" millions of tires to other parts of the nation and the world. The money from those tires fed a booming local marketplace in restaurants, auto dealerships, and a hundred other service businesses. By the end of the 1980s, however, nowhere near as many people were working in factories as had been before. So how could the service sector have grown?

As economists such as Shanahan were beginning to discover, however, this seeming paradox was one more aspect of conventional thinking that had been turned inside out by the rise of an entrepreneurial economy. A more accurate picture was slowly becoming visible, both in these economists' research and in the experience of companies such as those at Canal Place.

• Point one: It was manufacturing *employment* that was holding steady or declining, not manufacturing *output*. There weren't any numbers that measured the output of Akron's manufacturing companies as a group. But in the United States as a whole, factory productivity—output per worker—increased steadily during the 1980s. The mass production that was left after the shutdowns of the early 1980s, such as Goodyear's massive factories in the Southwest, utilized fewer and fewer workers. The craft production springing up in places such as Akron relied on relatively small groups of skilled workers using sophisticated machinery. But a manufacturing company's need for certain kinds of services—trucking, computer programming, advertising—depended on its output, not on its employment levels. In this respect, manufacturing could still be a healthy generator of service-industry jobs.

• Point two: The decline of big, integrated manufacturers and the growth of smaller ones changed the way a lot of service work was done. Unlike large corporations, small companies didn't have their own construction crews, accounting departments, advertising coordinators, data-processing managers, in-house engineers, benefits specialists, security services, graphic-design departments, or cafeterias. The proliferation of small manufacturing companies thus created a booming demand for all such services. Canal Place housed a restaurant, a day-care center, a commercial construction firm, a private security agency, and an electrical-contracting company. In the past, all could have been part of Goodrich; indeed, many of the people running these businesses were once on Goodrich's payroll, doing much the same jobs. But back then they would have been counted as part of the industrial work force; now they were part of the burgeoning service economy.

There was a snowball effect here as well. Big manufacturers cut back and small manufacturers grew, so small service companies found themselves with a new market. But service companies themselves needed services: every advertising agency needed a bookkeeper, every computer-programming firm restaurants to supply its employees' lunches. The result was the jump in service employment uncovered by Shanahan.

• Point three: Innovations in the service sector encouraged companies of all kinds to spend money on services that were unknown or scarce a decade ago. Bright Horizons Day Care Center, in Canal Place, wouldn't have been there (or anywhere else) in 1980. Neither would companies that wire personal-computer networks or install special telephone systems with voice-mail capabilities.

A young company that seemed to exemplify these trends was Enterprise Information Services, run by a man in his early fifties named David Gronauer. EIS was at the end of a long corridor in building 24 at Canal Place, and walking into its offices was like going back to the future. Canal Place itself was a relic of the industrial revolution. Many of the companies there, for all their up-to-date technology, were noisy metal-bending shops. At EIS, the soft hum of electronic equipment bespoke another kind of enterprise entirely.

Gronauer worked for Goodrich (later for Uniroyal Goodrich) for twenty-five years. All that time, he said, he had tried hard to interest the company in doing exactly what he was doing today. "But they wanted to cut costs, not grow. I couldn't talk them into doing anything." So, with $175,000 from savings and a mortgage, he bought some computer equipment and went out on his own. EIS offered a range of electronic-publishing services to a diverse list of clients: large and small manufacturing companies and service businesses. Its shop was a maze of Macintosh and IBM-compatible computers, laser printers, fax machines, and a device called a Linotronic 300R, which produced top-quality type electronically.

Gronauer's technology was by no means unique. Still, to someone brought up on the old cut-and-paste school of publication work, it was surprising to see what he could do and how fast he could do it. A customer might give him text and graphics for a company newsletter, brochure, or ad. He'd enter the text into a computer by means of a word processing program; use a graphics program and a page-making program to create page layouts on a computer screen; do a computer scan of any photographs; and print out proofs on a laser printer, for transmission by fax if the customer was in a hurry. Once the publication was edited and approved, he would put the whole thing into the Linotronic, which generates either a camera-ready positive or a film negative ready for the printer's platemaker.

Total working time might be no more than a few hours, and the time from start to finish only a day or two. "A lot of companies couldn't afford to do a nice-looking newsletter or annual report in the past," said Gronauer. "Now they can."

These three phenomena explained much of the growth in nationwide service employment over the past decade. Manufacturing hadn't disappeared, it had just been restructured; and the restructuring had produced a boom in service employment, which then fed on itself. But in an individual region such as Akron there was another element at work as well. More and more, it turned out, services could be "exported," just like tires and other manufactured products, and service businesses could thus form part of a region's economic base.

For some parts of the country, this has always been the case. New York City exports its financial services, Fort Lauderdale its tourism. Both industries bring in dollars from outside, and thus feed the local economy. Recently, though, researchers have been learning that other cities also export a significant portion of their services.

The discovery of this phenomenon is usually credited to a University of Washington geographer named William B. Beyers. Contemplating the Seattle region's economy, Beyers noticed the same trends that were visible in the Rust Belt: manufacturing employment down, service employment up. Rather than theorizing about the reasons (like Birch, Beyers wasn't an economist), he raised some money, hired some graduate students, and mounted a massive survey of 2,000 service-industry companies. What did they do? Who were their customers?

The finding that jumped out at Beyers was that *a substantial portion of these service companies did a lot of business outside the Puget Sound area.* Screening his initial sample, Beyers found 1,100 companies (somewhat more than half) that reported doing at least 10 percent of their business in other parts of the state or the nation. His researchers then studied this smaller group in depth and found an astonishing degree of national and even international orientation. Architects and engineers in the sample did nearly 40 percent of their business outside Washington State; computer-service firms did almost 50 percent. Adding up the numbers, Beyers calculated that the 1,100 companies accounted for 84,000 jobs, more than half of them attributable to nonlocal sales. "The number of jobs resulting from these exported services was [thus] larger than the number of export-tied manufacturing jobs in the Central Puget Sound region," he wrote. Undertaking a similar study in Akron, Shanahan and an associate found that business-service firms derived nearly 20 percent of their revenue, on average, from outside the Northeast Ohio region.

The scope of this phenomenon was new. It had been made possible not only by modern communications and transportation technologies but by the nature of today's service industries themselves. "I interviewed a man of about sixty-five," said Shanahan, "who used to run Goodrich's data-services operation. In the early seventies they spun out the operation. He kept Goodrich as a customer, but he also began doing data entry for the state of Pennsylvania, Ohio Bell, the *Encyclopaedia Britannica*. He employs between sixty and ninety people." The phenomenon also cast some of Canal Place's service businesses in a new light. For along with the restaurant, the day-care center, and the security firm—all conventional, locally oriented services—were some that could sell their wares anywhere.

One such firm was GPD Associates, an architectural and engineering firm, which occupied perhaps the classiest offices in the complex. Done in shades of gray and mauve, the offices indicated not only GPD's line of work (an architectural firm can't occupy a drab office) but its prosperity. "We've grown from thirty-five to seventy-five employees just in the last three years," explained David Granger, a partner. The firm's efforts were divided roughly equally among three categories: work on power plants, work on roads and bridges and other public projects, and private commercial work. Most of the power-plant projects were on the East Coast, while a significant number of the firm's other jobs were outside Akron. Microelectronics, of course, increased the productivity of such modern-day service firms. "We do all our private work and a portion of our public work on computer-aided design systems," said Granger. "And what a difference it makes! A guy goes out to do a survey with a hand-held computerized device. The device feeds information right into the computer, and the drawings come out of the CAD system."

Denny Oleksuk and Michael Owen, the managers of Canal Place, had made it clear that they wanted to encourage manufacturing in the buildings—the activity, after all, for which the complex had been designed. But business-service companies such as Granger's and Gronauer's were likely to be just as important as manufacturers. Unlike the stereotypical service businesses (hamburger joints and laundries), they were sophisticated, high-technology operations, as capable of generating wealth and employment growth as any goods-producing company.

Old ideas die hard.

If you saw the 1989 hit movie *Roger and Me,* you may have a picture of economic life in the Rust Belt much like the one most Americans had back in 1981 and 1982, when the factories were closing down.

If you missed the movie, here's a quick synopsis. Flint, Michigan—the birthplace of General Motors—was a city known for its automobile factories. In the mid-1980s GM closed some of its plants there, and threw some 30,000 people out of work. Filmmaker Michael Moore (who grew up in Flint), in pseudodocumentary style, sets out to "talk to" Roger Smith, the chairman of GM, about this devastation; predictably foiled at every turn, he contents himself with showing the audience the human cost of the plant closings. A high-school buddy of Moore's, who has suffered a breakdown after losing his job, shoots hoops at the local mental-health center. Innumerable Flint families are evicted from their homes. City officials and boosters, meanwhile, seem to be lost in fantasy. They set up a giant "AutoWorld" museum to attract tourists, and they host a series of visiting celebrities, who urge residents not to give up hope.

As was widely reported at the time, the movie wasn't a complete portrayal of reality, even in Flint. Faced with new competition, General Motors did indeed tear down plants and cut employment. And, as Paul Ingrassia of the *Wall Street Journal*'s Detroit bureau wrote, the company bore "plenty of blame for letting itself get so bloated that it had to discard workers like excess baggage from a sinking ship." But GM didn't exactly desert the city. In 1990 the company still employed about 45,000 people in Flint (a city of 150,000). It had automated and upgraded its facilities to the point where Flint workers could produce some of the highest-quality cars in the United States. GM had even begun to learn the value of labor-management teamwork. "Finally, management is letting our people use their minds as well as their hands," a local union official told Ingrassia. Moore was right on one count: Flint hadn't returned to its former prosperity. Nor had it witnessed the same outpouring of entrepreneurship as in Akron, partly because GM still employed so many people. But it wasn't nearly as bad off as *Roger and Me* pictured it.

Perhaps as unsettling as the lacunae is the filmmaker's apparent belief that Flint (and by implication every other city) cannot survive without the presence of some corporation such as GM. The only entrepreneur Michael Moore talks to in the movie is a poor, country-bred woman who sells rabbits (*Pets or Meat* says her hand-lettered sign). The only new company mentioned is a manufacturer of rollers to take lint off clothing. The audience is left thinking that things would be fine if—and only if—GM rebuilt its factories and staffed up at the old levels. Certainly "small business" couldn't be expected to become a prime source of employment.

In Akron, people were rejecting this old notion, partly because they had visible evidence of the change in the business landscape. In 1980, the huge complex of buildings on South Main Street had been occupied by a single giant company. In 1990 it was occupied by several dozen small ones. More important, there was a feeling of life, of growth, of economic vitality about the place. It was hard to think that Akron could be dying when so many thriving young companies were busily refurbishing this onetime symbol of decline.

The last time I spoke with them, Denny Oleksuk and Michael Owen were excited, because Canal Place had attracted a host of new tenants in the previous few months. There was a furniture refinisher and a photographic studio, an assembler of plastic products and a manufacturer of restaurant equipment. A company specializing in import and export of electrical components had fixed up its space so stylishly that a local law firm was thinking about moving in. A children's clothing manufacturer called North Coast Kids (a business, frankly, that I had pegged for early failure) was doing very well; it had recently come up with an innovative marketing strategy of selling direct to consumers through inexpensive kiosks in malls. And a company called Curtis Software (a perfect example of a 1990s service business) had moved a bevy of personal computers and modems into some newly renovated space. Curtis was providing computerized billing services to hospitals and clinics.

In 1991 Canal Place won first place in an "Excellence in Economic Development" competition sponsored by Arthur D. Little, the consulting firm. By then, close to a thousand people were at work in the big old complex, including the fourteen teachers who were taking care of the eighty or so children in the day-care center. That still left Oleksuk and Owen with a good deal of space to rent. But a lot of space had already been filled, and a lot of jobs created, in buildings that had once been consigned to the industrial graveyard.

Nobody was likely to make a hit movie about how Akron was making its way back from the tire-industry doldrums. But the city's recovery—and the gradual emergence of a different kind of economy—was no less dramatic for it.

6

The New Economy: Steel

I T WAS a muggy July day, and a transfer car filled with billets was making its way from one end of American Steel & Wire Corporation's billet yard to the other. When it arrived, the billets were picked up by an overhead crane and dumped onto the unscrambler, a kind of mechanized tilting platform that jockeyed them into position for their single-file entry into the gas-fired furnace. The billets—long, squared-off steel logs that were stacked by the hundred in American Steel & Wire's yard—were about five inches square in cross section, thirty-four feet long, and about a ton and a half apiece in weight. The mill on the other side of the furnace squeezed and stretched and rounded them into what is known in the steel business as wire rod, or just rod, which is to say a coil of precisely rounded steel a fraction of an inch in diameter and up to four miles long. "Rod" is what steel people call a semifinished product, meaning that it needs one more step before it can be made into a finished product. That step, which converts "rod" into "wire," involves drawing the steel through a ring-shaped diamond die, shrinking its diameter slightly and giving it a smoother, truer surface.

The process was simple enough but for the physics involved. Start to finish, each billet would be reduced in cross-sectional area from about twenty-five square inches to as little as four-hundredths of a square inch, a factor of 625. The steel would be lengthened by a corresponding factor. Because of the lengthening, each of the mill's twenty-five rolling stands had to operate at a higher speed than the one before, getting the ever-thinner steel in and out faster and faster. From inside the mill, these cumulative speed injections had a startling effect. The billet, glowing bright orange, seemed to meander out of the furnace. Then it hit the first rolling stand, where it got a jolt of velocity, and the second, where it began to travel still faster. In a few more seconds—now looking almost alive, a fiery snake amid the dark machinery—a thin strand of steel was flying through the rolls. Rocketing out of the last set, it could be traveling as fast as 14,000 feet a minute, or 160 miles an hour.

At such high speeds, tiny mechanical defects could spawn big problems. A roller guide out of alignment could send the high-speed steel straight up in the air, bending and curling it like a piece of ribbon candy. Failing so dramatic a breakdown, it could simply burn out a bearing in the rolling stand itself. To minimize such difficulties, alignments, temperatures, roller motors, and several other variables were monitored in a high glass-walled booth called the speed pulpit, which overlooked the rolling stands. A dozen workers stood below, ready to make adjustments between billets as necessary.

So intricate a process depended mightily on the hands and eyes of the mill workers. At American Steel & Wire, the most experienced pairs of both probably belonged to Ed Goldsmith, a burly man who, when I visited the company in mid-1990, was working the swing shift up in the speed pulpit. Goldsmith was born in 1940 and grew up in Youngstown, Ohio. Steel ran in his family. His grandfather had worked at the McDonald Works of U.S. Steel, also in the Youngstown area. His father had worked at Youngstown Sheet & Tube. In 1963, after four years in the navy, young Ed had decided to settle in Cleveland, and had found a job at what was then the Cuyahoga Works of U.S. Steel. He had started as a laborer; had gotten a promotion to pushout (ejecting the hot billets from the furnace); had been promoted again to rod gauger; and by the late 1960s had made roller. Roller was, and is, the highest non-management position in the mill. "He's your gang leader," explained Goldsmith, "and a little more than that, because he's right in there working with everybody else." Indeed, the job was all a steelworker might want. By 1983 Goldsmith was making good money, about $125 a day, plus generous overtime and fringes. He had been laid off a total of only six weeks over twenty years. The mill was a union shop, and Goldsmith was a member of Local 1298, United Steelworkers of America.

By 1983, however, there was trouble in the air. Ostensibly the United States was just emerging from the early-1980s recession. Wall Street was beginning to boom, and states such as Massachusetts and California to thrive. For steelworkers like Goldsmith, however, the economic outlook wasn't bright. The big steel mills had been closing their doors for several years already, and now the steel companies seemed to want to shut down more. U.S. Steel, like its competitors, was using the threat of closure to extract wage concessions from its union locals. Steel companies estimated their average labor costs— cash wages plus benefits—at about $17 an hour. At Cuyahoga Works, Goldsmith's local had already agreed to a wage-and-benefits cut totaling some $3 an hour. In December 1983 the company demanded another $2 cut to keep the plant open.

This time the local refused. "When we took that vote," Goldsmith remembered, "we knew we were taking a chance on them shutting it down. But we just felt, rather than take another cut like that, we were better off on the street looking for a job. You know, it would have eroded the attitude so bad. Here you are making $125 a day; now all of a sudden you're doing the same work for $90 a day. What's it going to do to your attitude? It can't do anything but take the attitude and morale right down to the bottom of the barrel." U.S. Steel, true to its word, closed the Cuyahoga Works a few months after the vote. Ed Goldsmith, a man then in his mid-forties, with a high-school education and no experience in anything but steel, found himself looking for work.

So far, Goldsmith's story was like many others. The nightly news in the early to mid-1980s was filled with images of laid-off employees, steelworkers among them. A number of books published since then have traced the abrupt decline of the American steel industry. Between 1975 and 1987 the largest steel companies closed twenty-four of their forty-seven mills. Steel-dependent communities in Pennsylvania, Ohio, and elsewhere had to find new industries or sink gradually into stagnation. A generation of steelworkers had to take early retirement, collect unemployment compensation, or set out in search of new work. The nationwide boom of the late 1980s brought no restoration. Domestic steel production in 1989—one of the industry's best years in recent memory—came to only 72 percent of 1979 output. The business as a whole employed only 124,000 wage earners, down from 342,000 ten years earlier.

Yet the familiar story, grim as it was, overlooked a curious paradox. While one segment of the American steel industry was declining, apparently inexorably, another segment was thriving. While the large companies were shrinking, a host of new ones was expanding, innovating, scouting out new markets or recapturing old ones. American Steel & Wire, a newly formed business, bought U.S. Steel's Cuyahoga Works in 1986 and promptly put Ed Goldsmith back to work at the job he knew best, rolling wire rod. It grew, stumbled a little, grew again. Moreover, AS&W was only one of many small steel companies that were competing successfully in a restructured industry—an industry in which the rules of business management and labor relations were seemingly being rewritten, and in which huge size seemed to hinder rather than ensure success.

I was visiting AS&W to learn what made it different from the big, old-line steel companies that had once dominated the industry.

AN INFLEXIBLE INDUSTRY

The simplest definition of steel is iron with most of the carbon removed. Taking out the carbon makes the metal both stronger and more malleable. Traditionally, a steel mill made iron from iron ore in a blast furnace. Then it converted the iron into steel in a so-called open-hearth furnace.

The process made economic sense only on a massive scale. The furnaces themselves were expensive items. So was the network of facilities required to assemble and process the raw materials. Early in the industry's history, pioneering engineers such as Frederick Wood capitalized on these economies of scale by building giant mills capable of carrying steel production from iron ore right through to finished product. Wood's Sparrows Point, Maryland, mill was built for about $7 million in the late 1880s, at a time when the average Maryland factory cost around $10,500. The facility covered about 400 acres. Yet materials moved efficiently from docks to furnaces to rolling mills, and a product—rails—"emerged within eyeshot of the blast furnaces where the ore was smelted," as Mark Reutter notes in his excellent history of Sparrows Point. This *integration* of the production process was new at the time, but it became the hallmark of the steel industry in the United States. In 1928 the Sparrows Point works, by then a part of Bethlehem Steel, included mills producing not only rails but fabricating and construction steel, two kinds of steel pipe, four kinds of sheet steel, tin plate (for cans), rod, and rod products such as nails. The word *works,* observes Reutter, came into being specifically to denote such sprawling facilities. Somehow neither *mill* nor *factory* was adequate to the descriptive task.

Integrated steel companies themselves grew correspondingly large. The biggest, of course, was United States Steel, incorporated on February 1, 1901; it included Andrew Carnegie's steel empire plus a host of other companies, and put something like two-thirds of the steel business under one corporate roof. U.S. Steel's share of the market declined over time, but only because other giant companies, such as Bethlehem, were growing. For most of the twentieth century, steel was a classic case of what economists call an oligopoly, an industry dominated by a few large companies. In 1958 Bethlehem, which was then the second-largest steel company, proposed to acquire Youngstown Sheet & Tube, then the fifth-largest. Upholding the Justice Department's challenge to the merger, the Southern District Court of New York pointed out that U.S. Steel and Bethlehem *already* controlled 45 percent of the nation's ingot capacity, and the top six companies as a group controlled more than two-thirds. To allow the merger, said the court, "would add substantially to concentration in an already highly concentrated industry and reduce unduly the already limited number of integrated steel companies."

For the steel companies, oligopoly led to a frustrating kind of prosperity. On the one hand, they were generally successful in doing what an oligopoly does best, which is to fix prices. Judge Elbert H. Gary, U.S. Steel's chairman from 1901 to 1927, regularly exhorted other companies in the industry to follow U.S. Steel's lead on prices. They regularly did so, and the practice proved so agreeable that it continued long after Gary's death. "U.S. Steel Corporation, as the unchallenged industry leader, in effect determined the industry's overall price structure," wrote Donald F. Barnett and Louis Schorsch, two analysts with long experience in steel. "Other large firms were generally more efficient, so that it was relatively easy for them to prosper under the umbrella of their unwieldy rival and leader." Because of the companies' domination of the marketplace—where else could customers get large quantities of steel?—prices could generally be set high enough to ensure profitability, regardless of market conditions. In the 1950s, when demand for steel was growing slowly, steel prices rose an average of 6 percent a year. Other wholesale prices only rose an average of 2 percent annually.

On the other hand, the companies could never, by their lights, seem to raise prices quite high enough. Accused of conspiratorial pricing, they could point to the fact that, measured by return on assets, steel did poorly by comparison with other large manufacturing industries; it outperformed average manufacturing returns in only two of the twenty years between 1940 and 1960. To be sure, a modern corporate raider would have found some opportunities for cost-cutting and thus profit boosting. In 1956, for example, Bethlehem Steel employed eleven of the eighteen highest-paid executives in the whole country, with chairman Eugene Grace pulling down the then-kingly sum of $809,000, considerably more than the head of General Motors. But even such bloat was overshadowed by the industry's dismal economics. Steel companies typically made a profit of about $12 per ton of steel in the mid-1950s. New mills at the time cost about $350 per ton of capacity. That figured out to a profit rate of about 3 percent.

From a steel executive's point of view, the industry could have done a good deal better but for two annoying obstacles. One was the government; the other was the union.

Government. The formation of U.S. Steel in 1901 may have allowed steel makers to regulate prices, but it also catapulted them into the public eye. Suddenly steel, like oil and a dozen other businesses, seemed to be the province of a monster trust engineered by big-money financiers for their own benefit. An antitrust suit brought by President Taft's Justice Department in 1911 failed. But the structure and functioning of the steel industry remained a hot political issue through the middle third of the twentieth century. In 1948, for example, the 10 percent price hike announced by U.S. Steel brought quick responses from Washington. Congress's Joint Economic Committee (JEC) immediately called a hearing on the increase. President Truman ordered investigations by his Council of Economic Advisers, by the Commerce Department, even by the FBI. "The [steel] firms," wrote historian Paul A. Tiffany, "became more apprehensive about the intentions of Washington and as a result more cautious in their marketplace response."

The pattern continued for years. The Celler committee (another congressional body investigating monopoly power) called steel makers on the carpet in 1950. Chairman Emanuel Celler, a Democrat from New York, said that the industry's earlier price increase "boldly points the need for a reexamination of the prerogatives of bigness." In 1952, with a strike threatening and the nation in the midst of the Korean War, President Truman seized the steel mills; he backed off two months later only after the Supreme Court disallowed the move. The JEC again launched hearings into steel price hikes in 1955, and the Senate's antitrust and monopoly subcommittee (led by the powerful Democrat from Tennessee, Estes Kefauver) mounted a hostile investigation in 1957. When John F. Kennedy attacked the steel companies for their 1962 price increase, he was carrying on a long and well-established tradition. The steel companies might form a powerful oligopoly, but they didn't enjoy complete freedom of action.

Labor. The American steel industry has never been known for amicable labor relations. An 1892 battle between Pinkerton guards and members of the Amalgamated Association of Iron, Steel, and Tin Workers at Andrew Carnegie's Homestead works left several dead and the union virtually destroyed. U.S. Steel adopted an antiunion policy from its inception, resisting a 1901 strike by the Amalgamated and forcing the union to cave in. In 1909 the company announced it would no longer recognize the union at all. As late as 1923 steelworkers typically worked eleven-hour or thirteen-hour shifts, plus a twenty-four-hour shift on alternate weekends. They got two holidays a year, Christmas and the Fourth of July; both were unpaid. Even so, union organizing stalled until the passage of the National Labor Relations Act in 1935. In 1937, U.S. Steel agreed to recognize the newly formed Steel Workers Organizing Committee (later the United Steelworkers of America). Several years and a good deal of bloodshed later, the other big companies signed union contracts, thanks largely to wartime pressure from the government.

Like the industry itself, the labor relations that evolved after World War II exhibited curious paradoxes. On the one hand, union-management relations remained unusually bitter. Contract negotiations frequently led to stalemates and strikes. Plant-level managers and union officials conducted "daily warfare," observed veteran *Business Week* labor reporter John Hoerr, "over such matters as discipline, job assignment, and the handling of worker grievances." On the other hand, the companies regularly acceded to generous wage boosts, eventually placing unionized steelworkers among the best paid blue-collar workers in the country. In 1949 steelworkers made only 18 percent more than the average U.S. manufacturing employee, and less than their counterparts in the auto industry. Ten years later they had passed auto workers, and were now making 39 percent more than the manufacturing average. By 1973 the differential was up to 50 percent.

Rigid job classifications and work rules—which stated exactly what a given worker would and would not be expected to do—came to be a hallmark of steel contracts, and were bones of contention at every negotiation. These problems, too, were tinged with irony. Job classification had been pioneered not by the union but by the companies. Influenced by the "scientific management" theories of Frederick W. Taylor, steel executives had broken down each job into its component parts; then they had assigned these narrowly defined jobs to particular workers, changing the assignments frequently. The practice allowed managers to hire unskilled immigrant laborers and quickly teach them what was expected of them. It also allowed managers to reward favorites and punish troublemakers. Predictably, classifications and work rules became a hot union issue; the union conducted a campaign to routinize and regularize them, hoping to eliminate pay inequities and favoritism. "The best thing that happened was that the union came in and everybody was established on their job," a retired steelworker told John Hoerr. "Now, when there was an advancement, you bid for the job, and if you had the seniority you got it."

But what protected the workers soon became a nightmare of red tape and contentiousness. Legal language spelled out exact requirements for thousands of jobs; there were "1,150 benchmark jobs within 152 representative classifications" in U.S. Steel's 1947 job-rationalization program, for example. A section in the contract prevented management from eliminating or changing *any* established labor practice unless it could demonstrate to the union's satisfaction that "underlying conditions" had changed. The union would rarely admit that underlying conditions had changed, particularly if doing so would enable management to eliminate jobs. Hoerr, who grew up in a steel town near Pittsburgh and worked in the mills as a young man, had firsthand experience with the featherbedding that resulted. In 1951 he had a job that required about ten minutes' worth of calculation every two or three hours; the rest of the time he slept and read. A friend had a job nearby stacking heavy lengths of pipe. "Once or twice, when he fell behind, I offered to help," Hoerr remembered.

" 'You'd better not, John,' he said. We both knew that union rules—and company rules, for that matter—forbade the crossing of job boundaries." Management, Hoerr added, was as fat as the work force. U.S. Steel had four levels of management in corporate head-quarters and six more levels of management in each mill.

Beset from without by the government and from within by the union, integrated steel makers could persuade themselves that they were doing the best they could under difficult conditions. How could they invest in new mills? Profit rates were low, and the politicians would scream if they tried to raise prices any more. And how could they bring in new technology, or introduce more efficient work practices, or do anything else that might lead to lower costs? The union would just throw up obstacles. Since everyone in the industry faced the same constraints, better to let things go on as they always had, jointly raising prices as much as possible and jointly giving away in wages as much as necessary. No one, after all, was going broke.

It was this attitude—at once contentious and complacent—that made it so difficult for the integrated steel companies to respond when the marketplace finally began to change. Beginning in the late 1950s, the giants began to face competitors who were playing by different rules—who paid more attention to cost-cutting and innovation and quality than to the government or the union. Some of these new competitors came from overseas. Others, to the everlasting surprise of the steel executives, were right here at home.

Competition from Imports. For much of the twentieth century, American steel facilities were larger and more productive than any other nation's. Steel executives thus supported free trade and did their best to take advantage of overseas markets. After World War II the steel makers' position in the world market seemed virtually invulnerable, because their mills hadn't been damaged by the war. Confident steel executives supported massive U.S. aid to both European and Japanese steel makers and contributed time and expertise to the rebuilding process.

As it happened, both Europe and Japan rebuilt their steel industries faster than anyone had expected, constructing efficient new mills that incorporated the latest technologies. Even so, imports into the United States hovered just above 1 million tons a year for most of the 1950s, typically amounting to only a percent or two of total steel usage. The year 1959, however, marked a turning point. Contract negotiations between the union and American steel makers that year broke down, and workers went out on what turned out to be a 116-day strike, until then the longest major strike in American history. (It was ended only when President Eisenhower invoked the Taft-Hartley Act's eighty-day cooling-off period and sent the strikers back to work; before the eighty days were up, the two sides had settled on terms generally favorable to the union.) Because of the strike, customers turned to overseas suppliers in droves, boosting imports in 1959 to 4.4 million tons.

Though imports dropped a little in the following couple of years, the tide had turned. "The big customers came back," a Bethlehem Steel manager later told John Strohmeyer, the former editor of the Bethlehem (Pa.) *Globe Times* and author of a book on the company. "But we began to lose the by-products—nails, field fence, and barbed wire. It was a nickel-and-dime impact at first but it started to affect the cost structure because we were now selling a smaller piece of the product.

"And soon we were competing with a market we could not match. Belgian barbed wire was being delivered on the docks at Baltimore at less money than it cost us to make it."

Interestingly, the United States continued to aid the steel industries of its allies and former enemies. The government sent $176 million in assistance to Japanese steel makers between 1957 and 1960, for example, accounting for about one-tenth of the total investment in Japanese steel during this period. The United States also sent technical experts and encouraged Japan to utilize so-called basic-oxygen furnaces, the newest and most efficient steel-making technology. During the 1960s Japan's steel output jumped more than fourfold, while U.S. domestic output grew only about 30 percent. Imports by 1970 came to about 14 percent of American steel consumption, with Japan now accounting for a noticeable share of the market.

Competition from the Minimills. There was trouble on the home front, too. Back in the 1930s a small Chicago-area rod producer called Northwestern Steel and Wire began experimenting with what was known as an electric furnace, a device that melted steel scrap with a high-voltage charge of electricity. Over the years Northwestern engineered significant improvements in the furnace, and by the late 1950s had developed facilities that could make certain kinds of steel from scrap more efficiently than the integrated producers could make it from iron ore. Soon a new generation of steel entrepreneurs began building companies to take advantage of this technology. The facilities they created were called minimills.

By far the best known of the minimill entrepreneurs was a Purdue University graduate named F. Kenneth Iverson, a folksy man with a fondness for photographing water birds in his spare time. In 1965, after a twenty-year career in the metalworking industry, Iverson found himself at the head of a sputtering company called Nuclear Corporation of America. It was a "hodgepodge of unrelated, unprofitable operating units," wrote my *Inc.* colleague Mark K. Metzger—a leasing business, a construction company, a nuclear instruments maker, on and on. Iverson sold off many of the units, focusing his attention on a division that fabricated steel joists. The division, he decided, needed its own source of steel. He knew about electric-furnace technology; he also knew of a group of minimill operators in northern Italy who were using electric furnaces to get a share of the European market. Raising $3 million in new capital, the company broke ground for its first mill in September 1968. By mid-1969 its employees were pouring steel.

Nucor, as the company came to be known, was one of the first minimill companies, and it would eventually be among the biggest. By 1990 it registered $1.5 billion in revenues and ranked number 263 on the Fortune 500. But the company's growth reflected, as well as contributed to, the growth of a new market segment. Minimills in the late 1960s accounted for about 5 percent of U.S. steel production. They existed more or less on the fringe of the marketplace, generally locating far from larger competitors and limiting themselves to regional markets. By 1980, however, the minimills as a group had increased their market share to 12 percent, and by 1989 to more than 20 percent. They had also moved away from the fringes of the market and begun challenging both the integrated companies and overseas competitors head-on. "The minimills have steadily gained on the integrated mills in terms of competitiveness," concluded a 1986 Brookings Institution study, "capturing more and more of each market they have penetrated, and moving on to the more sophisticated products formerly the province of the integrated companies. The minimills have not only pushed aside integrated U.S. producers but have also captured a larger share of the market once held by imports. Were it not for the soaring value of the U.S. dollar in the early 1980s, the minimills would have displaced even more imports."

The minimills were as different from the integrated mills as a young semiconductor company from RCA. By definition, minimills utilized electric furnaces and made steel from scrap, not from ore. They were smaller and more specialized than the integrated companies. A minimill might employ several hundred workers rather than several thousand. It typically produced only billets, rather than the full range of shapes produced at an integrated mill, and it rolled these billets into only a few final products, such as reinforcing bars for concrete. Mostly because they used scrap as their raw material, minimills could rarely turn out products with exacting quality specifications.

The minimills were also different kinds of organizations from their larger forebears. Nearly all were nonunion. Both blue-collar and white-collar work forces were kept as small as possible. A 1986 report on Nucor, for example, noted that it produced more than twice the steel per employee-hour that the integrated companies produced, and that the 4,000-employee company maintained a corporate staff of only seventeen, including Iverson. The minimills typically operated according to a management philosophy of worker involvement. Job descriptions were flexible, and teams of employees worked on solving production bottlenecks. A substantial part of employees' (and managers') compensation was tied to output; thus everyone had an interest in boosting productivity. Thanks to this incentive pay, minimill workers generally earned decent wages, although not what they would have earned in a unionized mill. Then, too, many of the minimill companies had profit-sharing arrangements or employee stock-ownership plans, thus allowing workers at all levels to capitalize on their growth.

The minimills succeeded in the marketplace not just because they happened on a good idea, but because they relentlessly pursued innovation and cost-cutting. "Most minimills use the newest technology," reported Brookings, "but they also tend to operate more efficiently in any given process—for example, tap-to-tap times, between pourings of heats or batches of molten steel, are much shorter and man-hours per ton much lower in minimill electric furnaces. This was not always the case. In the 1960s, the minimills' performance was relatively poor, but they have done far more to improve productivity and other efficiency measures than the integrated companies." Some of the improvements were startling. Tap-to-tap time, which measures how long it takes a mill to "mix" a batch of steel, averaged about five hours in 1975. Ten years later the average had dropped to only 1.5

hours. Costs declined, too. Between 1981 and 1985 (with overall prices for steel-mill products rising 8 percent) the cost of producing a ton of wire rod in a minimill *fell* 5 percent. The minimill cost was well below U.S. integrated companies' cost; it was even below Japanese companies' cost.

Over time, the minimills began expanding their horizons, moving into segments of the market dominated by the integrated companies. Raritan River Steel, a New Jersey minimill built in the late 1970s by a Canadian company, made wire rod of much higher quality than most minimills were capable of; by 1985 it was the leading producer of wire rod in the United States. Nucor had been a leader in the steel-making technology known as continuous casting, a process that allows a mill to bypass certain stages in the traditional process, and in mill automation. Now it pushed forward into other areas. In 1989 it opened a mill in Crawfordsville, Indiana, that produced flat-rolled steel, a market segment that until then had been the exclusive province of the integrateds. The mill utilized a new technology known as thin-slab casting; it could produce a ton of steel in 1.5 labor hours, compared with six labor hours in a traditional mill.

So imports and minimills were eating into the traditional steel producers' oligopoly. Even so, the integrated companies were big, rich organizations that seemed capable of responding to any competitive threat. The question was whether they could take the necessary steps.

Some steel executives denied that any response was required. "No one paid attention to the inroads of minimills," a senior Bethlehem engineer said to John Strohmeyer. "One of my assignments was to keep abreast of them. I would periodically report what the status, the product, and the tonnage were.

"The response was, 'If a guy comes on stream with 60,000 tons of raw steel a year, let's not worry about that.' But one guy here and one guy there and pretty soon you see the old customers disappear."

The integrateds also tried hard to downplay the threat from imported steel. In 1971 the president of Bethlehem Steel opined that "the long-range threat of foreign steel seems to be diminishing." Two years later the head of the industry's trade association said that Japanese companies' recent price hikes would drive American buyers away. Two years after that the president of Jones & Laughlin Steel Company wrote in the *Wall Street Journal* that "the era of cheap foreign steel has gone the way of cheap foreign oil, never to return."

Denial, of course, is seldom effective, and imports continued to take market share from domestic producers. Then again, maybe denial was as effective as anything. Everything else the big companies tried to do in response to the changing marketplace seemed to make the situation worse.

To fend off imports, for example, they sought protection from the government. As far back as 1969 the Nixon administration negotiated so-called voluntary restraint agreements with foreign steel producers to limit the amount of steel they could ship to the United States. "The fatal weakness of this program," wrote Barnett and Schorsch, "was that it limited the aggregate tonnage exported by the countries involved, so that many exporters simply shifted to higher value products, maintaining or even increasing the dollar value of their U.S. sales. . . . [Also,] the arrangement did not lead to any increase in U.S. investment or any reversal of the industry's competitive decline." Later the voluntary restraint agreements were replaced by what was known as a trigger price mechanism; any steel entering the United States below a certain price would immediately touch off a government investigation. That, of course, established a protective price floor for the domestic industry—and "ensured that prices in the American market would exceed those prevailing in world markets by an increasingly significant margin." Thus more foreign companies were eager to export their steel to the United States.

Another attempt to fend off imports was a contractual arrangement called the experimental negotiating agreement, or ENA, signed by the integrated producers and the United Steelworkers of America in 1973. The perpetual threat of strikes, reasoned the companies, scared off customers and encouraged them to rely on foreign rather than domestic steel producers. Under the ENA the union would relinquish its right to shut down the industry with a nationwide strike. In return, union members were guaranteed a 3 percent annual wage hike in addition to a cost-of-living increase. The union could bargain upward from the 3 percent figure, but the companies couldn't lower it.

The effects were dramatic. "To the steel companies' eternal regret," wrote John Hoerr, "the ENA turned out to be the most incredible money-making machine [for workers] ever invented in collective bargaining." The ENA covered steel contracts negotiated in 1974, 1977, and 1980. Between 1972 and 1982 the average steelworker's cash wage climbed from $4.27 an hour to $11.91, a 179 percent increase, considerably ahead of inflation. Nonwage benefits rose 344 percent. Other workers in this high-inflation decade did nowhere near as well. At the start of the agreement, steelworkers were making about 50 percent more in total compensation than the average manufacturing employee. At the end of it, they were making twice the average—with no corresponding increase in productivity. By raising costs so much, the ENA made the companies that much less competitive with overseas and minimill steel makers.

The one thing that might have saved the steel makers was a program of constant reinvestment and technological innovation, much like that pursued by the minimills. Oligopolists that they were, however, the steel companies had never found it necessary to stay on the technological cutting edge. Indeed, they had long erred greatly on the side of caution. In the 1920s an engineer named John Butler Tytus came up with a new flat-rolling process, an innovation "ranked by experts as among the greatest breakthroughs in basic steelmaking." Most of the integrated companies didn't adopt the new technology for several years. In the 1950s the integrateds expanded their capacity with open-hearth furnaces instead of the newer and more efficient basic-oxygen furnaces, a program described by *Business Week* as creating 40 million tons of "the wrong kind of capacity." When the companies finally began installing basic-oxygen facilities, in the 1960s, they generally ignored the other major steel-making improvement of recent decades, the continuous caster. By 1975 Japanese companies made nearly one-third of their steel with continuous casters, while the comparable figure for American companies was about one-tenth.

Like a lot of big, complacent U.S. corporations, the steel makers had no structures or incentives designed to encourage innovation. Steel companies as a group spent less on research and development, and employed fewer scientists and engineers, than nearly every other industry. The proportion of revenues spent on R&D actually declined between 1960 and 1980. One student of the industry summed up the situation in the early 1980s: "Compared to the largest Japanese companies, the world's most efficient steel producers, the integrated U.S. producers suffer from significantly outmoded capacity, poor location and layout, mismatched products and markets, and significant technological backwardness in energy productivity, resource utilization, and finishing capability."

By the late 1980s there were at least a few signs that the big steel makers were finally learning to compete in the new marketplace, albeit at an extraordinary human cost. Bethlehem, for example, shed some 50,000 employees between 1981 and 1988. But the 33,000 workers that remained were now working for a profitable, efficient company; Bethlehem had finally begun pouring money into technological improvements, and at some plants could now produce high-quality steel for less than Japanese steel makers. (According to *Business Week*, the customer rejection rate on Bethlehem's automobile sheet steel dropped from 8 percent in 1981 to 0.08 percent in 1988.) USX Corporation, as U.S. Steel was renamed, had also invested in steel making technology, despite its widely publicized efforts to diversify out of the steel business. The company's Gary Works, which lost an estimated $250 million a year in the early 1980s, generated profits of more than $300 million in 1988. The industry that hadn't turned a collective profit since 1981 began making money again in 1987. Even labor relations seemed to mellow a little. Integrated companies such as LTV Steel and National Steel, in cooperation with the union, were experimenting with labor-management participation teams, involving workers in solving production problems in the mills. USX itself began experimenting with a team approach, though in this case the motive seemed to be to circumvent the union rather than work with it. "We want worker cooperation, but we don't want to broker it through the union," a USX executive told *Business Week*.

But the big steel companies' apparent revival seemed iffy. It depended in part on continuing import restraints, in part on the economic boom of the 1980s, and no one was sure what the future held. A 1988 *Wall Street Journal* article was headlined, "Big Steel Is Back, But Upturn Is Costly And May Not Last." Not quite a year later the industry was still thriving—but the *Journal* headlined another story, "Steel Industry Boom Seems Set to Go Bust."

By 1990, at any rate, it was plain that the fate of the industry no longer depended wholly on the biggest companies. The minimills themselves were a powerful and dynamic force, accounting for more than one-fourth of steel shipments. In addition, the industry that had once been so well integrated (the same companies that melted steel had also made finished and semifinished products such as wire rod) had now *dis*integrated. Newer, smaller American companies, taking advantage both of new technologies and of the new style of labor relations pioneered by the minimills, were elbowing their way into market niches abandoned by the once-giant producers. A seemingly old and tired industry was proving receptive to small-scale entrepreneurship.

REBIRTH OF A MILL

At *Inc.*, we began hearing about entrepreneurship in the steel industry early in the decade. A colleague traveled to Youngstown, Ohio, in 1984, looking for examples of unemployed workers setting up businesses of their own. He returned with an even better story: a onetime U.S. Steel executive named David Houck had put together a company to reopen part of the company's recently shuttered McDonald Works. Houck's new business, McDonald Steel, had already put 125 people back to work rolling specialty shapes on two of U.S. Steel's mills. Over the next few years we learned that Houck wasn't alone. In Johnstown, Pennsylvania, for example, a group of former U.S. Steel managers had teamed up with a local investor to buy the Johnstown Works, a facility that had produced mill rolls, castings, and other heavy pieces for the giant steel maker. Johnstown Corporation, as the new company was called, had a payroll of some 540 by 1988, with annual sales over $35 million.

It was right about then, 1988 or so, that we began hearing about Tom Tyrrell.

Tyrrell (the name is pronounced TEER-ll) was president of a new company called American Steel & Wire, in Cleveland. By all indications this was no ordinary venture, and Tyrrell no ordinary entrepreneur. *Esquire* listed him in its 1988 "register" of people to watch. "The young company Tom Tyrrell runs has a special feel to it," said the magazine, likening it to a Silicon Valley start-up. *Fortune* mentioned Tyrrell in an article called "What the Leaders of Tomorrow See." Tyrrell was a manager who had "mastered the concept of the learning organization," said writer Brian Dumaine; he was a man who "sounded more like a born-again preacher than a CEO." In 1990 we invited Tyrrell to a staff lunch at *Inc.*, where he talked virtually nonstop for more than two hours. His manner wasn't boastful, but he expressed little doubt as to the importance of what he was doing. His company, he said, was symbolic not only of where the steel industry was headed but of what American manufacturers had to do to compete in a global market. It was a high-tech operation in a low-tech business. It was a participatory, egalitarian, cooperative organization in an industry in which bureaucracy and bitter antagonism between labor and management had been the time-honored rules. It was learning to produce wire rod of a quality that no other company in the United States was then capable of, and was thus preparing to recapture markets that had been utterly dominated by Japanese producers. It was a harbinger of the revival of American steel.

Tyrrell invited us to visit his company. I took him up on the invitation, and in July spent several days wandering around the mill and talking with Ed Goldsmith and a dozen other employees about the company they were building.

The company was in Cuyahoga Heights, just a few minutes' drive from downtown. It did not, I have to say, look like any other new business I have seen. Some of the company's huge mill buildings dated back to 1910 and looked it: they were great gray shedlike structures surrounded by weedy acres of industrial wasteland. The large headquarters building (AS&W didn't come close to filling it up) was of brick and concrete, with an art-deco facade. Inside, it was reminiscent of a 1940s-vintage public school, with tiled walls and wired-glass hallway doors.

The facilities had been known as the Cuyahoga Works when they were owned by U.S. Steel. By happy coincidence, they had been neither cannibalized nor dismantled when the giant company had shut them down in 1984. A man named Jim Thomas, the plant manager at the time, had hoped to raise money to buy the mill from U.S. Steel, so he had ordered the machinery and equipment carefully mothballed. Even the electricity had remained on: U.S. Steel's contract with the electric company called for a fixed price regardless of usage, so it was never shut off. Thomas's venture, however, didn't get off the ground, and by 1986 the rumor was that U.S. Steel planned to demolish the facilities and take a $24 million tax write-off.

The Cuyahoga Works had only one chance for survival. Two Cincinnati investors, who were looking to buy up short-line railroads, had discovered one that served the abandoned facility. The investors didn't know much about steel, but they knew the railroad would be a lot more valuable if the mill were open and functioning. So they began investigating. They met with U.S. Steel, and toured the well-preserved facility. They explored sources of funding, such as the state of Ohio's Department of Development. The state, they figured, would be interested in the jobs that could be brought back to the area if the mill were reopened.

But even if they could get the money together and negotiate a favorable deal, they would need an experienced steel executive, someone who could not only come in and roll steel but who had the savvy to negotiate the industry's treacherous late-1980s marketplace. The head of U.S. Steel's realty division, a man who had once been the general manager for rod and wire sales, had a suggestion. If they were seriously interested in running a rod mill, he said, there was one man they had better get in touch with as soon as they could. His name was Tom Tyrrell.

Thomas N. Tyrrell is an intense, voluble man with brown hair and small features, whose modest stature is augmented by a bushy, carefully styled hairdo. He is also a man who has organized his life (retrospectively, at least) into a coherent story, which he occasionally refers to as a "book" he has been writing. Chapter one for Tyrrell took place in the Chicago area. Born in 1945, he was the oldest of six children. His father, Thomas W., never made it through the first year of high school, and supported his sizable family mainly by working nonstop. "When I was five," said Tyrrell, "he was working cleaning out drums at a paint company during the daytime. He was working the switchboard at Sears at night; and on the weekends he worked at a gas station. I remember we'd drive into the gas station on Sunday, so I'd get a chance to see him. During that time—when I was five, six—he also built the house that we lived in. He and his brothers and his father were all bricklayers. They physically built the whole house."

Tyrrell, too, grew up working. As a child he sold soda to construction workers, returning to the construction site at night to collect the bottles and thereby pocket the deposits. In high school and college he held a variety of jobs at the paint and can company his father was then working for; he loaded boxcars, painted pallets, worked the can lines, did typing and secretarial work, even filled in for a credit manager who had quit abruptly. Graduating from Elmhurst College, in Illinois, in 1967, he took a job with Bethlehem Steel and was assigned to the company's famed Loop program, generally regarded as one of the best training programs in the industry. A year later he was posted to a sales job in Greensboro, North Carolina.

Tyrrell decided that this chapter of his life should last five years. "I had a five-year plan to get out of Greensboro. Every year I would try to evaluate myself as closely as I could, to see how I was doing. I always wanted to be the youngest on any job. Then I could keep moving up, to where I could be in the higher echelons of the company at a relatively young age. And that's the way it worked. Four years and ten months later I joined the rod and wire division and moved to Bethlehem. That's when I really got into the rod and wire business and began to understand it."

The Bethlehem chapter also lasted five years, but by now the plot was taking some unexpected turns. Bethlehem Steel's priorities lay in flat-rolled steel, and Tyrrell grew frustrated with the company's lack of commitment to his division. Rod and wire was making money, but wasn't seeing a corresponding reinvestment in new facilities and equipment. Tyrrell himself wasn't sure he wanted to move up at the pace the giant company seemed to expect. "In his last performance appraisal," his former boss told a reporter, "I said if Tom continued to progress in the same areas and at the same speed in our department that . . . he would eventually become a key player at Bethlehem— possibly the president. But he felt it would take an inordinate amount of time to become a VP, and he didn't want to wait." Instead of waiting, in 1978 Tyrrell wrote a letter to the president of Raritan River Steel, the New Jersey minimill company that was planning a new rod mill. He was hired as vice-president of marketing and over- saw a sales effort that garnered the young company a 25 percent share of its market in eight years.

As Tyrrell recounts his story, all the chapters right through the sojourn at Raritan were just so much preparation. His ultimate goal was to build a rod mill on the Great Lakes, and to make rod of the highest quality. That was a market niche in the steel industry that seemed unfilled, and that Tyrrell figured he could do a good job of filling. Raritan itself had a reputation for making high-quality rod, but as its production volume grew, its quality, in Tyrrell's view, began to slip. Also, Tyrrell couldn't believe that steel companies had to be quite the caldrons of labor-management hostility that most of them were. Managed right, he figured, they could be organizations in which everyone pitched in to get the job done, and in which everyone benefited. The Japanese had succeeded in the steel business partly because of their relentless attention to quality, and partly because of their relatively harmonious labor relations. An American company couldn't transplant Japanese methods wholesale. But maybe it could develop a better way of operating than the integrated companies had ever demonstrated.

Fueled by such ambitions, Tyrrell was more than ready to run his own show. When he got a phone call in late 1985 from a Cincinnati investor who asked if he wanted to be involved in reopening a rod mill in Cleveland, it was like a young Luciano Pavarotti being asked if he wouldn't mind playing the lead in an opera or two.

From the first of April 1986 on, Tyrrell lived in Cleveland, working out of the Cuyahoga Heights steel facility, and tried with the Cincinnati investors to put together a deal to resurrect the mill. He admits now to "a little naïveté" in his estimate of how easy it would be; in fact it was a Herculean set of tasks, with one obstacle after another thrown into his path. Negotiations with U.S. Steel went slowly. The state of Ohio, from which Tyrrell was requesting a low-interest loan, dragged its feet. Some political maneuvering moved matters along, and by May the deputy director of the state's department of development was announcing a seed-money loan of $4 million. Since several banks were reported to be interested in providing more money, the deal seemed all but done. "Last week," wrote a local columnist on May 26, "it was announced that the [Cuyahoga] plant would reopen by midyear, and that 430 new jobs were on their way to Ohio." The mill would be run by the newly formed American Steel & Wire Corporation, Tom Tyrrell, president.

Back at the office, however, Tyrrell was sweating. The works alone was costing upwards of $30 million, he knew, and many millions more would be needed before the company could begin rolling steel. The state money was only a drop in the bucket, and the Cincinnati investors were putting only a little cash into the venture. Worse, the banks that had professed themselves interested were getting cold feet. In late April the bank Tyrrell had been counting on to lead a loan consortium backed out. He scrambled to find others; typically, he would get a favorable response at first, then a no after a few weeks of negotiating. When he announced the creation of the company, in May, he had no bank. May became June and still he had no bank. U.S. Steel had signed a letter of intent to sell the Cuyahoga Works to American Steel & Wire, but the commitment ran out June 30.

At that point, so it seemed, the fledgling company's luck turned. An associate of Tyrrell's found himself delayed at the Baltimore airport. He got to talking with a fellow traveler, who happened to work for a new commercial-finance arm of Westinghouse. Soon thereafter Tyrrell and his chief financial officer were on their way to visit Westinghouse, and in three weeks they had a commitment for $40 million. The *t*'s were crossed and the *i*'s dotted just before the end of June. Along with the Cuyahoga Works (the new company's flagship plant), American Steel & Wire got two other mills: a rolling mill in Joliet, Illinois, and a tiny facility in Cleveland that made specialty wire for the Defense Department.

But there were more hurdles still to come. American Steel & Wire had no facilities for making its own raw steel; it would have to buy steel billets from a mill, then roll them into rod. The logical supplier of billets was U.S. Steel's mill in nearby Lorain, Ohio, and indeed a supply contract was written into the agreement with the big steel maker. Knowing that U.S. Steel had negotiations with the United Steelworkers of America scheduled for August 1—and figuring that there might be a strike—Tyrrell put in orders for large quantities of billets. He was planning on having his mill ready for operation by September 15, and he wanted to ensure a steady supply of material. Until then, the longest steel strike in history had been the 1959 strike, 116 days. Tyrrell figured this one for a maximum of seventy-five days.

Sure enough, the Steelworkers went out in August. They were still out in September; still out in November. Tyrrell's new company refused to lay off any of its newly hired workers, but it was hemorrhaging money. The sales staff, which had found a host of ready customers, had to return $25 million in orders, saying that American Steel & Wire couldn't fill them. Buyers scoured the world for billet sources, but couldn't always obtain the high-quality billets that the Lorain Works could have provided. Tyrrell began rolling low-quality, industrial-grade rod, exactly what he hadn't wanted to do. The strike dragged on through December and January. When it ended, on January 31, it had lasted 184 days. When American Steel & Wire's first fiscal year ended, the following June, the company had lost close to $9 million.

Yet Tyrrell had been right: there was indeed a market for a rod mill in the Great Lakes area. Many customers that had been left stranded in 1984, when U.S. Steel had shut down the Cuyahoga Works, were glad the facility was reopened, and began buying. By the end of its second fiscal year, in June 1988, American Steel & Wire's sales had jumped to $158 million, with a profit of more than $8 million. The company had a payroll of about 450, including 100 or so at the Joliet mill and a couple of dozen at the specialty-wire facility. "Steel Firm Rebounds in Two Years," read a headline in the Akron *Beacon Journal*.

To keep on growing and making money over the next several years, Tyrrell felt, American Steel & Wire would have to focus on two goals. First, it couldn't get mired in the labor-management animosity and rigidity that had dragged the industry down in the past. On the contrary, it would need a system of labor relations that allowed for flexibility and teamwork. As in any young business, workers would have to work different jobs, pitching in where they were needed and working together in teams to solve problems. The company would have to run lean. It couldn't afford any superfluous bodies on the payroll, and it would have to pay relatively low base wages, with supplements from profit sharing or stock ownership when the company was doing well.

Second, the company would have to improve the quality of its product, and eventually establish a reputation for the highest-quality rod in the country. Plenty of mills produced wire rod. But few companies outside of Japan produced rod of the quality necessary for a wide variety of applications, such as the production of engine bolts and other high-reliability industrial fasteners. (Cuyahoga Works had itself once produced high-quality rod, but U.S. Steel, like other integrated companies, had ceded the market to imports.) Tyrrell's experience had convinced him that many American customers would buy steel from a domestic supplier if they could get quality that was equivalent to the Japanese. He also expected a large market to develop from Japanese "transplant" companies, such as the new Honda plant in Marysville, Ohio. But Japanese buyers wouldn't be satisfied with less than Japanese-style quality.

Neither of these objectives, it turned out, would be easy to attain.

Labor Relations. When American Steel & Wire was being formed, Tyrrell and United Steelworkers district leader Frank Valenta danced a courteous *pas de deux* through the newspapers. "Whether it's union or nonunion is of no concern to us," Tyrrell told a reporter, stopping short of saying that the Steelworkers would be welcomed with open arms. Valenta, for his part, said of Tyrrell and his associates, "They have real sincerity and honesty and want the plant in business." But pretty soon the two men began needling each other in the press. Valenta complained that the company was hiring too many older workers (who already had union pensions) and not enough younger ones (who might be more interested in bringing a union into the plant). Don't blame me, Tyrrell retorted; it was blue-collar employees themselves who were doing the hiring. Finally Valenta told a reporter that of course he planned to organize the plant; the only question was when.

By 1989 the Steelworkers had mounted a serious organizing campaign and had persuaded 51 percent of AS&W's Cuyahoga employees to sign cards requesting a union-representation election. It quickly became plain that Tyrrell wasn't neutral at all on the question of unionization. On the contrary, he threatened that the company would "go back to ground zero" on wages, benefits, and its no-layoff policy if the workers voted the union in. What he didn't say, but what was clear to anyone who knew the history of the steel industry, was that he feared the company couldn't compete if it were unionized. As a young company in a chancy marketplace, it could pay workers well if it was making money, but it couldn't afford the high fixed wages that any self-respecting union would promptly press for. Nucor had prospered partly because it had kept all of its plants nonunion. Then, too, though the Steelworkers had developed a reputation as one of the more cooperative unions in the country, there was no guarantee that a collective-bargaining contract would ever allow the kind of managerial flexibility that Tyrrell felt was necessary. Even a hint of rigid rules and job classifications could hamstring the company's operations.

The campaign was acrimonious. Shortly before the scheduled election day—May 5, 1989—the union filed charges of unfair labor practices with the National Labor Relations Board. The company, the Steelworkers charged, was threatening wage cuts if the union won, and promising wage hikes if the union lost. That was illegal. "The employees for the most part are now fearful of having the union represent them," an organizer claimed. American Steel & Wire officially declined comment. The NLRB launched an investigation. In a lawyerly settlement a short while later, the company admitted no wrongdoing but agreed to post a notice saying it wouldn't engage in any unfair labor practices.

It did, however, keep the pressure on the union. With the election now rescheduled for October 5, the company distributed profit-sharing checks to workers on September 30. The union, too, stepped up its campaign. "We expect to win," said the Steelworkers chief organizer a few days before the election. If they did, Tyrrell's methods and managerial approach would plainly be in jeopardy.

Quality. While it was struggling with the unionization issue, AS&W was facing another major problem: quality control.

To anyone unfamiliar with the metal, steel is steel. Those who make and use the material know that it is as variable as lumber. It comes in different grades, with different metallurgical compositions. Slight variations in the way it is heated or cooled impart different characteristics to the final product. A billet may have seams or other surface imperfections, and these defects will create defects in the rod that the billet is rolled into. High-quality rod (the kind that Tyrrell had set out to make) must be free of such defects. It must also be manufactured to rigorous specifications. An engine-bolt maker, for example, may require steel with a precise chemical composition and a precise degree of hardness. The rod from which the bolt is made must fit within exacting size and roundness tolerances. Meeting all such specifications requires careful attention to the manufacturing process. A malfunctioning rolling stand, or improper cooling procedures, will compromise the final product.

Tyrrell's first step toward high-quality rod was a major renovation of the rod mill itself, a ground-up rebuilding that cost some $20 million. With technical assistance from Japan's Kobe Steel, American Steel & Wire modernized its furnace, installed an elaborate computerized monitor-and-control system, added new rolling stands, incorporated new laser gauges, and updated a dozen other aspects of its production process. Before, the mill had been capable of producing rod sized within industry-standard tolerances of fifteen-thousandths of an inch. Now it would be capable of so-called half-standard production, meaning tolerances within eight-thousandths. That put it in the same quality ballpark as the Japanese. Not incidentally, it would also be capable of handling larger billets and processing more steel per hour, thus lowering the company's costs.

But there was another task facing Tyrrell, and it came upon him a little before he was ready for it. To understand it, you need to understand the revolution that was taking place in manufacturers' quality-control procedures.

The easiest way to make sure a piece of steel (or any manufactured part) is built right is to inspect it. Gauge it, analyze it, check it for defects. Inspection systems traditionally were manufacturers' first (and sometimes their only) line of defense against poor quality. But inspection has its limitations. You generally can't inspect every piece. If you find a bad one, you don't know how many others are bad. In the past, inspection was typically performed in batches, well after each batch was produced. So the inspector could rarely tell what caused the problem.

During the late 1980s a fundamentally different approach to quality control began to permeate many different manufacturing industries, including those that bought steel from the likes of AS&W. One precept of this new approach, which was already widely utilized in Japan, was to track and measure the variables that went into a production process as well as the products coming out of it. If everything on the input side was functioning right, the theory ran, then the product would be produced right, too. A second precept was to gauge and analyze the product *as it was being produced,* so the production process could be quickly stopped and modified if it wasn't working properly. Finally, all this measurement—of both input and output—was to be written down. That way there would be a record of how, and under what conditions, every item was produced.

Large U.S. manufacturers attempted to implement these precepts in their own factories, and to instill them in the smaller companies on which they depended for parts and materials. Ford Motor Company, to take only one example, instituted an extensive quality-assurance program, not only for its own operations but for its suppliers and its suppliers' suppliers, the latter category including American Steel & Wire. The program spelled out exactly what each manufacturer was expected to measure, control, and record. A producer of bolts might have to provide full statistical documentation for each batch, indicating size and roundness variation, with the measurements taken while the bolt-making machine was in operation. A producer of the wire rod used in making the bolts wouldn't be asked just to measure and analyze the steel. It would also be asked to measure and record furnace times and temperatures, cooling procedures, and so on, for each billet. Ideally, every single coil—like every single bolt—would be produced according to a rigid set of specifications, and a written record would show that every variable along the way had stayed within the specifications. Ultimately (so the theory ran) the car itself would be an assembly of nearly perfect materials and parts. Any defect that did creep in would be traceable to its original manufacturer.

American Steel & Wire had not yet developed a full statistical-process-control system, as the new approach was known, when it completed the rod-mill renovation. But it sold plenty of steel to customers that supplied Ford as well as other big manufacturers, and Tyrrell knew it was only a matter of time before it would have to develop such a system. Then, right about the time of the union vote, Ford showed up.

You have ninety days, said the automaker. At the end of that time we'll plan to do a quality audit of your plant. If your procedures score satisfactorily, we'll award you what we call Q101 status.

Q101, Tyrrell knew, was the first step toward qualifying for Ford's so-called Q1 ranking, which assured the automaker of extraordinarily strict quality-control procedures. Anyone who didn't have a Q1 ranking by 1992 wouldn't be selling anything to Ford, or to any of Ford's suppliers. No other rod maker yet had Q101 status, let alone Q1. If American Steel & Wire could satisfy Ford, it would ensure not only the company's survival but a fittingly high reputation in the industry.

A DIFFERENT KIND OF COMPANY

Both the union election and the Ford visit took place in the fall of 1989, not long after American Steel & Wire had closed the books on its second full year of operation. By that time, Tyrrell had established a company whose very structure seemed to help it navigate the choppy waters it was confronting.

For one thing, he had muddied the conventional distinction between employees and owners. Every worker was expected to buy at least $100 worth of stock in the company. "If anybody didn't want to buy stock," he liked to tell reporters, "we didn't have a job for them." To encourage more stock purchases Tyrrell made shares available to employees at deep discounts. When Ed Goldsmith started out, in 1986, he bought 1,200 shares at 10 cents a share. When the company sold stock to the public, in 1988, Goldsmith's shares were worth $9 each. Nor were the workers treated like second-class owners. Company managers held regular small-group meetings every quarter to explain the business's financial situation in detail to employees. An intricate profit-sharing arrangement distributed about 20 percent of American Steel & Wire's pretax profits to workers. Like most young enterprises, the company paid out no regular dividends to other shareholders.

Tyrrell was also blurring the distinction between blue-collar employees and managerial employees. Until recently, this was one of the more visible class distinctions in American industry. Blue-collar ("hourly") workers dressed in work clothes, ate out of lunch buckets, punched time clocks. They were laid off as a matter of routine when business was poor, then were called back when business picked up. They were unlikely to get much in the way of fringe benefits unless they belonged to a strong union, in which case their fringe benefits would be spelled out in rigorous detail. Managers—and most white-collar office employees—were paid salaries, had more control over their time, typically got more generous fringes, and were rarely subject to routine layoffs.

Traditional companies such as the integrated steel firms had gone to great lengths to reinforce these status distinctions, with devices ranging from different colored hard hats to reserved parking spaces. American Steel & Wire abolished all such trappings. Hard hats were all the same color, with everyone's first name printed in big letters on the front. Everyone working in or visiting the mill wore the same blue smock. No one got a special parking place; no one other than the outside salespeople was given a company car. There were no time clocks, since everyone was on salary. Fringe benefits were the same for all.

In Tyrrell's mind, the most important of these egalitarian commitments was his pledge not to lay anyone off in a business downturn. Rather than letting 10 percent of the work force go, he asked, why not reduce everyone's hours 10 percent? The effect on costs would be the same, but the effect on morale would be incalculably different. "What happens when you do that? No one's happy, getting less pay. But they all have a job, and they're all in it together, and when you come back everyone comes back together. If you ever lay somebody off, you've probably lost that person for life. Even if he comes back, you've lost him here." Tyrrell pointed to his head. "And every person that works with him thinks, Am I next? So his mind's not on the job.

"I want everyone thinking this is all there is; that the best job they can get is here and that this is a company that will take care of them. We benefit in the good times, by sharing the profits. In the bad times, if we hit them—well, are the workers responsible for the problems? The plant people are typically the ones that suffer, but they know they're not responsible for what the market does."

Finally, Tyrrell created an elaborate series of structures to make sure that employees had a voice in the running of the business—that they had the chance to develop and implement ideas for change, to express grievances, even to arbitrate disputes. Among these structures:

Concerns committees for each unit of the company were charged with taking up and resolving employee concerns about company policies. Composed of representatives from various departments (but open to anyone who wanted to attend), they met regularly to discuss matters ranging from safety issues to the company's attendance policy. Essentially, the committees were a formal method of addressing the communications breakdowns that occur in any large organization. They could address written questions to any manager, and were entitled to written responses.

An *employee council* made up of specially trained blue-collar volunteers was the court of last resort for individual grievances or disputes with managers. A worker who had been fired, for example, could take his cause either to Tyrrell or to the employee council; if he chose the latter he'd get a formal, confidential hearing, complete with an advocate provided by the company's human-resources staff. Among the cases described to me were these: A worker who had been fired for chronic absenteeism and lateness was put on probation by the council, which took into account a set of unusual family problems. A worker who had been fired for fighting had his termination upheld by the council. A worker who had sought full salary while off on basic training for the military reserves had his request denied by the council. The council met, on average, about once a month. It overturned management decisions in not quite half of its cases.

Customer value teams were shop-floor committees that met regularly to discuss problems or improvements in the production process. These, as it turned out, were among the most significant of Tyrrell's innovations; we'll see below how they worked in practice. In concept, they were much like the quality circles or team-based production systems instituted by a lot of American companies during the 1980s. The idea was simply to involve employees at all levels in solving the inevitable bottlenecks and inefficiencies of a complex manufacturing operation.

Such structures have been visible throughout American business history, in a variety of contexts. They were typical of what was known as the American Plan, in the 1920s, when companies such as General Electric experimented with works councils made up of representatives from labor and management.* More recently, they have turned up in a variety of newly revitalized manufacturing companies. But American Steel & Wire's structures were particularly interesting precisely because of the legacies Tyrrell's young company had to confront. The steel industry was a realm of bitter labor-management antagonism. ("You've got people in here that are carrying their fathers and their grandfathers on their backs," said Tyrrell.) American steel makers had ceded the high ground of quality to Japanese competitors, and were now trying to win it back. The question was whether Tyrrell's approach to management would help.

In the fall of 1989, one conclusion became apparent: for better or worse, the United Steelworkers of America would not be playing a role in American Steel & Wire's fate. Curiously, for an election whose outcome had seemed in doubt to both sides, there was no doubt whatever in the workers' minds. They voted by a whopping margin—181 to 40—against the union.

What neither side had counted on was the employees' faith in the new system of management and the antipathy that some of them felt toward the union. "This place doesn't need a union," a worker told a reporter the day after the vote. "Everybody here is an owner." When I visited several months later, I talked with several workers individually and informally, no managers in sight, and promised them anonymity if they requested it. Not one had a good word to say about the union. One former member spoke bitterly of having been on layoff from a previous job with U.S. Steel for five years and of getting no help from the union when he needed it. Another described how he and his partner helped each other, even though they were responsible for different jobs. "I have an understanding of the whole process," he said. "If the union were here, I couldn't even do his job."

Such views evidently carried the day, even among the employees who had signed cards requesting a union election. Ed Goldsmith, a union member for twenty-one years, argued forcefully against the

*In most companies, American Plan systems didn't survive the Depression. Beset by grim conditions, companies cut wages and let workers go. Workers felt they had been suckered and were then more receptive to the industrial unionism and us-against-them philosophy of the new Congress of Industrial Organizations (CIO).

union. He pointed out that, in the old days, U.S. Steel's Cuyahoga payroll had been padded with unnecessary workers, some of them there at the union's insistence. The rod mill, for instance, was run with a twenty-three-man crew, compared with a fourteen-man crew under American Steel & Wire. Now, Goldsmith argued, the employees shared in AS&W's profits, so they had no interest in any union-enforced payroll padding.

Goldsmith was also worried that, with a union in the mill, the powerful effect of peer pressure would work the way it used to under U.S. Steel, rather than the way it was working now. "There's nothing more motivating than to have your buddy come up and say, If you don't get off your ass and do your job, you're going to be out of here. And they'll do that. They'll get on you, and dog you, until you start doing your job. Under U.S. Steel it was do as you're told and no more. And no one said anything—that was a unionized situation, and you don't run your brother down." It was this new atmosphere, Goldsmith figured, that was allowing American Steel & Wire to boost its production and make money. The old atmosphere had led U.S. Steel to close the mill.

The process of improving quality procedures took a little longer to resolve than the issue of union representation. But it, too, typified the company's approach to management.

"Ford's Q101 program involved a 200-point audit," explained Craig L. Young, who at the time was working as a quality-assurance manager. "We might have scored about 80. And you needed a minimum of 140 to qualify." Most of the items AS&W would have "failed" didn't relate to the production process itself; the company had plenty of steel-industry veterans on board and was rolling rod of generally high quality. But it was weak in the area of systems and procedures. It could provide little documentation of its operations, or traceability if anything went wrong. It had no manual of standard operating practices. It had very little in the way of continuous measurement and tracking during the production process. U.S. Steel, said Young, had destroyed all its own practices-and-procedures manuals when it shut down the mill, for fear of later liability problems should somebody else try to follow them. When American Steel & Wire started up, people weren't writing things down systematically or consistently. So a procedure that was followed on one shift might or might not be followed on the next.

Part of what Ford wanted was a set of manuals specifying standard procedures. That could have been provided by any reasonably competent group of quality engineers. But Ford also wanted to know that employees on every shift were actually following the procedures. "So we got the employees to write up the procedures themselves," said Young. "They wrote them down; then we, the engineers, red-penned and critiqued them, and sent them back for rewrite. The guys weren't used to doing that. It had always been done by the boss."

In some cases, the very act of writing things down led the company to discover problems. Young remembered an example from the part of the mill where rod is turned into wire. In the wire mill, the coils of steel went into a cleaning tank, which needed to be kept at a certain temperature. If the temperature was off by too much, any coating that was to be applied to the wire wouldn't adhere well.

"The guys said, We can hold it to plus or minus five degrees," said Young. "I said, Show me. So we began keeping track, and then we looked at the charts. They couldn't hold it to plus or minus twenty-five degrees. We just weren't as good as we thought we were. So we began checking it once a day; then once a turn [shift]; then twice a turn. Now they're closer to plus or minus five degrees."

When Ford returned for its quality audit, in early 1990, American Steel & Wire's Cuyahoga mill scored 161 out of a possible 200—well above the 140 cutoff, and the second-highest score registered by a rod mill anywhere in the country.

I got a sense of just how important this was when I visited one of American Steel & Wire's customers, in nearby Mentor, Ohio. RB&W, as the company was called, was one of the largest suppliers of industrial fasteners in the United States, counting Ford and other big manufacturers among its customers. (If the concept of "industrial fasteners" stumps you, think for a moment of all the bolts, screws, nuts, and other fasteners in an automobile, or indeed in any complex machine. Most of these are engineered products: that is, they're built to precise specifications for a particular application.) To make the fasteners, RB&W bought a lot of steel rod.

Until 1988 it had bought rod from a variety of suppliers, large and small. That year, it set out to reduce the number of these suppliers from twenty to three. High steel quality was a necessary condition for making the cut. RB&W had once operated the way most manufacturers did, with what was known as an acceptable quality level of 2 percent. Two out of every 100 coils of rod, for example, could be rejected and sent back without jeopardizing the supplier's business relationship. Now, however, it was trying to catch up to the market-place's new expectations, and had set an objective of zero defects. To qualify for RB&W's business, a supplier would have to institute rigorous quality-assurance procedures at its own plant.

American Steel & Wire made RB&W's cut, thanks in large part to its own efforts toward boosting quality. It was a sign that AS&W had come a long way toward putting its manufacturing system "in control" by the new standards.

In the past, steel companies were institutions that didn't change much. Individual executives such as Tyrrell might jockey for position and scramble up the corporate ladder. (If Tyrrell had been born a decade or two earlier, he would probably have spent his whole career with Bethlehem.) Individual workers such as Goldsmith could work their way through the blue-collar ranks and hope that their union won them a few more dollars every year in wages and benefits. But the corporation as a whole seemed immutable. Steel was made one day pretty much the way it had been made the day before. Job descriptions, if not the individuals filling those jobs, varied little. It was a system that provided a great deal of security and, for many, a good living. In Woody Allen's phrase, 98 percent of success consisted of showing up. It was as true of the companies as it was of individuals.

American Steel & Wire, like most companies in the late 1980s, was operating in a fundamentally different environment. Success wasn't guaranteed from one year to the next. Quality standards continued to tighten, which meant that the company had to be con-stantly on the lookout for ways to improve its production process. Japanese companies could still provide wire rod of substantially higher quality (though not at lower cost) than American Steel & Wire. Also, there was no predicting where new competition would come from. A change in exchange rates or in government policies governing imports could make the American market more attractive to overseas competitors. Domestic companies might decide to invade American Steel & Wire's niche; after all, it had cost Tyrrell a rela-tively modest amount, by steel-industry standards, to get into the business he was in. Market demand itself was uncertain. A traditional steel company seeking to supply the auto market could go after GM or Ford or Chrysler, knowing that all three would be buying plenty of steel. American Steel & Wire, by contrast, had to allocate its marketing efforts among suppliers to a dozen different auto companies, including several Japanese transplants. The company's success would depend in part on the success of its target customers.

A largely static marketplace could be served by a largely static kind of organization. A fast-changing, competitive, uncertain marketplace must be served by an organization that learns to change and adapt. As American manufacturers have begun to realize, this is the connection between the quality revolution and employee involvement of the sort practiced by American Steel & Wire. A problem with a customer's order has to be solved immediately. An opportunity to improve the production process has to be seized quickly. A top-down organization can't move fast enough. The only organization that can is one in which everybody is thinking about how to change things.

American Steel & Wire's so-called customer value teams were the front-line troops in this struggle for constant improvement. Each work unit was likely to have its own team, usually no more than six or eight people from various levels within the unit. Charged expressly with problem solving, they undertook three sorts of tasks:

1. *They fixed—or made plans to fix—the innumerable glitches that crop up in the production of steel*. I walked around the mill one afternoon with Rick Teaman, an amiable middle-aged man who was then working in the company's human-resources department but had once been a manager in the rod mill. As we walked he rattled off improvements that customer value teams had suggested and implemented just in the past year or two. The transfer car that carried billets from the yard to the unscrambler used to run on propane and was always breaking down; it was now powered by a stationary motor that sat at one end of the track it ran on. The mill used to have trouble with the "peel bar" that pushed each billet out of the furnace; the team and two managers investigated a different system in use at AS&W's Joliet mill, then modified it for use in the Cuyahoga mill.

Ed Goldsmith could recite a similar series of improvements that had been made by the rod mill's customer value team. But what seemed to excite him most was how different the system was from the way things worked under U.S. Steel. "At U.S. Steel they had a suggestion program. You took this suggestion form, and you put down what your idea was for the improvement. After you put your idea down, it went first through your immediate supervisor, then the general manager, then it went through engineering. Engineering would decide whether it was a good idea or not, and whether it was feasible moneywise." The whole thing, he added, could take months. The employee was never told what had happened to his idea, nor why it might not be implemented.

Goldsmith continued. "Now, if you've got an idea, it can be implemented in 15 minutes. Sure, if it costs money, you've got to work up your figures, come up with the documentation to justify the cost, and give it to the appropriate management. But the majority of things that come out of CVT aren't expensive." He cited as an example the installation of rollers in the pipes that receive newly rolled steel and turn it 90 degrees so that it can enter the spiral "laying head" pipes that transform it into a coil. The 90-degree pipe would sometimes scratch the surface of the steel, and people were wondering whether installing a roller and bearing in the pipe would prevent the scratching. Goldsmith had been thinking about just that problem, and had an idea how to install the devices. One morning he and some coworkers tried it out; they cut a notch in the 90-degree pipe and put in a roller and bearing. In less than an hour the pipe was ready to run. The roller and bearing helped some, and eventually Goldsmith's group installed two more rollers. That solved the problem.

"You're asked to use your head here," concluded Goldsmith. "In the old days, you were supposed to check your brains at the gates."

2. *They looked into customers' complaints and problems, and changed things so that the problems didn't crop up again.* Traditionally, blue-collar workers stayed put, on the factory floor, and did what they were told. At American Steel & Wire, customer value teams traveled to customers' shops and consulted with the people who were actually using their steel to figure out how to resolve problems. Here, too, nearly everyone in the company seemed to be able to cite examples. Ben Marty, a salesman, recounted the story of a claim submitted by Cuyahoga Bolt and Screw, a fastener manufacturer down the street from American Steel & Wire. The customer bought a kind of wire known as cold-heading quality wire from AS&W, then fed it into bolt-making machines that cut, shaped, and threaded the steel.

One spring day Cuyahoga called to complain that there were gouges on the inside of three coils of wire, and that the gouges had fouled up the bolt-making machines. Marty and some wire-mill employees went to take a look. "I wouldn't have known what caused it," said Marty. "But I had Gary Robbins with me, and he's the worker that had actually drawn the material." The wire-drawing machine he had been working on, said Robbins, had a loose bolt, and he realized that the bolt had caused the gouges. Such face-to-face contact, of course, has at least two effects. Everyone understands the source of the foul-up, including the customer, who then has reason to believe it won't happen again. The responsible employee sees the effect of a malfunctioning machine and understands that it's his problem, not just the company's. More generally, a potential source of friction between supplier and customer is turned into a problem-solving session. Everyone feels good because a puzzle has been solved and responsibility ascertained. Without such a resolution, it's easy to imagine a welter of charges and countercharges, both between the two companies and within American Steel & Wire itself.

3. *They acted as vehicles for any number of organizational ideas, suggestions, complaints, and questions.* The CVTs, like parent-teacher organizations and other participatory groups, weren't all alike. "Some teams flounder around, finding themselves," acknowledged Regis Dauk, the company's vice-president of human resources. "The best developed is the one down at our TOW plant. You ought to take a look at that."

The TOW plant (a small wire mill that produced a highly specialized product) was something of an anomaly within American Steel & Wire. (One can only guess how much of an anomaly it had been within U.S. Steel, which owned it until 1986.) The letters of the acronym stand for Tube-launched, Optically tracked, and Wire-guided, adjectives that refer to a particular kind of antitank missile. A soldier launches the missile, then watches an image of the target in a computerized viewfinder. His motions in keeping the target in the cross hairs are transmitted by a thin wire to the missile itself, which adjusts its course accordingly. For more than twenty years, the mill had been supplying this wire to missile maker Hughes Aircraft, which in turn supplied the Department of Defense.

The eight members of the TOW plant's CVT had been elected from a list of volunteers by the plant's two dozen employees. They typically met twice a month and were paid $15 apiece extra for each meeting. The chairman, a talkative young man named Bobby Unger, was responsible for preparing the agenda, which was passed out two days ahead of the meeting. Nothing like this, everyone agreed, had ever happened or would ever have happened when the plant was owned by U.S. Steel. "The only time anyone met was when something went wrong," one supervisor cracked. "The suggestion plan was OK, but it could take a year and a half before a suggestion was implemented."

For a business reporter, sitting in on the TOW plant's customer value team meeting was a startling experience, a little like seeing a shadow cabinet of blue-collar employees discussing the management of the company. Dennis Derbin, who had recently attended a meeting of the companywide steering committee for employee concerns, opened with a report of what he had learned: sales figures for the month before, anticipated changes in the marketplace, how the rod mill was coping with some recent quality problems, and so on. Chairman Unger then chipped in with a report on a meeting he had attended about the company's business plan. He recounted details of a loan package that had recently been put together by American Steel & Wire. He outlined profit-and-loss figures for each division of the company and explained their impact on employees' profit-sharing checks. He went through a series of policy issues, such as the company's interest in finding more women employees. "Send your wives and daughters down there," said Unger. "They really want women in blue-collar jobs."

Most companies share very little such information with their employees. At TOW, however, very little seemed to be off-limits. Although part of the time was taken up with run-of-the-mill suggestions (e.g., better ventilation in the locker room), the team had also worked on some far-reaching reforms. It had drawn up and approved a new pay ladder for TOW employees that spelled out the time period and other requirements for progressing from entry-level wages to the plant's top pay level. It had mapped out a series of procedures that allowed employees to train and qualify for new jobs. Most dramatically, the CVT had undertaken a while back to evaluate the plant's managers, just as blue-collar employees were evaluated *by* the managers. Dennis Derbin reported that other divisions of the company wanted to know more about this system; they, too, were thinking of implementing it.

The workers on the customer value team were under no illusions as to the extent of their power. They had been agitating for a raise in the overall pay scale, for example, and had so far been unsuccessful; in the meeting they talked about ways to push their case still harder. But the disagreement had the earmarks of a family argument rather than an us-against-them dispute typical of traditional labor-management relations. The team had asked for a written response from the company to their request for a raise, and most people seemed content to wait for the letter before taking another step. "Maybe we'll have to question the letter," said Kenny Ferjutz, "but last time around they brought up some things we didn't think of." After the meeting, Bobby Unger complained to me, "It's not hard to get heard in this company; it's just hard to get what you want." But he then proceeded to tell me how he had dropped in on the company's chief financial officer to talk over some personal problems he was having with the Internal Revenue Service, and how the CFO had telephoned the company's lawyer on the spot; both the CFO and the lawyer had then spent 45 minutes of company time reviewing Unger's problems and offering advice.

"To me that meant—my God, companies don't work like this. Under U.S. Steel you couldn't even go out of the building during working hours. They've gained our trust. I've made friends with people I'd never have met before. You can walk into any meeting, say whatever you want, and not have to worry. There's problems—I'm not saying there's not. But you always have an outlet."

In 1990 American Steel & Wire still had many, many miles to travel on the journey that Tom Tyrrell had mapped out. In quality alone, there were avenues that the company hadn't even begun to explore. After Ford's Q101 audit came the possible upgrade to Q1, which would be that much more demanding upon the company's system. No steel company in AS&W's sector of the marketplace had yet qualified for Q1 status. The quality of steel offered by the Japanese was still unmatched by American companies. "They are as far ahead of us," said AS&W's quality-assurance chief, "as we are ahead of our domestic competitors." There was unexplored terrain in labor relations as well. Not all of the customer value teams worked as well as the TOW plant's; not all the potential in the systems Tyrrell had set up had been realized. The union would doubtless be back, too. "Everybody started here with the understanding that the company started up on a five-year plan," said Ed Goldsmith. "I said [to the workers], 'You told the man you'd give him five years, and in all fairness he should get the five years. If you give him five years and you still aren't happy, then take another look at the union.'" The five years would be up in 1991.

The financial side of the business continued to be shaky, in large part because the original Cincinnati investors insisted that the company take out big new loans in 1990 to pay themselves and other shareholders a "special dividend" of $3.25 a share. American investors are frequently criticized for being shortsighted, and the Cincinnati group seemed to be living up to that reputation. The costs of the new financing, among other factors, left the company at just below break-even level in fiscal 1990, which ended in the middle of the year. The market going into the fall was soft. All in all, it was not a good time for a steel company to be deeply in debt.

For all the uncertainty, though, I couldn't shake an eerie feeling: this must have been what it was like in Japan thirty years ago, when companies were experimenting with new systems and learning to make a product that was better than anyone else's. Now it was the Japanese who were the world leaders and the Americans who were catching up. Unexpectedly, the fastest movers on our own track were small entrepreneurial companies such as Tyrrell's, not the giant steel companies that had once dominated the industry. Thanks to American Steel & Wire, Ed Goldsmith and at least a few others like him had jobs rolling steel. This time, like Japanese workers, they were expected to use their heads as well as their hands.

Afterword

Living in
the New Economy

A QUICK SUMMATION:

For the quarter-century after World War II, we Americans lived amidst a remarkably stable business landscape. The economy's key industries were typically dominated by a few giant corporations. Each employed tens or hundreds of thousands of people; each exerted enormous influence over its markets. Over time, they seemed only to grow bigger and more powerful. People who worked for—or bought from—Ford, Firestone, RCA, or AT&T had no reason to doubt that all such companies would be around, looking much the same, for decades to come.

The events of the 1970s and especially the 1980s upset this placid landscape. Macroeconomic turmoil—the energy crises, inflation, deregulation, and so on—undermined the stability of the marketplace. International competition, particularly from Japan, grew fierce. A wholly new technology, microelectronics, gave birth to a raft of new industries, and altered the way goods were produced and services delivered in old industries. Twenty years ago there were no cellular telephones and no automatic teller machines, let alone desktop computers.

Facing an uncertain environment and stiff new competition, the giant corporations flailed about. They slashed their payrolls, shutting down or selling off whole divisions, and contracted out what they had once done for themselves. They scrambled to get into newer, more profitable industries, leaving behind those they considered out of date. Many of the companies oozed red ink. A few were taken over and dismantled.

Meanwhile—partly in response to the corporate cutbacks, partly in response to new technologies and market opportunities—thousands upon thousands of new businesses came into existence. Some of these new companies grew very big very quickly. Most remained relatively small. Even so, it wasn't "small business" in the traditional sense that was flourishing. Unlike the neighborhood stores and job-shop manufacturers of the past, the new companies were oriented toward growth. They were technologically and managerially sophisticated, typically leading their larger competitors into new markets rather than following them.

This proliferation of new companies arguably saved America's economy from disaster. Newer, smaller businesses created many of the 18 million private-sector jobs added during the 1980s. They gave a massive boost to Akron and a hundred other cities around the country, regions that had depended heavily on big manufacturers and were left without visible means of support when the giants cut back or departed. They introduced innovations of all sorts, technological and nontechnological, in old-line industries such as trucking and new ones such as telecommunications. They helped maintain a competitive American presence in such global markets as semiconductors and steel. Some pioneered new ways of doing business, redefining relationships among companies and among managers and employees.

A tumultuous decade, the 1980s brought a good deal of economic pain. Yet the new companies provided a good deal of economic opportunity—not just the wealth that went to successful entrepreneurs but the excitement, challenge, and chances for advancement that many people found to be part of a growing young enterprise. How you perceived the trade-off depended, of course, on where you were economically: your age and education, your occupation and region, the company you worked for. But there was little doubt that the new business world offered much to many—and that the U.S. economy was better adapted to the world marketplace at the end of the decade than it had been at the beginning.

For all that, living and working in this new business world took—and will continue to take—some getting used to. The economic stability that Americans once took for granted was gone. We could no longer count on big companies for what they used to provide.

For much of the post-World War II era, people could build lives around the existence of the large corporations. They could go to work for a company after high school or college and expect to stay with the same firm for the next forty years if they wanted to. Blue-collar workers could join a union, even go out on strike, confident that the company could and probably would meet some of their demands—and would still be around to pay them a pension on retirement. Towns and cities could take at least part of their economic support for granted. Who expected Pittsburgh's steel mills to shut down?

By the beginning of the 1990s, big companies could not promise this kind of stability any longer, and the people who worked for them knew it. Kodak restructured, and several thousand jobs disappeared. Digital Equipment Corporation—one of the most successful computer companies in history—couldn't seem to keep up with the changing marketplace, and in early 1991 announced its first layoffs ever. General Electric continued to sell off some of its subsidiaries and to buy up others. Nor were markets and industries likely to stabilize in the foreseeable future. American companies would be facing more competition from other countries, not less. They would continue to do business in a world that was economically and technologically and politically unpredictable. They would continue to face competitive challenges from entrepreneurs.

But the new entrepreneurial companies held no prospect of long-term stability, either. Quite the contrary: even successful new companies typically grew in fits and starts, as David Birch showed. They expanded into new market niches, then consolidated or even shrank as they were beset by competition. And even the biggest of the new companies didn't have the kind of market power that Galbraith once saw as characteristic of the large corporation. Federal Express (81,000 employees in 1990) faced brutal competition, both from other delivery services and from new technologies such as fax machines.

Then, too, smaller companies in general rarely have the financial resources to weather serious setbacks. If things get too bad, they just go out of business. Successful ones may be sold, split up, or otherwise restructured, thereby throwing people out of work. My own employer, *Inc.*, has prospered for more than a decade. But my job depends not just on the magazine's continuing profitability; it also depends on the health, strategic decisions, and personal proclivities of the company's owner. I might hope to work at *Inc.* for the rest of my career. I'd be a fool to count on doing so. So it is with most small companies.

The decline of unions was both a symptom and a cause of this lack of security, at least so far as blue-collar workers were concerned. In 1970 about 20 million workers—28 percent of the wage-and-salary work force—belonged to unions. Two decades later the figures were 17 million and 17 percent. (Since public-employee unions were growing, the drop in private-sector union membership was even steeper.) Much of the decline corresponded to the shift in the labor force. Employment in the biggest industrial companies, historically the most fertile ground for union organizing, dropped. Employment in smaller manufacturing companies and service establishments, traditionally harder for unions to organize, grew. Also, unions' ability to win benefits was constrained by the new competitive environment. Instead of negotiating wage increases, they were frequently reduced to haggling over wage concessions. Pressing for job security, they ran into stone walls of opposition. The International Union of Electrical Workers, for example, won a not-quite-three-percent wage increase from General Electric in 1988, down from 5 percent in the previous contract. But it failed to get a promise from GE not to reduce factory work force levels. That year, according to the Bureau of National Affairs, only seventy-five of 1,060 union-negotiated labor contracts contained any provisions at all relating to job security.

A second sign—and second cause—of the lack of security was the appearance of what was known, rather chillingly, as the contingent work force. "Contingent workers, loosely defined, include part-timers, leased employees, temporary workers, business services employees, and the self-employed," wrote Gene Koretz in *Business Week*. "Their common denominator is that they do not have a long-term implicit contract with their ultimate employers, the purchasers of the labor and services they provide." Leased employees, if you're not familiar with the term, are employees nominally on the payroll of an employee-leasing company, who are then contracted out to a "regular" employer for whom they will perform tasks. Both employee-leasing and temporary-employment agencies boomed in recent years; the latter began supplying their clients with accountants, engineers, and other professionals as well as with secretarial and clerical help. Business services was also a booming sector of the economy, in part because the travel agents and benefits planners that had once been on corporate payrolls were now likely to be working in small, independent firms, serving customers both large and small.

According to estimates, contingent workers accounted for about one-fourth of the labor force by the end of the 1980s. Indeed, some experts saw a two-tier, or "core and periphery," system evolving: companies would have a small central staff, augmented as required by temps, part-timers, and other contingent workers. Contingent workers were generally paid less than regular full-time workers, and got fewer benefits. They could also be eliminated at the stroke of a pen. "When you hire someone on, you've made a commitment to them to take care of them for the rest of their lives," an executive of Owens-Corning Fiberglas Corporation told Amanda Bennett of the *Wall Street Journal*. Unable to live up to that commitment (the company let go 20 percent of its employees in the mid-1980s), Owens-Corning began using more and more temporary and contract workers.

During the boom years of the later 1980s, the lack of job security wasn't as scary as it might have been. New companies were expanding, and most people who lost one job could usually find another, albeit not always at the same level. In a stagnant economy or recession, however, the effects were likely to be devastating. Unemployment in past recessions consisted in fair measure of factory workers laid off for the duration. However painful they might be, layoffs were at least expected, and the workers had the promise of a job to go back to when things picked up. Unemployment in the new economy, by contrast, was likely to be spread more widely, and without assurance of a job to return to.

Large corporations provided other benefits in the past as well. They offered health insurance, often company-paid. They set up pension funds. People who worked a long time for a big company could thus count on a measure of financial security as well as stable employment. Smaller companies typically provided fewer benefits, and most didn't even attempt to guarantee a pension. Some offered profit-sharing and stock-ownership plans, but those only benefited employees of companies that did well. Besides, as people changed jobs more frequently, they were likely to lose whatever benefits they had accrued. By 1990 the only jobs offering the security once provided by the Fortune 500 were civil-service jobs. That may explain why some 100,000 people showed up in New York City to take an exam for 2,000 openings—as sanitation workers.

•

It would be foolish to mourn the good old days, when giant U.S. corporations dominated the world economy and could guarantee stable work for millions of Americans. Nobody can bring back the old régime, either economic or technological. And to do so would sacrifice much of the innovation and dynamism we gained from the proliferation of growing companies in the past ten years. Besides, the old days were pretty good for Americans precisely because they were pretty bad for everybody else. European and Japanese companies, let alone enterprises in developing nations, could seldom compete with the big U.S. multinationals. Incomes in other industrial countries (again, not to mention developing ones) remained low relative to our own. The emergence of a competitive international economy reflects the fact that Japan, European countries, and a host of others can now hold their own (or better) in competition with the United States. From the point of view of humankind, that is a net plus.

But if the American economy is to provide its citizens with a rising standard of living and at least a little peace of mind, then we as a nation have a tightrope to walk. We'll need a highly dynamic business world, one characterized by high levels of innovation, technical progress, and entrepreneurship. That's the only way we'll create enough opportunities to counterbalance the lack of stability. We'll also need social programs that provide people with a measure of financial security, even if they find themselves working for a dozen different employers in the course of a career, with periodic stretches of unemployment in between.

Governments, both state and federal, can help on both counts.

Encouraging Dynamism. One method of stimulating innovation and new-company creation is not to protect U.S. industries from imports. Steel companies, textile and apparel makers, semiconductor companies, and a host of others have been clamoring—and will continue to clamor—for tariffs and other import restrictions. But restrictions not only raise prices to consumers, they allow businesses to avoid or postpone innovations that could increase their efficiency. Goods and services cost more than they need to, and U.S. companies fall farther behind overseas competitors.

Our trouble, in the past, is that we confused protecting people (who should be protected) with protecting companies and industries (which shouldn't). If American steel can't compete with Japanese or Korean steel, we as a nation are better off importing it. But the people who worked for our steel companies needed much more help in making the transition to a new life than they (or any other displaced group of workers) ever got.

Then, too, we frequently underestimate the extent to which innovative American companies *can* compete in world markets. Some of the old-line steel companies went out of business when faced with competition from imports. But minimills such as Nucor, and specialty producers such as American Steel & Wire, were taking on all comers. The same was true in semiconductors. National Semiconductor and Advanced Micro Devices were hard hit in the 1980s by Japanese competition. But Cypress and Weitek and Altera and a dozen other smaller, more flexible companies did just fine. The United States will probably never dominate world trade as it once did. That doesn't mean we can't hold our own.

I don't mean to understate the difficulties of managing international trade in today's environment, nor do I mean to take a rigid ideological stance in favor of free trade. Volumes have been written on this subject, and I can't do it justice here. Considerations of national security enter the picture. So do other countries' policies. Japan, in particular, is notorious for not allowing other nations' companies free access to its markets, and reciprocal restrictions on our end may at times be a useful tool in negotiating more equitable trade arrangements. Still, when trade barriers have no effect other than to protect inefficient American companies, they should be abolished.

A second method of encouraging dynamism is to foster the creation of new businesses. In recent years state governments have experimented widely with this difficult art, and have registered some successes. Ohio's state government made an early loan to American Steel & Wire, and provided it with a grant for employee training. Though both were small compared to the company's need for capital, they helped persuade private lenders that the venture was serious and reputable. Pennsylvania undertook a host of measures to foster new companies. One of the best known was the so-called Ben Franklin Partnership, which provided a variety of financial aids and technical-assistance programs for entrepreneurs.

The state that probably went the farthest in this direction was Michigan, under Democratic governor James Blanchard. Elected in 1982, with Michigan's economy in a tailspin, Blanchard first took several steps to improve the general business climate for new and small companies. He lowered unemployment taxes for new employees; rewrote the state's securities laws to make it easier for companies to issue stock in Michigan; and appointed a small-business ombudsman. Then he developed a series of far-reaching programs. The Michigan Venture Capital Fund began investing 5 percent of the state's pension-fund money in new businesses (and in privately managed venture-capital funds). The Michigan Strategic Fund offered incentives for banks to make loans to promising but risky enterprises, and provided capital for several Business and Industrial Development Corporations, or BIDCOs, designed to help undercapitalized businesses get loan money. The state funded two technology research institutes, and it set up the so-called Michigan Modernization Service, which helped small companies cope with the difficulties of introducing new technologies. The service, wrote David Osborne, "is an institution that can help small manufacturers upgrade their production technologies, retrain their workers, revamp their labor management systems, find new markets, even launch new companies. With an annual budget of almost $5 million . . . the Michigan Modernization Service is one of the nation's most comprehensive and sophisticated industrial extension systems."

Osborne, a writer who studied state programs all over the country, called his book on the subject *Laboratories of Democracy,* after Justice Louis Brandeis's often-quoted hope that the states would serve precisely that function. As the phrase suggests, successful programs could be adopted by the federal government. A survey of state efforts to encourage entrepreneurship would surely turn up some that would work on a national scale. American agriculture, after all, is the envy of a lot of countries. It owes its success, in part, to the land-grant colleges and the federally financed Agricultural Extension Service. An administration that saw part of its mission as helping to spawn new companies could come up with and sponsor similar initiatives.

What's required, as Osborne argues, is that the government and the private sector work in concert, not in opposition; that the government view its proper role as working *with* business, not simply regulating it (as liberals prefer) or giving it a free hand (as conservatives propose).

In American political dialogue, encouraging a dynamic economy is frequently subsumed by the traditional conservative agenda of being kind to business. Yet the two shouldn't be confused. Cutting capital-gains taxes, for example, is said to benefit investment. What we need to encourage, though, isn't "investment" in general (which is frequently no more than speculation) but investment in new technologies and new companies. Compared with this narrow but important objective, an across-the-board capital-gains reduction is a blunt instrument. Similarly, it is said that government should ease its regulations on business. But a persuasive argument can be made that some regulations—occupational health and safety rules and pollution restrictions—not only improve Americans' quality of life, they force companies to be more innovative. "Without advanced regulations," writes Michael E. Porter, of the Harvard Business School, "U.S. industry will lose the innovation race in the affected industries and U.S. products will not sell well to sophisticated consumers abroad. Stringent standards for products, environmental quality, and the like not only serve the public good but are vital to economic success."

Mitigating the Effects of a Dynamic Economy. Implicit in the notion of encouraging dynamism is that businesses—sometimes a lot of businesses—will be allowed to fail. From a purely economic standpoint, capitalism works best when a company that can't keep up fails and its slot in the marketplace is taken by a more innovative company. The economist Joseph Schumpeter called this process creative destruction, and hailed it as the great engine of technological development. During the 1980s we saw Schumpeter's process at work. Jobs, companies, sometimes whole communities were devastated. But dozens of new industries and thousands of new companies came into being, and the communities that spawned them prospered.

But even creative destruction is still destruction, and the people who lose their jobs need to be taken care of until they can find new ones. In a dynamic economy what economists call frictional unemployment will rise: people will find themselves between jobs more frequently than in the past. Individual careers will be less likely to consist of work for one or two employers. And with technological change continuing apace, more and more people are likely to need retraining at some point (or points) in their working lives. This suggests at least three additional roles for government.

First: The unemployment compensation system will play an increasingly important role in providing income security, and not just for factory workers or poorly educated "fringe" workers. Unemployment compensation is typically paid only to those who can show they're actively looking for work; it should be paid as well to those who are pursuing state-approved adult education or training programs. Economist Lester Thurow has proposed an "individual training account," consisting of a subsidy for non-college-bound youth equal to what governments at various levels provide in subsidy for the college-bound. The young worker could cash in the subsidy over his or her career at any approved training program.

Second: Since people can't count on their employers to provide health insurance or pensions, government will have to step in. The need for some kind of national health insurance is likely to grow more pressing. (Witness the fact that businesspeople have begun to lead the chorus for reform.) So is the need for measures to encourage individual saving for retirement, in the manner of the late lamented individual retirement accounts.

Third: In general, employees will need plenty of protection in the new competitive environment. Workplace health and safety regulations will need to be strictly enforced; so will laws ensuring equitable and nonexploitative treatment. The trick will be to accomplish these ends without getting innocent companies bogged down in a morass of regulations or lawsuits. Trade associations and unions could play a role here, establishing "fair play" standards and making sure that member (or unionized) employers abide by them. Too few American businesspeople have learned a simple truth: The way to keep government off your back is to make sure that government has no reason to get on it in the first place.

We've entered a new economic era. Americans over thirty grew up in an age not only when the United States dominated the world economy, but when large, seemingly permanent companies dominated the business landscape. We took those companies for granted; indeed, many of us thought our society's major problem was finding some way to regulate their worst abuses. The marketplace did it for us. But it left us with an economy that, while full of opportunity, could no longer guarantee us the kind of security we assumed was our birthright.

In the future, our job as a society will be to cultivate, and learn to take advantage of, the opportunities provided by our newly dynamic entrepreneurial economy—and to mitigate both its excesses and its probably chronic instability. To that end, government will have to work with business, and business with government. The kind of dynamism symbolized by the growth of new companies is a powerful tonic; it should help America compete in the global marketplace, and it should continue to stimulate innovation and growth. But if these objectives are accomplished at the expense of people's well-being and sense of security, the new economy will be doomed to fail.

Acknowledgments

I COULDN'T have written this book without help from many sources.

I particularly want to thank the scores of people who agreed to be interviewed and to help me understand their ideas or learn about their companies. Their names appear under the chapter headings in the Notes section.

Several people helped me in a more general way; they, too, deserve special thanks.

Nancy Lyons and Jim Case read the entire manuscript and offered many fruitful suggestions. They aren't responsible for the infelicities that remain.

George Gendron, editor in chief of *Inc.* magazine, gave me the job that led to this book, then gave me time off from that job to finish it. Bo Burlingham and other editors at *Inc.* helped shape some of the material in the book.

Jesse Fried and J. D. Connor provided me with many hours of diligent research.

John Brockman, my agent, and Alice Mayhew, of Simon & Schuster, made it possible for me to turn a vague idea into what I hope is a coherent argument.

My children, Brendan and Liam, saw me through thick and thin. Writing a book involves plenty of both. My wife, Quaker Case, read every chapter and provided endless amounts of intellectual, emotional, and logistical support, despite a demanding career of her own. I couldn't have begun the book, let alone completed it, without her help.

Pizarro, the cat, was a faithful muse, except when she leaped from the floor onto the computer keyboard.

Notes

Interviewees and other sources of information are listed below. Articles from *Barron's, Business Week, The Economist, Forbes, Fortune, Inc., Industry Week, The New York Times,* and *The Wall Street Journal* are not separately cited. Most chapters draw on some or all of these publications.

CHAPTER ONE: DISCOVERY

This chapter draws heavily on interviews with David Birch and many others, including Thomas Gray, Bruce Phillips, Catherine Armington, Dennis Jacques, James Blanchard, Zoltan Acs, William Brock, David Evans, Charles Brown, James Hamilton, John Jackson, Sammis B. White, Lisa Binkley, William McMahon, Jeffrey Osterman, and Tim Sheehy. Thanks, too, to Bo Carlsson, William Dennis, William Dunkelberg, Reid Gearhart, Bruce Kirchhoff, Jonathan Leonard, David Mills, Paul Reynolds, Mark Roberts, and William Shepherd.

Additional facts and examples were taken from the following books and studies:

Zoltan J. Acs and David B. Audretsch, "Editors' Introduction," *Small Business Economics* 1, No. 1 (1989).

Catherine Armington and Marjorie Odle, "Small Business—How Many Jobs?" *The Brookings Review* (Winter 1982).

Lisa S. Binkley, William F. McMahon, Jeffrey D. Osterman, and Sammis B. White, "The Changing Economic Structure of West Allis, Wisconsin, 1979–1987," Urban Research Center, University of Wisconsin–Milwaukee, 1989.

David L. Birch, "The Job Generation Process," MIT Program on Neighborhood and Regional Change, 1979.

———, "Who Creates Jobs?" *The Public Interest* (Fall 1981).

———, "The Small Business Share of Job Creation: Lessons Learned from the Use of a Longitudinal File," MIT Program on Neighborhood and Regional Change, 1983.

———, "Share of Jobs vs. Job Creation: A Flow Analysis," MIT Program on Neighborhood and Regional Change, 1983.

———, *Job Creation in America* (New York: The Free Press, 1987).

Samuel Bowles, Richard C. Edwards, and William G. Shepherd, eds., *Unconventional Wisdom: Essays on Economics in Honor of John Kenneth Galbraith* (Boston: Houghton Mifflin Company, 1989).

William A. Brock and David S. Evans, *The Economics of Small Businesses* (New York: Holmes and Meier, 1986)

———, "Small Business Economics," *Small Business Economics* 1, No. 1 (1989).

Charles Brown, James Hamilton, and James Medoff, *Employers Large and Small* (Cambridge: Harvard University Press, 1990).

John Kenneth Galbraith, *The New Industrial State* (Boston: Houghton Mifflin Company, 1967).

———, *Economics and the Public Purpose* (Boston: Houghton Mifflin Company, 1973).

James Hamilton and James Medoff, "Small Business Monkey Business," *The Washington Post,* April 24, 1988.

Charles H. Hession, *John Kenneth Galbraith and His Critics* (New York: New American Library, 1972).

Robert Howard, "Can Small Business Help Countries Compete?" *Harvard Business Review* 68 (November–December 1990).

John E. Jackson, "Seeing the Trees Through the Forest: The Changing Michigan Economy, 1978–1987" (draft provided by the author).

Bruce A. Kirchhoff and Bruce D. Phillips, "Are Small Firms Still Creating the New Jobs?" George Rothman Institute of Entrepreneurial Studies, Fairleigh Dickinson University, April 1991.

David Nussbaum and Sammis White, "Employment Change in Suburban Milwaukee, 1979–1987. The Winner: Waukesha County," Urban Research Center, University of Wisconsin–Milwaukee, 1989.

Werner Sengenberger and Gary Loveman, "Smaller Units of Employment: A Synthesis Report on Industrial Reorganization in Industrialised Countries," discussion paper, International Institute for Labour Studies, Geneva.

Myron E. Sharpe, *John Kenneth Galbraith and the Lower Economics* (White Plains, N.Y.: International Arts and Sciences Press, 1973).

Michael B. Teitz, Amy Glasmeier, and Douglas Svensson, "Small Business and Employment Growth in California," Working Paper No. 348, Institute of Urban and Regional Development, University of California, Berkeley, 1981.

Sammis B. White and Jeffrey D. Osterman, "Is Employment Growth Really Coming from Small Firms?" Urban Research Center, University of Wisconsin–Milwaukee, 1990.

President Jimmy Carter's "Erosion of Confidence" speech can be found in *Vital Speeches of the Day,* August 15, 1979. John Mitchell's speech to the Georgia Bar

Association is quoted in Morton Mintz and Jerry S. Cohen, *America Inc.* (New York: The Dial Press, 1971).

CHAPTER TWO: THE END OF THE CORPORATE ERA

Thanks to my father, Everett N. Case, who read this chapter in manuscript.

The economic statistics in the chapter are taken largely from the *Statistical Abstract of the United States* and *The Economic Report of the President,* both published each year by the U.S. Government Printing Office in Washington, D.C. Information about the Fortune 500 is taken from the directories published each April by *Fortune* magazine.

Additional facts and examples were drawn from the following books and studies:

William J. Abernathy, Kim B. Clark, and Alan M. Kantrow, *Industrial Renaissance* (New York: Basic Books, 1983).

Jack Baranson, project director, "Sources of Japan's International Competitiveness in the Consumer Electronics Industry," Developing World Industry & Technology Inc., Washington D.C., June 1980.

Richard J. Barber, *The American Corporation* (New York: E.P. Dutton, 1970).

John Brooks, *The Takeover Game* (New York: E.P. Dutton, 1987).

Martin Feldstein, ed., *The American Economy in Transition* (Chicago: University of Chicago Press, 1980).

Tom Forester, ed., *The Microelectronics Revolution* (Cambridge, Mass.: MIT Press, 1981).

David Halberstam, *The Reckoning* (New York: William Morrow & Company, 1986).

Max Holland, *When the Machine Stopped* (Boston: Harvard Business School Press, 1989).

John E. Jackson, "Economic Development in Michigan: Choosing an Economic Future," Center for Political Studies, Institute for Social Research, University of Michigan, 1987).

Michael C. Jensen, "Eclipse of the Public Corporation," *Harvard Business Review* 67 (September–October 1989).

James Lardner, *Fast Forward* (New York: W.W. Norton, 1987).

Frank R. Lichtenberg and Donald Siegel, "The Effects of Leveraged Buyouts on Productivity and Related Aspects of Firm Behavior," discussion paper, U.S. Bureau of the Census, Center for Economic Studies, July 1989.

"Life in Tomorrow's America: Costlier, Less Exciting, But Maybe Better, Too," *U.S. News & World Report,* July 5, 1976.

Jeff Madrick, *Taking America* (New York: Bantam Books, 1987).

Ira C. Magaziner and Robert B. Reich, *Minding America's Business* (New York: Harcourt Brace Jovanovich, 1982).

James E. Millstein, "Decline in an Expanding Industry: Japanese Competition in Color Television," in John Zysman and Laura Tyson, eds., *American Industry in International Competition* (Ithaca: Cornell University Press, 1983).

Michael J. Piore and Charles F. Sabel, *The Second Industrial Divide* (New York: Basic Books, 1984).

Robert B. Reich, *The Next American Frontier* (New York: Times Books, 1983).

———, *The Resurgent Liberal* (New York: Times Books, 1989).

Robert B. Reich and John D. Donahue, *New Deals* (New York: Times Books, 1985).

Steven A. Schneider, *The Oil Price Revolution* (Baltimore: The Johns Hopkins University Press, 1983).

Harvey H. Segal, *Corporate Makeover* (New York: Viking, 1989).

J.-J. Servan-Schreiber, *The American Challenge* (New York: Atheneum, 1968).

"Adam Smith" (George J. W. Goodman), *Paper Money* (New York: Summit Books, 1981).

Robert Sobel, *RCA* (New York: Stein & Day, 1986).

David Vogel, *Fluctuating Fortunes* (New York: Basic Books, 1989).

CHAPTER THREE: NEW BUSINESS

The story of Kennedy Die Castings is based on interviews over a two-year period with the following people: Paul Kennedy, Bob Kennedy, Francis Kennedy, Michael Quarrey, Jim Girouard, Terry Trainor, Rick Selby, John McMahon, and Jim Ferguson. I'm grateful to the Kennedy family for allowing me access to the company. I'm also grateful to Stanley Works manager John Wiedemann for allowing me to accompany Kennedy's "99 Knife" team (Jose Gonzalez, Van Le, Jose Marrero, Wilson Ramos, and Rafael Torres) on a tour of Stanley's Eagle Square plant in Shaftsbury, Vermont.

The story of Thrislington Cubicles appeared in somewhat different form in *Inc.,* April 1989. Elizabeth Conlin provided additional research for the story; it was she who talked with Joel Koenig of Touche Ross (now Deloitte & Touche) and Peter Walmsley of Du Pont. I interviewed the following people: Gregory Braendel, Jack Dunsmoor, Jo Strate, Bo Rostrom, Tim Haase, Dennis Hines, Robert A. Swan, Robert H. Van der Linde, Kevin Nicusanti, Donald Duffey, Bob McCoy, Peggy Braunz, Harold Reichwald, Bob Kilbourne, Michael Fahringer, Howard McAloney, Barbara Sherman, Harris Parsons, Shirlea Bellwood, Bob Buce, Bob Kliesch, Joe Duzynski, Bob Edward, Dick Stumbaugh, John Muir, Cynthia Kolke, and Miles O'Dwyer.

Others who provided me with information used in this chapter include David Birch, Phil Pachulski, Mark S. Smith, Jim Hanahan, Tom Scholl, and Malte von Matthiessen.

Additional facts and examples were drawn from the following books and studies:

David L. Birch and Susan J. MacCracken, "The Role Played by High Technology Firms in Job Generation," MIT Program on Neighborhood and Regional Change, 1984.

Steve Coll, *The Deal of the Century* (New York: Atheneum, 1986).

John Kenneth Galbraith, *Economics and the Public Purpose* (Boston: Houghton Mifflin Company, 1973).

Robert J. Gaston, *Finding Private Venture Capital for Your Firm* (New York: John Wiley & Sons, 1989).

Susan Rachel Helper, *Supplier Relations and Technical Change: Theory and Application to the US Automobile Industry* (Harvard University Ph.D. dissertation, 1987, available from UMI Dissertation Information Service, Ann Arbor, Michigan).

Gary Jacobson and John Hillkirk, *Xerox: American Samurai* (New York: Macmillan Publishing Company, 1986).

Larry Kahaner, *On the Line* (New York: Warner Books, 1986).

Michael Malone, *The Big Score* (New York: Doubleday & Company, 1985).

Milton Moskowitz, Robert Levering, and Michael Katz, *Everybody's Business* (New York: Doubleday, 1990).

Douglas K. Smith and Robert C. Alexander, *Fumbling the Future* (New York: William Morrow & Company, 1988).

Michael B. Teitz, Amy Glasmeier, and Douglas Svensson, "Small Business and Employment Growth in California," Working Paper No. 348, Institute of Urban and Regional Development, University of California, Berkeley, 1981.

U.S. Small Business Administration, Office of Advocacy, *Small Business in the American Economy* (Washington, D.C.: U.S. Government Printing Office, 1988).

John W. Wilson, *The New Venturers* (Reading, Mass.: Addison-Wesley Publishing Company, 1985).

CHAPTER FOUR: THE NEW ECONOMY: CHIPS

I owe particular debts of gratitude for this chapter to AnnaLee Saxenian, who generously shared both her ideas and her research experience, and to Charles F. Sabel, who took the time to recount his own intellectual biography and to read the chapter in draft form. Portions of the chapter appeared in different form in *Inc.,* July 1988 and August 1990.

Many people in Silicon Valley spoke with me at considerable length, and I regret I couldn't include all the fascinating stories they told me. They include Rodney Smith, Paul Newhagen, Clive McCarthy, Stan Kopec, Erik Cleage, and Jim Sansbury of Altera; Arthur Collmeyer of Weitek; T. J. Rodgers of Cypress Semiconductor; Gordon Campbell of Chips and Technologies; William Hogan and Kathy Lee of MasPar; Eric Larson of Hewlett-Packard; Robert Graham of Novellus Systems; Gary Kennedy of Orbit Semiconductor; Michael Hackworth of Cirrus Logic; John Adler, G. Venkatesh, and Paul Hansen of Adaptec; Mike Bruzzone and Isaac Levanon of Arche Technologies Inc.; Ron Johnson and others at RJ Associates; and Dan Hutcheson of VLSI Research Inc. Mary Curtis, Melanie Taylor, John Hamburger, Gavin Bourne, Jerry Steach, Steven Schick, Paula Jones, and especially Susan Cain Franson were helpful in arranging interviews.

This chapter draws on articles in *Electronics, Electronic Business, Electronic Buyers' News, Electronic Engineering Times, Business Month, Venture,* and *The Harvard Business Review,* as well as the usual sources in the business press.

Additional facts and examples were drawn from the following books and studies:

Alfred D. Chandler, *The Visible Hand* (Cambridge, Mass.: Harvard University Press, 1977).

Electronics Panel, Committee on Technology and International Economic and Trade Issues, Office of the Foreign Secretary, National Academy of Engineering, "The Competitive Status of the U.S. Electronics Industry" (Washington, D.C.: National Academy Press, 1984).

Charles H. Ferguson, "The Competitive Decline of the U.S. Semiconductor Industry," written testimony for the Subcommittee on Technology and the Law, U.S. Senate Judiciary Committee, February 26, 1987.

George Gilder, *Microcosm* (New York: Simon & Schuster, 1989).

Dirk Hanson, *The New Alchemists* (Boston: Little, Brown & Company, 1982).

Michael S. Malone, *The Big Score* (New York: Doubleday & Company, 1985).

Michael J. Piore and Charles F. Sabel, *The Second Industrial Divide* (New York: Basic Books, 1984).

Clyde V. Prestowitz, Jr., *Trading Places* (New York: Basic Books, 1988).

Charles F. Sabel, "Flexible Specialization and the Re-Emergence of Regional Economies," in P. Hirst and J. Zeitlin, eds., *Reversing Industrial Decline* (Oxford, U.K.: Berg, 1988).

AnnaLee Saxenian, *The Political Economy of Industrial Adaptation in Silicon Valley,* unpublished Ph.D. dissertation, Massachusetts Institute of Technology, 1988.

———, "Regional Networks and the Resurgence of Silicon Valley," *California Management Review* 33 (Fall 1990).

———, "The Origins and Dynamics of Production Networks in Silicon Valley," Working Paper No. 516, Institute of Urban and Regional Development, University of California, Berkeley.

Semiconductor Industry Association, "Performance of the U.S. Semiconductor Industry, 1975 to 1985" (SIA, 1986).

Semiconductor Industry Association, "Key Facts and Issues" (SIA, 1989).

U.S. Department of Commerce, *A Report on the U.S. Semiconductor Industry* (Washington, D.C.: U.S. Government Printing Office, 1979).

CHAPTER FIVE: THE NEW ECONOMY: RUST BELT

This chapter draws heavily on interviews with Dennis K. Oleksuk and his colleague Michael Owen, and on research by James L. Shanahan and W. Richard Goe.

I'm also grateful to everyone else in Akron who took the time to talk with me: Robert Bowman, Richard Young, Deborah Victory, and Dale Gibbons of the Akron Regional Development Board; James Phelps, Bill Jasso, and David DeShon of the mayor's office; George Knepper and Daniel Nelson of the University of Akron;

Robert Fawcett of the Edison Polymer Innovation Corporation; David DeVore and James Bartlett of Primus Venture Partners; Peter Geiger and Larry Pantages of the Akron *Beacon Journal;* Stuart Lichter of Covington Capital Corporation; Randall Eberts of the Federal Reserve Bank of Cleveland; Canal Place tenants David Granger, Allen Ross, Dave Gronauer, John Cole, Gregory Gibson, Dan Lang, Robert Winer, Alan Robbins, Richard Fasenmyer, Ron Piekarski, John McKenna, N. Kevin Green, Russ Nofsinger, Karen Rupert, and Julie Schafer; also Michael LeHere, S. Lee Combs, Charles Stephenson, Lawrence Saulino, Robert Flaherty, John Bodis, Bruce Bowers, Claudia Bowers, Barbara Hiney, Robert Reffner, Jack Jeter, Richard Moore, and Alan Woll.

Additional facts and examples were drawn from the following books and studies:

William B. Beyers, et al., *The Service Economy: Export of Services in the Central Puget Sound Region* (Seattle: Central Puget Sound Economic Development District, 1985).

————, *The Service Economy: Understanding Growth of Producer Services in the Central Puget Sound Region* (Seattle: Central Puget Sound Economic Development District, 1986).

Barry Bluestone and Bennett Harrison, *The Deindustrialization of America* (New York: Basic Books, 1982).

"The Firestone Tire and Rubber Co." Booklet prepared for Firestone's twenty-fifth anniversary in 1925, provided to me by Jack W. Jeter of Jeter Systems Corporation.

W. Richard Goe and James L. Shanahan, "Analyzing the Implications of Service Sector Growth for Urban Economies," unpublished paper, October 1988.

————, "Producer Services, Trade, and the Social Division of Labor," unpublished paper, May 1989.

————, "Understanding the Growth of the Service Economy in Northeast Ohio," unpublished paper, July 1989.

David Halberstam, *The Reckoning* (New York: William Morrow & Company, 1986).

James S. Jackson and Margot Y. Jackson, *The Miller The Quaker and The Square* (Akron: Bookhound Press, 1984).

John E. Jackson, "Economic Change in Michigan, 1978–1984," unpublished paper, 1985.

George W. Knepper, *Akron: City at the Summit* (Tulsa: Continental Heritage Press, 1981).

Daniel Nelson, "Managers and Nonunion Workers in the Rubber Industry: Union Avoidance Strategies in the 1930s," *Industrial & Labor Relations Review* 43 (October 1989).

"100 Years of the Pneumatic Tire," various authors, *Tire Business*, August 1988.

James L. Shanahan, "The Future Economy of Akron, Ohio: Moving in the Right Direction," unpublished paper, November 1988.

James L. Shanahan and W. Richard Goe, "Akron, Ohio: Regional Economy at the Turning Point," in Richard D. Bingham and Randall W. Eberts, eds., *Economic Restructuring of the American Midwest* (Boston: Kluwer Academic Publishers, 1990).

CHAPTER SIX: THE NEW ECONOMY: STEEL

Thanks to the following people at American Steel & Wire Corporation for the time they spent talking with me: Tom Tyrrell, Ed Goldsmith, Regis Dauk, Mike Blake, John Asimou, Craig Young, Rick Teaman, Jay Massey, Bill Scott, Walter Robertson, Bob Meyer, Corky Meserole, Dave Zenker, Dave Gooch, Tom Moraca, Ben Marty, Ray Belcher, Mike Dempsey, Dwain Novak, Joe Kuzma, John Warnock, John Stout, George Hendricks, Kenny Hyczwa, Ron Lieb, Dave Miller, Bob Unger, and other members of the TOW plant customer value team. Thanks also to Gerald Breen of Cuyahoga Bolt and Screw, and Jack Lohrman and Brian Murkey of RB&W Corporation. Additional facts about AS&W were drawn from reports in the local press, particularly the *Cleveland Plain Dealer* and *Crain's Cleveland Business*.

The decline of the American steel industry is a story told in a number of recent books. I relied primarily on the following:

Zoltan J. Acs, *The Changing Structure of the U.S. Economy: Lessons from the Steel Industry* (New York: Praeger Publishers, 1984).

Donald F. Barnett and Robert W. Crandall, *Up from the Ashes* (Washington, D.C.: The Brookings Institution, 1986).

Donald F. Barnett and Louis Schorsch, *Steel: Upheaval in a Basic Industry* (Cambridge, Mass.: Ballinger Publishing Co., 1983).

John P. Hoerr, *And the Wolf Finally Came* (Pittsburgh: University of Pittsburgh Press, 1988).

William T. Hogan, S.J., *Minimills and Integrated Mills* (Lexington Books, 1987).

Mark Reutter, *Sparrows Point* (New York: Summit Books, 1988).

John Strohmeyer, *Crisis in Bethlehem* (Bethesda, Md.: Adler & Adler, 1986).

Paul A. Tiffany, *The Decline of American Steel* (New York: Oxford University Press, 1988).

Additional facts and examples were drawn from the following books and studies:

Walter Adams and James W. Brock, *The Bigness Complex* (New York: Pantheon Books, 1986).

Daniel Bell, *The End of Ideology* (New York: The Free Press, 1960).

Michael Borrus, "The Politics of Competitive Erosion in the U.S. Steel Industry," in John Zysman and Laura Tyson, eds., *American Industry in International Competition* (Ithaca: Cornell University Press, 1983).

Alfred D. Chandler, *The Visible Hand* (Cambridge: Harvard University Press, 1977).

Ira C. Magaziner and Robert B. Reich, *Minding America's Business* (New York: Harcourt Brace Jovanovich, 1982).

Michael J. Piore and Charles F. Sabel, *The Second Industrial Divide* (New York: Basic Books, 1984).

AFTERWORD

David Osborne, *Laboratories of Democracy* (Boston: Harvard Business School Press, 1988).

Index